Getting Started in
Options

FOURTH EDITION

Michael C. Thomsett

John Wiley & Sons, Inc.

New York • Chichester • Weinheim • Brisbane • Singapore • Toronto

Copyright © 2001 by Michael C. Thomsett. All rights reserved.

Published by John Wiley & Sons, Inc.

Published simultaneously in Canada.

This publication is designed to provide accurate and authoritative information in regard to the subject matter covered. It is sold with the understanding that the publisher is not engaged in rendering professional services. If professional advice or other expert assistance is required, the services of a competent professional person should be sought.

Library of Congress Cataloging-in-Publication Data:

ISBN 0-471-40946-4

Printed in the United States of America.

10 9 8 7 6 5 4 3 2 1

Getting Started in
Options

Contents

Acknowledgments   vii

Introduction
    An Investment with Many Faces   1

Chapter 1
    Calls and Puts   15

Chapter 2
    Opening, Closing, and Tracking the Option   63

Chapter 3
    Buying Calls   97

Chapter 4
    Buying Puts   119

Chapter 5
    Selling Calls   144

Chapter 6
    Choosing the Right Stock   179

Chapter 7
    Selling Puts   229

Chapter 8

Combined Techniques   247

Chapter 9

Choosing Your Own Strategy   291

Glossary   313

Index   323

Acknowledgments

I want to thank the many readers of the three previous editions who took the time to write and offer suggestions for improving the book. Their letters have helped add to the clarity of examples, definitions, and explanations, which ultimately helps all other readers.

Further thanks and gratitude go to Linda Rose Thomsett, whose continued support and encouragement have made this book a work of enjoyment and a challenge worth accepting with energy and enthusiasm.

An Investment with Many Faces

The people who get on in this world are the people who get up and look for the circumstances they want, and if they can't find them, make them.
—George Bernard Shaw, *Mrs. Warren's Profession*, 1893

The value of familiarity cannot be emphasized too greatly. The well-understood investment makes decisions easier and more comfortable.

When most people think about investments, the first idea that comes up is the stock market. The majority of investors know more about stocks than most other alternatives. They may also be familiar with bonds, real estate, and other mainstream ways to invest. The popularity of mutual funds makes that choice an easy one because most investors know how they work. They understand the mechanics of buying and selling mutual fund shares, they understand the jargon of mutual funds, and they are comfortable with the workings of the fund's management in the market as a whole.

Familiarity with a form of investing gives it an air of legitimacy among investors. The most comfortable (and therefore logical) way to begin investing is, for most people, to buy shares of stock directly or through a mutual fund. Some first-time investors are so confident that they understand what they are getting into that they might not be aware of the many forms of risk to which they expose themselves. Those risks can be learned about and managed through the acquisition of experience, which means that learning often is accompanied by the "pain of discovery"— or, in the market, the loss of money.

So for any investor embarking upon new ground, there are a few essentials that everyone needs to possess *before* actually parting with money. These include knowledge about how the investment works, comfort with the language unique to that investment, and an understanding of the risks involved (as well as the willingness to take those risks).

This observation is basic. It applies to all types of investments, whether in the stock market directly or through mutual funds; in real estate; in commodities and futures; and, of course, in options. When you buy your own home, you also buy personal security and long-term appreciation. Those are attributes unique to home ownership, because you also live in the home with your family. You insure your investment, and you benefit from real estate appreciation and fixed long-term payments that increase your equity. There is no pressure to make moment-to-moment decisions to sell or hold. Of course, you have unique risks as well in buying your own home. You might need to move and be forced to sell when the market is soft. The neighborhood could change, affecting your family's safety as well as property values. Changes in interest rates could make your mortgage a poor deal over the long term. Like stock market investors, buyers of real estate—whether for home ownership or for investment—can educate themselves in the attributes of the investment, the market, the language of real estate, and the risks involved.

Learning about markets and risks improves your chances of success, and makes you a wiser investor. Wisdom translates to profits more often than ignorance does, in any market. Information is the key to smart decision-making. In widely popular markets like the stock market, there is plenty of information out there, and it is easy to find. If you have access to the Internet, you will have no problem educating yourself. In fact, your greatest problem will be in trying to decide which information to use and which to throw out. If anything, there is far too much information to sift through. Investors who develop knowledge through research can master popular markets with relative ease. The availability of helpful information helps bring new investors into markets. For example, the incremental growth of mutual funds in recent years is phenomenal and has also been healthy for investors. Widespread investment by informed people creates a healthy, robust market. The more knowledge there is in the hands of the general public, the better it is for everyone who places their money at risk.

Just as well-informed investors make markets healthier and better for everyone involved, the reverse is also true. Poorly informed investors make markets unhealthy and dangerous. For example, a popular trend on the Internet is day trading. While it is true that some speculators can make fast money through high-risk speculation, the majority will lose. Lacking the awareness of the high risks involved, many inexperienced investors concentrate only on the promise of fast money. A gamble is not the same as an investment, and day trading is not for the inexperienced—in spite of the many promotions to the contrary. When investors do not understand markets, they cannot really understand the level of risk to which they are exposed. Every potential profit has a corresponding potential for loss. This is one of the basic realities of all investment—the inescapable relationship between potential for gain and risk of loss. So in any market, the experienced investor creates for himself or herself both a profit goal *and* a bail-out point meant to minimize losses. For example, smart investors in the stock market know that they stand a chance to win or to lose, so they approach this potential risk/reward situation with a thorough understanding. They diversify their capital among several dissimilar investments, and then they monitor their portfolios by watching trends and reading the financial news.

Some markets are too exotic for mainstream tastes. They may contain risks too high, require too large a dollar amount of capital, or depend too heavily on detailed technical knowledge. So the average investor would not be well-advised to try those markets. Only a small number of highly skilled specialists can participate successfully in such markets.

Some markets fall somewhere in between these extremes. They are not broadly understood like stocks or real estate. Yet, with knowledge, many investors can find these markets accessible, and they can participate in ways that are profitable. Typically, such markets are poorly understood by the general investing public. From a lack of understanding, risks are exaggerated or overstated; and the complexity may be emphasized, when in fact it is only a matter of terminology that confuses or frightens would-be investors.

The options market is one such market. It is not broadly understood, and most investors who have heard about options see the market as high-risk and dangerous. Lack of knowledge creates fear and apprehension, and appropriately so. Remember, though, this basic rule for *all* forms of investing:

> No one should ever invest in *any* market without first becoming educated as to that market's risks, opportunities, rules of trading, and terminology.

You probably have heard people describe the options market as too risky or complicated. Certainly, aspects of option investing fit these descriptions, but so do aspects of virtually every form of investing. The truth is, options can take many forms, some high-risk and others extremely conservative.

The way that you go into the options market should be determined by your own personal profile as an investor, including the kinds of risks you are willing and able to assume. One of the guidelines for investment advisers is called the "know your customer" rule. Stockbrokers and financial planners are supposed to know each customer's level of sophistication, financial situation, and risk tolerance. Similar rules should apply to the customer. Use the "know your investment" rule before you invest. And if you use the services of a stockbroker or financial planner, also use the "know your adviser" rule. Make sure your adviser knows the market before giving you advice.

The "know your investment" rule is a good place to start. When you hear the word "options," what is your reaction? Many people have rejected the idea of investing in options out of hand because they associate it with complexity and high risk. They believe that options are appropriate only for high-rolling speculators willing to take extraordinary risks. This is not necessarily true. The options market can be utilized in many ways and includes many different strategies. Options can be used to hedge other investment positions, or even as a form of insurance against the risk of loss in a stock investment. You will be able to overcome apprehension about options by gaining knowledge about the full range of investment possibilities. Learning about a market leads to informed judgments.

If, upon learning about options, you decide that the market is not right for you, that will be an informed judgment rather than an opinion without basis. Rejecting a potential market without first learning about the risks and the range of possibilities is a lost opportunity. Any market could be beneficial to you; how will you know unless you investigate?

You are not alone if you are uncertain about exactly how options work. This is a relatively new investment alternative. Options were first traded publicly in 1973. The stock market has been around for centuries in one form or another, so the rules for trading stocks have been refined and fine-tuned over many years. However, options have a short history in comparison. This disparity makes it difficult to compare the options market to the stock market as it has been used traditionally. Other differences make any comparisons inapplicable; although options and stocks are connected to one another, they are vastly different in many important ways.

Still, the risk element needs to be explored because, like the stock market, options are subject to their own set of rules, including potential for gain as well as limitations; profit opportunities as well as risks; timing considerations and the need for close monitoring. You might ask, "If options are not as risky as I have heard, why don't more people take part in option trading?" The answer is twofold. First, the relatively brief history of the market has kept it out of the public eye, at least in the past. Second, while the various strategies involved in option trading are not as complex as many people think, the language of options is highly specialized. When language is overly technical, the average person gets a sense of alienation and intimidation—in other words, it creates fear. Unfortunately, the terminology of the options market is far from user-friendly. One of the main features of this book is that it carefully presents *ideas* behind the terminology as each new term is introduced, supported further with examples, explanations, and charts.

Because options are new in comparison to the stock market, we cannot see how an option investor would have fared in 1929 or in the 1950s. But again, because there are so many variations to option investing, it is likely that in any market involving extreme bull or bear tendencies some option investors will have a tidy profit, while others will lose. We can only apply our understanding of options and how they are used in the market as we see it today. Many investors can relate to this. If your parents invested in stocks and believed that stocks were the way to go, then you probably have a good understanding of the stock market as well as an appreciation for its value. However, it is less likely that your parents have been long-term option market participants. The market is too young.

The market continues to evolve and change. The introduction of index options, in addition to stock options, has given investors many new and different ways to participate in the options market. The United States stock exchanges are undergoing pilot programs in a multiyear project to convert from trading in 16ths of a dollar to a decimal system. Decimalization, as this process is being called, will make it easier for all investors to understand stock and option listings.

While these changes are underway, we can expect yet more developments in all markets as online trading becomes the most common method by which investors buy and sell. Within a few years, the traditional broker/client relationship will probably be completely different than it has been in the most recent past. In this changing environment, the use of options in your portfolio can be significant and can serve many purposes.

Options today can be used in numerous applications. This book emphasizes the strategic use of stock options for publicly traded stocks, either for speculation or for one of the more conservative and less risky approaches. On the speculative side, options represent pure risk, operating as a form of side bet on a stock's near-term future price movement. On the conservative extreme of the risk spectrum, options can be used as insurance to protect against losses in stock investments, enabling you to hedge a position so that any loss is offset by a corresponding gain. In between these two extremes, a broad range of possible strategies and combinations can be employed. To decide how you can best use options in your investment portfolio—or to first determine whether options are even suitable in your situation—you need to go through a four-step process of evaluation:

1. *Master the terminology of this highly specialized market.* Recognize that it is not the complexity of the investment, but rather the complexity of the language, that makes it difficult for new investors to understand what is going on. The language of options is foreign even to seasoned stock market investors, because many ideas utilized in the options market are not common in the stock market. Options traders have developed a shorthand method of communicating ideas in order to communicate with one another quickly.

2. *Study the options market in terms of risk.* Break down each proposed idea and strategy (or combination of strategies) in terms of the risk level you are willing and able to assume. Don't expect one profile to fit everyone. Your situation is unlike anyone else's, so a proposed strategy that works well for someone else may not always work as well for you. Many investors and speculators use a broad range of strategies involving options, and not always in the same way. Because of the range of possibilities, it is likely that one investor will use dissimilar and even opposing strategies at the same time, within the same portfolio. (For example, you might have several different stocks in your portfolio and, based on their current status, you may decide to apply two different option strategies, one to each stock.)

This means that a broad range of risks often is found within a single portfolio. Because different option strategies may be applied at the same time, an overall risk assessment is not always easy to identify. Investors who use options have more types of risk associated with their portfolios than stock market investors have. Traditional stock market investors buy shares, hold them for a period of time, and then sell. This sequence of events—buy, hold, sell—is familiar to most people, and is known as a "long" position.

Some investors "go short," meaning they begin the series of events by selling as an opening transaction. So the short seller reverses the traditional sequence to sell, hold, buy. The short seller believes the value of the stock will fall, so the position can be closed by buying the stock back for less per share than the short seller sold it for. Obviously, in this situation, a much different risk profile is in effect. The long position has a risk that is limited (a stock can go down only to zero and no lower in the very worst case), but the short position has a potentially unlimited risk, because there is no limit to how high a stock's value can climb.

Certain option strategies can be very helpful to short sellers. The broader your investment strategy, the broader a corresponding option strategy will be as well. In other words, if you are mixing up long and short positions and speculating with stocks in other ways, then options may be used to protect positions, to limit risks, and even to enhance potential gains. The same argument has to be applied to risk, however: As you expand your exposure through the mix of stock investment strategies, a corresponding level of risk is expanded as well.

You will need to define yourself in terms of risk. Are you a high-rolling speculator willing to take very high risks or a very conservative investor who wants to insure against every possible contingency? Chances are you are somewhere in between these extremes; most people are. Just as you decide carefully how to buy and sell stocks as defined by what you consider to be acceptable risks, you will need to apply the same level of judgment for identifying the risks associated with each option strategy.

3. *Observe the market.* Learn how to read option listings as well as stock listings in the financial press and on the Internet. Track the rise and fall of option values over time, and note how option pricing reacts to price and volume changes in the broader market and in the stock itself. What factors besides stock prices affect option values? When does time work for you and when does time work against you? By identifying the important elements affecting and influencing option values, you will be equipped to analyze each option strategy and select the ones that best suit your requirements.

4. *Set a risk standard for yourself.* This is the most critical step in any form of investing. You need to have specific goals for yourself. Without goals, you cannot know when to buy or sell, why you are investing in the first place, or even when a particular strategy is appropriate. Everything is defined by goals—even when to bail out of a losing position—and goals dictate the timing of decisions and the use of the right strategies. The decisions you make and how well they are clarified by your personal standards and goals ultimately determine your success as an investor.

This four-part process can be applied to any form of investing, and not just to the options market. Even when you buy shares of stock, these four steps are useful and important—because they define the purpose of investing itself. Successful investing depends on the development of a thorough working knowledge of the market, an intimate comprehension not only of the mechanics of buying and selling, but of the more subtle degrees of risk unique to a particular market. After identifying risks, you need to further your control over your investment portfolio by developing methods for the intelligent market tracking and trend watching that investors need to perform. In addition, your own changing circumstances should prompt a review of your investing goals and risk standards, and of the assumptions that you bring to your investment management approach. For example, if you purchase a home, marry or divorce, or have children—all major life events—then you are also likely to need a review of your risk tolerance and personal investment goals. Going through these phases as part of a responsible investment program is what differentiates successful investors who consistently earn profits through hard work from those who sometimes are just lucky.

You have a great advantage over the option investor and speculator of the mid-1970s. Today, inexpensive Internet access to gain information and sophisticated access to the market to place trades have made option investing a powerful and effective alternative for many people. Before the World Wide Web, investors depended on brokers for up-to-date information about option and stock pricing, and even that information was often too old to be useful. Today, you can find free information on dozens of Internet sites with only a 20-minute delay—a technological miracle by the standards of the 1970s. With access to information once available only to stockbrokers, who were accessible only a few hours per day, you now can trade on your own without paying brokers for advice you often do not need, and access is available virtually 24 hours per day. As an option trader, you are less likely to need advice from a broker, because it is the nature of the options market that its players must have knowledge of their own. By the time you are through studying the information in this book, you will understand the options market far better than most brokers.

Not many years ago, all stock market investing was inconvenient and remote, so delays up to several hours were not uncommon. In the options market, a lengthy delay between placing an order and its execution can have drastic consequences. In the past, the limited number of brokers available to place orders and the slow information systems meant that serious option investing was available only to those few people who had a direct line to the floor of the exchange. The combination of automated access and widespread availability of good information means that more people than ever before can take advantage of the opportunities in option investing. At the same time, you have access to option trading information immediately, so that you do not suffer from the mistakes common in the past due to outdated communications systems, inadequately trained brokers giving poor advice, or the lack of good information for the beginning investor.

Still, technical speed and convenience are not enough. If you use a broker's services, that broker should be an expert in options. Many brokers understand the language and the mechanics of trade execution, but are poorly equipped to advise you. It is more likely that you will benefit from using a dependable, reasonably priced online service charging a flat fee per trade. You simply do not need a broker's advice today, with the vast amount of investment information online. A broker who is able to help you master the techniques of option trading could be a valuable resource, but it is quite likely that in a short period of time you will outgrow the broker and find it makes sense to trade through a discount brokerage firm that charges for placing trades but offers no advice. Remember, a commission-based broker makes a living by convincing you to execute trades. The commission is paid when you buy and sell, and the broker gets his or her commission whether you make a profit or suffer a loss. If your broker is not more knowledgeable than you are about the options market, then your best interests are not being well served. Given the nature of options trading—where fast action sometimes is essential and the volume of trading can be quite high—the use of a commission-based broker is not only cumbersome, but more often than not unnecessary.

Whether you use a broker's help or invest on your own, you will need to master the techniques and terminology of the options market before you will be ready to make your move. This book is designed to introduce you to this highly specialized market; to show how opportunities in options trading can be maximized; and to help you define your personal goals and risk tolerance standards in order to make the most of your investment dollars. This book does not recommend any one course of action, nor even that you should become an options investor. Everyone is different. To make a broad assumption or a single recommendation would violate the very principle upon which this book is based. This book does attempt to carefully and thoroughly define options terminology, to explain options investing in a manner that makes sense, and to present strategies that you might be able to put to work for yourself. Each chapter is presented in a step-by-step format, a building-block approach to the topic. It combines the introduction of terminology with practical examples and, when helpful, an accompanying graph or chart showing how a particular strategy works. The purpose in this approach is to help you master the topic in real terms and to show what can be achieved (or risked) with the strategy—so that the information is practical rather than theoretical. Risk profiling in this book shows through graphs the maximum potential profit and loss that can be realized in a particular strategy. The identification of profit zones and loss zones brings the information to life in a way that is readily understood.

In many cases, discussions involve the cost of an option, sales price, and profit, but exclude calculation of brokerage and trading costs. Each time you buy or sell an option, you will be charged a transaction fee, in the same way that you pay for buying or selling stock. The trading cost is left out of examples intentionally for two practical reasons. First, every brokerage fee is different and ever-changing, both through the Internet and in the old-fashioned method of trading. Second, commission rates also vary by the volume of trading involved. For example, the fee for a single option trade will invariably be greater than the fee (on a per-unit basis) for a set of 5, 10, or 20 options. As a general rule, the rate decreases as more units and larger dollar amounts are involved. So a single option example could be applied in higher multiples with the same result, but commission rates would vary widely. As you go through the examples in this book, be sure to modify the outcomes to allow for brokerage fees as they will apply in your own case.

In order for any strategy to work well, it needs to be appropriate, comfortable, and affordable. These ideas are not commonly expressed in books about investing but, in fact, they are of great importance to you when you come to the decision point. So they should be in your mind at all times as you make decisions about how and where to invest your money. No one idea is going to be appropriate, comfortable, or affordable for everyone, and options are no exception to this observation. No matter how easy, practical, or foolproof an idea seems in print, and no matter how well it works on paper, remember that when you put real money at risk, it changes everything. Your decisions should feel right to you. Investing in any manner should be not only profitable, but enjoyable as well. Too many would-be investors make their decisions on the basis of advice from others—friends, family members, brokers, or books—without researching on their own, and without studying the attributes and risks involved with the decisions. They overlook the importance of research as being necessary to apply information in a *real* situation, using *real* money and taking *real* risks. Analysis by itself is not enough, while action without analysis is nothing more than poor planning and unacceptable risk.

You have the best chance for success by first gathering the facts that you need to make intelligent decisions. Mere profit is not worth the effort if it is obtained at the expense of your peace of mind and personal sense of satisfaction. Success in the market is a combination of personal accomplishment and financial gain. Anyone who has invested on the advice of others knows the uneasiness of making a profit but not really knowing why, or suffering a loss and feeling that one should have been better informed. Part of the accomplishment in the journey toward becoming a competent and successful investor is the satisfaction you get through mastering a difficult and complex market. Then *you* are in control. By applying information to your situation, you will have mastered one of the many possible avenues to becoming a successful and knowledgeable investor.

Chapter 1

Calls and Puts

I know of no more encouraging fact than the unquestionable ability of man to elevate his life by a conscious endeavor.
—Henry David Thoreau, *Walden*, 1854

Most people are familiar with two types of investing: equity and debt. There is a third method, however, and that third method is far more interesting than the other two, because its attributes are unlike any that most people are familiar with—a troubling set of differences that can also be called a promising set of opportunities.

To lay a little groundwork, let's be sure that the popular equity and debt differences are properly understood. An *equity investment* is the purchase of a share in the ownership of a company. The best-known example of this is the purchase of stock through the stock market. Each *share* of stock represents part of the capital, or ownership in the company.

The second broad form is a *debt investment*, also called a debt instrument. This is a loan made by the investor to the company or government, which promises to repay as a contractual obligation. The best-known form of debt instrument is the bond. Corporations, cities and states, and the federal government finance

equity investment
an investment in the form of part ownership, such as the purchase of shares of stock in a corporation.

share
a unit of owner-ship in the capital of a corporation.

debt investment
an investment in the form of a loan made to earn interest, such as the purchase of a bond.

their operations through bond issues, and investors in bonds are lenders, not stockholders.

When you buy 100 shares of stock, you are in complete control over that investment. You decide how long to hold the shares, and when to sell. Stocks provide you with tangible value, because they represent part ownership in the company. Owning stock entitles you to dividends if they are declared, and gives you the right to vote in matters before the board of directors. (Some special nonvoting stock lacks this right.) If the stock rises in value, you will gain a profit. If you wish, you can keep the stock for many years, even for your whole life. Stocks, because they have tangible value, can be traded to other investors over public exchanges, or they can be used as collateral to borrow money.

When you own a bond, you also own a tangible value—not in stock but in a contractual right with the lender. Your contract promises to pay you interest and to repay the amount loaned by a specific date. Like stocks, bonds can be used as collateral to borrow money. They also rise and fall in value based on the interest rate a bond pays compared to current rates in today's market. In the event of the lender's bankruptcy, bondholders usually are repaid before stockholders as part of their contract, so bonds have that advantage over stocks.

The intent of this brief rundown is to introduce you to a *third* method of investing—one whose features might seem alien at first. For the purpose of understanding how an investment works, we can take some comfort by understanding the tangible values associated with both stocks and bonds. Stocks earn dividends and bonds yield interest on a predictable schedule, and they have long-term value. Stocks last for as long as we own them, and bonds remain in effect until maturity date. Most investors take pause at the thought of putting money into an investment that has no tangible value, and that literally evaporates into worthlessness after a few months. Imagine an intangible investment that is guaranteed to be worthless—in fact, one that will cease to exist—in less than one year. To make this question even more interesting, imagine that the value of this intangible investment is virtually guaranteed to decline just because time passes by.

These are some of the features of options, the subject of this book. Taken by themselves, these attributes certainly do not make the market look very appealing. The attributes just described make options seem far too risky for most people, but there are good reasons for you to read on. Not all methods of investing in options are as risky as you might think. Some are quite conservative. However you might use options in the future, the many strategies available make them one of the more interesting ways to invest.

Smart Investor Tip You have a lot of choices with options. Some strategies are high-risk, and others are very conservative. Options give you a rich variety of choices.

An *option* is a contract that provides you with the right to execute a stock transaction—that is, to buy or to sell 100 shares of stock. This right includes a specified, fixed price per share that is good until a specified date in the future. When you own an option, you do not gain any equity in the stock, and neither do you have a debt position. You have only a contractual right to buy or to sell 100 shares of a company's stock.

option
the right to buy or to sell 100 shares of stock at a specified, fixed price and by a specified date in the future.

Since you can always buy or sell 100 shares of stock at the current market value, you might ask: "Why do I need to purchase an option to gain that right?" The answer is found in the fixed stock price that you get with the option contract. That is the key to the option's value. Stock prices are dynamic; they rise and fall, often substantially. This price movement is unpredictable, which makes stock market investing interesting. When you own an option, the price at which you can enter into a stock transaction is frozen for as long as the option remains in force; so no matter how much price movement takes place, as an owner of the option you have fixed the price for your purchase or sale of stock; and that fixed price, when compared to the market price of the stock, ultimately determines what the option is worth as time passes.

Some important restrictions come with the option. The right to buy or sell stock at the fixed price is never indefinite; in fact, time is a critical factor. An option exists for only a few months. When the deadline has passed, the option becomes worthless and it ceases to exist. Because of this, the value of an option falls as the deadline approaches, in a predictable manner. Each option also applies to only a single stock, and cannot be transferred between different stocks. Finally, each option applies to exactly 100 shares of stock, no more and no less. Stock transactions usually occur in blocks divisible by 100, called a *round lot*, and that has become the standard trading unit on the public exchanges. In the market, you have the right to buy an unlimited number of shares that you want, assuming they are available for sale and that you are willing to pay the price the seller is asking. However, if you buy fewer than 100 shares in a single transaction, you are charged a higher commission. An odd-numbered grouping of shares is called an *odd lot*.

So each option applies to 100 shares, conforming to the commonly traded round lot—whether you are operating as a buyer or as a seller. There are two types of options. First is the *call*, which grants its owner the right to buy 100 shares of stock in a company. Every option relates to the stock of only one corporation and to its price per share. When you buy an option, it is as though someone is saying to you, "I will allow you to buy 100 shares of this company's stock, at a specified price, at any time between now and a specified date in the future. For that privilege, I expect you to pay me a price."

That price is determined by how attractive an offer is being made. If the price per share of stock specified in the option is attractive (based on the current price of the stock), then the price will be higher than if the opposite were true. The more attractive the fixed option price in comparison with the stock's current market price, the higher the cost of the option will be. Each option's value changes according to the changes in the price of the stock. If a stock's value rises, the value of the call option will follow suit and rise as well. And if the stock's market price falls, the option will react in the same manner. When an investor buys a call and the stock's market value rises after the purchase, the investor profits because the call becomes more valuable. The value of the option is really quite predictable—it is affected by time, of course, and also is related directly to the value of the stock.

round lot
a lot of 100 shares of stock or of higher numbers divisible by 100, the usual trading unit on the public exchanges.

odd lot
a lot of shares that is fewer than the more typical round lot trading unit of 100 shares.

call
an option acquired by a buyer or granted by a seller to buy 100 shares of stock at a fixed price.

Smart Investor Tip The value of an option is affected by movement in the stock's market value as well as by the passage of time. These changes are predictable; option valuation is no mystery.

The second type of option is the *put*. A put is the opposite of a call, because it refers to selling rather than to buying. The put contract grants its owner the right to sell 100 shares of stock in a specified company's stock. When you buy a put, it is as though someone is saying to you, "I will allow you to sell 100 shares of this company's stock, at a specified price per share, at any time between now and a date in the future. For that privilege, I expect you to pay me a price."

It is confusing at first to remember the attributes of calls and puts. You can buy either; but a call gives you the right to buy stock, and a put gives you the right to sell stock. So whereas you can buy either type of option, the right itself varies. The distinction is made easier to remember if you keep in mind that a call buyer believes that the stock's value will go up, and a put buyer believes that the stock's value will go down. If the investor's belief turns out to be true, then the investor will profit. So no matter which direction the market moves in a particular stock, you can make a profit in calls or in puts—as long as your prediction is correct.

Smart Investor Tip Buyers of options can make money whether the market rises or falls; the tricky part is knowing ahead of time which direction the market will take.

If an option buyer—dealing either in calls or in puts—is correct in estimating changes in *market value*, then the investor will earn a profit. Market value, of course, is the price value agreed upon by both buyer and seller, and is the common determining factor in the auction marketplace. However, when it comes to options, you have one additional obstacle besides predicting the direction of movement: The change has to take place by the deadline that is attached to every option. You might be correct about a stock's prospects in the long term, but

 put
an option acquired by a buyer or granted by a seller to sell 100 shares of stock at a fixed price.

 market value
the value of an investment at any given time or date; the amount a buyer is willing to pay to acquire an investment and what a seller is also willing to receive to transfer the same investment.

options relate only to short-term value and change. That is the critical point: Options are finite. Unlike stocks, which you can hold for as long as you want and need to, or bonds, which are repaid by a contractual date, options cease to exist and lose all of their value within only a few months. Because of this daunting element to option trading, time is often the determining factor in whether a buyer realizes a profit or a loss.

Smart Investor Tip It is not enough to accurately predict the direction of price movement. For option buyers, that movement needs to occur within a very short period of time.

Why does the option's market value change when the stock's price moves up or down? First of all, remember that the option is only a right, and that it has no tangible value of its own. That right is contracted for 100 shares of a specific stock *and* for a specific price per share. Consequently, if the option buyer's timing is poor—meaning the stock's movement doesn't happen by the deadline—then the buyer does not realize a profit.

When you buy a call, it is as though you are saying, "I am willing to pay the price being asked to acquire a contractual right. That right provides that I may buy 100 shares of stock at the specified fixed price per share, and this right exists to buy those shares at any time between my option purchase date and the specified deadline." If the stock's market price rises above the fixed price indicated in the option contract, the call becomes more valuable. Imagine that you buy a call option giving you the right to buy 100 shares at the price of $80 per share. Before the deadline, though, the stock's market price rises to $95 per share. As the owner of a call option, you have the right to buy 100 shares at $80, or 15 points below the current market value.

The same scenario applies to buying puts, but with the stock moving in the opposite direction. When you buy a put, it is as though you are saying, "I am willing to pay the asked price to buy a contractual right. That right provides that I may sell 100 shares of the specified stock at the indicated price per share, at any time between my option purchase date and the specified deadline." If the stock's price falls below that level, you will be able to sell 100 shares *above* current market value. For example, let's say that you buy a put option providing you with the right to sell 100 shares at $80 per share. Before the deadline, the stock's market value falls to $70 per share. As the owner of a put, you have the right to sell 100 shares at the fixed price of $80, which is $10 per share above the current market value.

The potential value in an option is in the contractual right that it provides. This right is central to the nature of the option, and each option bought or sold is referred to as a *contract*.

THE CALL OPTION

A call is the right to buy 100 shares of stock at a fixed price per share, at any time between the purchase of the call and the specified future deadline. This time is limited. As a call *buyer*, you acquire the right, and as a call *seller*, you grant the rights of the option to someone else. (See Figure 1.1.)

Let's walk through the illustration and apply both buying and selling as they relate to the call option:

1. *Buyer of a call.* When you buy a call, you hope that the stock will rise in value, because that will result in a corresponding increase in value for the call. If the call has more market value, it can be sold and closed at a profit; or the stock

 contract
a single option, the agreement providing a buyer with the rights the option grants. (Those rights include identification of the stock, the cost of the option, the date the option will expire, and the fixed price per share of the stock to be bought or sold under the right of the option.)

 buyer
an investor who purchases a call or a put option; the buyer realizes a profit if the value of stock moves above the specified price (call) or below the specified price (put).

FIGURE 1.1 The call option.

seller
an investor who grants a right in an option to someone else; the seller realizes a profit if the value of stock moves below the specified price (call) or above the specified price (put).

can be bought at a fixed price below current market value.

2. *Seller of a call.* When you sell a call, you hope that the stock will fall in value, because that will result in a corresponding decrease in value for the call. If the call has less market value, it can be purchased and closed at a profit; or the stock can be sold to the call buyer at a price above current market value (although no one would be likely to buy stock above market price); or the call option can expire worthless. (More information on selling calls is presented later in the book, in Chapter 5.)

You can sell options before you buy, and then close the position later by buying. This backwards sequence is difficult to grasp for many people accustomed to the more traditional buy, hold, sell pattern. The seller's approach is to sell, hold, buy. Remembering that time is running for every option contract, the seller, by reversing the sequence, has a distinct advantage over the buyer. Time is on the seller's side. The reversed pattern is not unique to options, but occurs in stocks, and even in other investments.

Smart Investor Tip Option sellers reverse the sequence by selling first and buying later. This strategy has many advantages, especially considering the restriction of time unique to the option contract. Time benefits the seller.

Example: You own a house that you rent out. The present tenant has expressed an interest in buying the house from you; however, the tenant does not have enough cash for a down payment. So you enter into a contract called a lease with an option to buy (a lease option). The contract specifies that the monthly payment has two parts. First is the monthly rent, and second is a prepayment to be applied toward a future down payment to purchase the house. The purchase price is agreed to by contract and fixed at $125,000, and the tenant agrees that the deal will be closed within three years from the contract date. If the tenant decides not to buy the house within that time frame, the accumulated deposit will be returned. However, as long as the lease option contract is in effect, you agree that you will not sell the house to anyone else.

Three years later, real estate prices have risen dramatically and the house is now worth $150,000, or $25,000 more than the fixed lease option price. The tenant has the right to buy the house for $125,000. You might approach the tenant and say, "I would like to cancel your option to buy my house. I offer to return all of your deposit, plus an additional $10,000 if you will agree to cancel your option." The tenant might respond, "I am still interested in buying the house at the agreed-upon price. If I go elsewhere, I would have to pay $150,000 for a comparable property. However, I will agree to cancel my option if you will pay me $15,000."

This example is typical of a call option. Because the market value of the house increased during the option period, the owner had an incentive to pay in order to cancel the agreement. The tenant was in the position of knowing that values had risen and that consequently the lease option appreciated in value. Keep the distinction in mind between the contract and the property: The contractual right grew in value as the result of the property's increase in value. The contract had no tangible value, but its contractual value changed due to changes in the property's tangible value.

In the example, the option's terms were negotiated between the landlord (seller of the option) and the tenant (buyer of the option). Because the property increased in value, the option became a valuable asset. As long as both sides are able to agree on a price to cancel the option, the contract can be nullified. In this case, the tenant had the choice of either getting the property for $25,000 below market value or taking a profit on the option.

The arguments would be different if the house's market value fell. For example, let's say that the lease option specified a price of $125,000, but the value of the house fell to $110,000 by the end of the three-year term. The tenant would then have no incentive to pay $125,000, so the option would have no market value.

Listed options—those traded publicly on exchanges

like the American Stock Exchange, Chicago Board Options Exchange, and Philadelphia Stock Exchange—are not negotiated in the same manner. Due to the high daily volume in option trading each day, listed option prices are established strictly through *supply and demand*. Those are the forces that dictate whether market prices rise or fall for stocks. As more buyers want stocks, prices are driven upward by their demand; and as more sellers want to sell shares of stock, prices decline due to increased supply. The supply and demand for stocks, in turn, affect the market value of options. The option itself has no direct fundamental value or underlying financial reasons for rising or falling; its market value is related entirely to the fundamental and technical changes in the stock.

Smart Investor Tip The market forces affecting the values of stocks in turn affect market values of options. The option itself has no actual fundamental value; its market value is formulated based on the stock's fundamentals.

The orderly process of buying and selling stocks, which establishes stock price values, takes place on the exchanges through trading that is available to the general public. This overall public trading activity, in which prices are established through ever-changing supply and demand, is called the *auction market*, because value is not controlled by any forces other than the market itself. The auction market operates strictly through supply and demand on the part of the collective market. Increased demand for stocks drives up stock prices; and increased desire to sell shares of stock, or a growth in the supply, softens the market in a particular stock and drives prices downward.

The auction market for stocks directly affects the market values of options. As long as the price of a stock rises above the fixed price specified in the call option contract, that option will also grow in value along with the stock. And as long as the stock's price falls below the fixed option price, the value of the corresponding call will fall as well. The option is directly tied to the stock's value. Thus, the forces of supply and demand affect stock prices, and option values change as a result.

supply and demand the market forces that determine the current value for stocks. A growing number of buyers represent demand for shares, and a growing number of sellers represent supply. The price of stocks rises as demand increases, and falls as supply increases.

auction market the public exchanges in which stocks, bonds, options, and other products are traded publicly and in which values are established by ever-changing supply and demand on the part of buyers and sellers.

Options themselves have little or no direct supply and demand features, but their values respond to changes in the corresponding stock's value. There are two primary factors affecting the option's value: First is time and second is the market value of the stock. As time passes, the option loses market desirability, because the deadline approaches after which that option will lose all of its value; and as market value of the stock changes, the option's market value follows suit.

Smart Investor Tip   Option value is affected by movement in the price of the stock and by the passage of time. Supply and demand affect option valuation only indirectly.

The owner of a call enjoys an important benefit in the auction market. There is always a *ready market* for the option at the current market price. That means that the owner of an option never has a problem selling that option, although the price reflects its current market value.

ready market
a liquid market, one in which buyers can easily sell their holdings, or in which sellers can easily find buyers, at current market prices.

This feature is of critical importance. For example, if there were constantly more buyers than sellers of options, then market value would be distorted beyond reason. To some degree, distortions do occur on the basis of rumor or speculation, usually in the short term. But by and large, option values are directly formulated on the basis of stock prices and time until the option will cease to exist. If buyers had to scramble to find a limited number of willing sellers, the market would not work efficiently. Demand between buyers and sellers in options is rarely equal, because options do not possess supply and demand features of their own; changes in market value are a function of time and stock market value. So the public exchanges place themselves in a position to make the market operate as efficiently as possible. They facilitate trading in options by acting as the seller to every buyer, and as the buyer to every seller.

How Call Buying Works

When you buy a call, you are not obligated to buy the 100 shares of stock. You have the right, but not the obligation. In fact, it is reasonable to say that the vast majority of call

expiration date
the date on which an option becomes worthless, which is specified in the option contract.

underlying stock
the stock on which the option grants the right to buy or sell, which is specified in every option contract.

exercise
the act of buying stock under the terms of the call option or selling stock under the terms of the put option, at the specified price per share in the option contract.

buyers do *not* actually buy 100 shares of stock. You have until the *expiration date* to decide what action to take, if any. You have several choices, and the best one to make depends entirely on what happens to the market price of the *underlying stock*, and on how much time remains in the option period.

You have three scenarios relating to the price of the underlying stock, and several choices for action within each.

1. The stock's market value rises.
2. The stock's market value does not change.
3. The stock's market value falls.

Market Value of Underlying Stock Rises In the event of an increase in the price of the underlying stock, you can take one of two actions. Either you can *exercise* the option and buy the 100 shares of stock below current market value, or, if you do not want to own 100 shares of that stock, you can sell the option for more money than you paid for it and take a profit on the difference.

The value in the option is there because the option fixes the price of the stock, even when current market value is higher. This fixed price in every option contract is called the *striking price* (or strike price) of the option. Striking price is expressed as a numerical equivalent of the dollar price per share, without dollar signs. The striking price is normally divisible by 5, as options are established with striking prices at five-dollar price intervals. (Exceptions are found in some instances, such as after stock splits.)

Example: You decided two months ago to buy a call. You paid the price of $200, which entitled you to buy 100 shares of a particular stock at $55 per share. The striking price is 55. The option will expire later this month. The stock currently is selling for $60 per share, and the option's current value is 6 ($600). You have a choice to make: You may exercise the call and buy 100 shares at the contractual price of $55 per share, which is $5 per share below current market value; or you may sell the call and realize a profit of

$400 on the investment (current market value of the option of $600, less the original price of $200).

Smart Investor Tip In setting standards for yourself to determine when or whether to take profits in an option, be sure to factor in the cost of the transaction. Brokerage fees and charges vary widely, so shop around for the best option deal based on the volume of trading you undertake.

Market Value of Underlying Stock Does Not Change It often happens that within the relatively short life span of an option, the stock's market value does not change, or changes are too insignificant to create the profit scenario you hope for in buying calls. You have two alternatives in this situation. First, you may sell the call before its expiration date (after which the call becomes worthless). Or second, you may hold onto the option, hoping that the stock's market value will rise before expiration, resulting in a rise in the call's value as well at the last minute. The first choice, selling at a loss, is advisable when it appears there is no hope of a last-minute surge in the stock's market value. Taking some money out and reducing your loss may be wiser than waiting for the option to lose even more value. Remember, after expiration date the option is worthless. An option is a *wasting asset*, because it is designed to lose value as expiration approaches. By its limited life attribute, it is expected to decline in value as time goes by. If the market value of the stock remains at or below the striking price all the way to expiration, then the *premium* value—the current market value of the option—will be much less near expiration than it was at the time you purchased it, even if the stock's market value remains the same. The difference reflects the value of time itself. The longer the time until expiration, the more opportunity there is for the stock (and the option) to change in value.

Example: You purchased a call a few months ago "at 5." (This means you paid a premium of $500.) You hoped that the underlying stock would increase in market value, causing the option to also rise in value. The call will ex-

striking price
the fixed price to be paid for 100 shares of stock specified in the option contract, which will be paid or received by the owner of the option contract upon exercise, regardless of the current market value of the stock.

wasting asset
any asset that declines in value over time. (An option is an example of a wasting asset because it exists only until expiration, after which it becomes worthless.)

premium
the current price of an option, which a buyer pays and a seller receives at the time of the transaction. (The amount of premium is expressed as the dollar value of the option, but without dollar signs; for example, stating that an option is at 3 means its current market value is $300.)

pire later this month; but, contrary to your expectations, the stock's price has not changed. The option's value has declined to $100. You have the choice of selling it now and taking a $400 loss or holding the option hoping for a last-minute increase in the stock's value. Either way, you will need to sell the option before expiration, after which it will be worthless.

Smart Investor Tip The options market is characterized by a series of choices, some more difficult than others. It requires discipline to apply a formula so that you make the smart decision given the circumstances, rather than acting on impulse. That is the key to succeeding with options.

Market Value of Underlying Stock Falls As the underlying stock's market value falls, the value of all related calls will fall as well. The value of the option is always related to the value of the underlying stock. If the stock's market price falls significantly, your call will show very little in the way of market value. You may sell and accept the loss or, if the option is worth nearly nothing, you may simply allow it to expire and take a full loss on the transaction.

Example: You bought a call four months ago and paid 3 (a premium of $300). You were hoping that the stock's market value would rise, also causing a rise in the value of the call. However, the stock's market value fell instead, and the option followed suit. With less than one month until expiration, it is now worth only 1 ($100). You have a choice: You may sell the call for 1 and accept a loss of $200; or you may hold onto the call until near expiration. The stock could rise in value at the last minute, which has been known to happen. However, by continuing to hold the call, you risk further deterioration in the call premium value. If you wait until expiration occurs, the call will be worthless.

This example demonstrates that buying calls is risky. The last-minute rescue of an option by sudden increases in the value of the underlying stock can and occasionally does happen, but usually it does not. The limited life of the option works against the call buyer. The entire amount invested could be lost. The most significant advantage in speculating in calls is that instead of losing a larger sum in buying 100 shares of stock, the loss is limited to the relatively small premium value. At the same time, you could profit significantly. The stockholder, in comparison, has the advantage of being able to hold stock indefinitely, without having to worry about any expiration date.

Example: You bought a call last month for 1 (premium of $100). The current price of the stock is $80 per share. For your $100 investment, you have a degree of control over 100 shares, but without having to invest $8,000. Your risk is limited to the $100 investment; if the stock's market value falls, you cannot lose more than the $100, no matter what. In comparison, if you paid $8,000 to acquire 100 shares of stock, you could afford to wait indefinitely for a profit to appear, but you would have to tie up $8,000.

Example: You gain control over 100 shares at $80 per share. You achieve this control by purchasing a single call option at 1 ($100). Your potential loss is limited to $100, and your potential gain is limited only by time itself. By using this strategy and accepting the limitation of time, you do not need to tie up $8,000. For the benefit of control available over a short amount of time, you need to commit significantly less capital.

Smart Investor Tip For anyone speculating over the short term, option buying is an excellent method of controlling large blocks of stock with minor commitments of capital.

In some respects, the preceding example defines the difference between investing and speculating. The very idea of investing usually indicates a long-term mentality and perspective. Because stock does not expire, investors enjoy the luxury of being able to wait out short-term market conditions, hoping that over several years the company's fortunes will lead to profits—not to mention continuing dividends and ever-higher market value for the stock. There is no denying that stockholders enjoy clear advantages by owning stock. Speculators, in comparison, risk losing all of their investment, while also being exposed to the opportunity for spectacular gains. Rather than considering one method as being better than the other, think of options as yet another way to use investment capital. Option buyers know that their risk/reward scenario is characterized by the ever-looming expiration date.

Smart Investor Tip　The limited life of options defines the risk/reward scenario, and option players recognize this as part of their strategic approach. The risk is accepted because the opportunity is there, too.

To understand how the speculative nature of call buying affects you, consider the following two examples.

Example when stock price rises: You buy a call for 2 ($200) that provides you with the right to buy 100 shares of stock for $80 per share. If the stock's value rises above $80, your call will rise in value dollar for dollar along with the stock. So if the stock goes up $4 per share to $84, the option will also rise four points, ($400) in value. You would earn a profit of $400 if you were to sell the call. That would be the same amount of profit you would realize by purchasing 100 shares of stock at $8,000 and selling those shares for $8,400. (Again, this example does not take into account any brokerage and trading costs. Chances are that fees for the stock trade would be higher than for an option trade because more money is being exchanged.)

Example when stock price falls: You buy a call for 2 ($200) that gives you the right to buy 100 shares of stock at $80 per share. By the call's expiration date, the stock has fallen to $68 per share. You lose the entire $200 investment as the call becomes worthless. However, if you had purchased 100 shares of stock and paid $8,000, your loss at this point would be $1,200 ($80 per share at purchase, less current market value of $68 per share). Your choice, then, would be to sell the stock and take the loss or continue to keep your capital tied up, hoping its value will eventually rebound. Compared to buying stock directly, the option risks are more limited. Although stockholders can wait out a temporary drop in price, they have no way of knowing when the stock's price will rebound, or even if it ever will do so. As an option buyer, you are at risk for only a few months at the most. One of the risks in buying stock is the "lost opportunity" risk when capital is committed in a loss situation while other opportunities come and go.

In situations where an investment in stock falls, stockholders can wait for a rebound. During that time, they are entitled to continue receiving dividends, so their investment is not entirely in limbo. If you are interested in long-term gains, then a temporary drop in market value is not catastrophic; it might even be expected. Some investors would see such a drop as a buying opportunity, and pick up even more shares. The effect of this move is to lower the overall basis in the stock, so that a rebound creates even greater returns later on.

Anyone who desires long-term gains such as this should not be buying options, which are short-term in nature, and which do not fit the risk profile for long-term investing. The long-term investor is aware of the permanence of stock and of its secondary value. For example, the stockholder can use stock as collateral, which options buyers cannot do. Options, lacking tangible value, cannot be pledged like stock.

Smart Investor Tip A long-term investor can hold stock indefinitely, and does not have to worry about expiration. If that is of primary importance to someone, then that person probably will not want to buy options.

The real advantage in buying calls is that you are not required to tie up a large sum of capital or to keep it at risk for a long time. Yet, you are able to control 100 shares of stock for each option purchased as though you had bought those shares outright. Losses are limited to the amount of premium you pay.

Investment Standards for Call Buyers

People who work in the stock market—including brokers who help investors decide what to buy and sell—regularly offer advice on stocks. If a stockbroker or financial planner is qualified, he or she may also offer advice on buying options. Several important points should be kept in mind when working with a broker, especially where option buying is involved:

1. The broker might not know as much about the market as you do. Just because someone has a license does not mean that he or she is an expert on all types of investments. Even brokers with expertise in the stock market might be completely ignorant about the workings of the options market. One rule for all options investors is: Be your own expert and don't depend on others to give you working strategies.

2. Don't expect a broker to train you. Remember, brokers earn their livings on commissions and placement of orders. That means their primary motive is to get investors to buy and to sell. The broker is not a teacher and, while many capable brokers are glad to provide guidance about the market, that should not be expected as part of the service.

3. There are no guarantees. Risk is found everywhere and in all markets. While it is true that call buying comes with some specific risk characteristics, that does not mean that buying stock is safe in comparison. It all depends on timing, on the market, and on future changes that you cannot know about today. Whenever you invest money, you will face risk. It is a mistake to believe that a broker's reassurances are guarantees that your money is safe.

4. Options are highly specialized instruments, and everyone involved with them should design a program that includes a series of strategies suitable to their own requirements. With that in mind, it often does not make sense to work with a broker at all. You are better off working with a discount broker who offers a transaction service but no advice. This approach is becoming increasingly popular as more investors realize that brokerage advice often is self-serving and unnecessary. In theory, a broker is paid for giving out advice. But in the options market, things change so quickly that strategies need to be individualized. A broker's advice for options investing may not be helpful and, in fact, could be contrary to your best interests.

Smart Investor Tip Anyone who wants to be involved with options will eventually realize that a broker's advice is unnecessary and could even get in the way of a well-designed program.

Brokers are required by law to ensure that you are qualified to invest in options. That means that you should have at least a minimal understanding of market risks, procedures, and terminology, and that you understand what you will be doing with options. Brokers are required to apply a rule called *know your customer*. The brokerage firm has to ask new investors to complete a form that documents the investor's knowledge and experience with options; the firms also give out an options *prospectus*, which is a document explaining all of the risks of option investing.

know your customer
a rule for brokers requiring the broker to be aware of the risk and capital profile of each client, designed to ensure that recommendations are suitable for each individual.

Smart Investor Tip You can get a copy of the options prospectus, called "Characteristics and Risks of Standardized Options," online at www.cboe.com/resources/odd.

The investment standard for buying calls includes the requirement that you know how the market works, and that you invest only funds that you can afford to have at risk. Beyond that, you have every right to decide for yourself how much risk you want to take. Ultimately, you are responsible for your own profits and losses in the market. The role of the broker is to document the fact that the right questions were asked before your money was taken and placed into the option.

prospectus
a document designed to disclose all of the risk characteristics associated with a particular investment.

How Call Selling Works

Buying calls is similar to buying stock, at least regarding the sequence of events. You invest money and, after some time has passed, you make the decision whether to sell. This is the case whether involving shares of stock or a call. But with a call, you may sell the call at a profit, or you may exercise it and buy shares of stock. The transaction takes place in a predictable order. Call selling doesn't work that way. A seller begins by selling a call, and later on buys the same call to close out the transaction.

Many people have trouble grasping the idea of selling *before* buying. A common reaction is, "Are you sure? Is that legal?" or "How can you sell something that you don't own?" It is legal, and you can sell something before you buy it. This is done all the time in the stock market through a strategy known as *short selling*. An investor sells stock that he or she does not own, and later places a buy order, which closes the position.

short selling
a strategy in the stock market in which shares of stock are first sold, creating a short position for the investor, and later bought in a closing purchase transaction.

The same technique is used in the options market, and is far less complicated than selling stock short. Because options have no tangible value, becoming an option seller is fairly easy. A call seller grants the right to someone else—a buyer—to purchase 100 shares of stock at a fixed price per share and by a specified expiration date. For granting this right, the call seller is paid a premium. As a call seller, you are paid for the sale but you must also be willing to deliver 100 shares of stock if the call buyer exercises the option. This strategy, the exact opposite of buying calls, has a different array of risks than those experienced by the call buyer. The greatest risk is that the option you sell might be exercised and require you to sell 100 shares of stock far below the current market value.

When you are an option buyer, the decision to exercise or not is entirely up to you. But as a seller, that decision is always made by someone else. As an option seller, you can make or lose money in three different ways.

Market Value of Underlying Stock Rises In this instance, the value of the call rises as well. For a buyer, this is good news. But for the seller, the opposite is true. If the buyer exercises the call, the 100 shares of stock have to be delivered by the option seller. In practice, this means you are required to pay the difference between the option's striking price and the stock's current market value. That means the seller loses money. Remember, the option will be exercised only if the stock's current market value is higher than the striking price of the option.

Example: You sell a call that specifies a striking price of 40 ($40 per share). You happen to own 100 shares of the subject stock, so you consider your risks to be minimal in selling a call. In addition, the call is worth $200, and that amount is paid to you for selling the call. One month later, the stock's market value has risen to $46 per share and the buyer exercises the call. You are obligated to deliver the 100 shares of stock at $40 per share. This is $6 per share below current market value. Although you received a premium of $200 for selling the call, you lose the increased market value in the stock, which is $600. Your net loss in this case is $400.

Example: Given the same conditions as in the previous example, let's now assume that you did not own 100 shares of stock. What happens if the option is exercised? In this case, you are still required to deliver 100 shares at $40 per share. Current market value is $46, so you are required to buy the shares at that price and then sell them at $40, a loss of $600 on the stock, offset by the $200 premium for selling the call—net loss is $400.

The difference between these two examples is that in the first case you owned the shares and could deliver them if the option were exercised. There is even the possibility that you originally purchased those shares below the $40 per share value, producing some profit. So the so-called loss exists only regarding the call transaction, which prevents you from benefiting from the stock's full price appreciation. In the second example, you have a genuine loss because you have to buy the shares at current market value and sell them for less.

Smart Investor Tip   Call sellers have much less risk when they already own their 100 shares. They can select calls so that upon exercise the stock investment will still be profitable.

Market Value of Underlying Stock Does Not Change In the case where the stock's value remains at or near its value at the time the call is sold, the value of the call will fall over time. Remember, the call is a wasting asset.

While that is a problem for the call buyer, it is a great advantage for the call seller. Time works against the buyer, but it works for the call seller. You have the right to close out your sold call at any time before expiration date. So you can sell a call and see it fall in value, and then buy it at a lower premium, with the difference representing your profit.

Example: You sell a call for a premium of 4 ($400). Two months later, the stock's market value is about the same as it was when you sold the call. The option's premium value has fallen to 1 ($100). You cancel your position by buying the call at 1, realizing a profit of $300.

Example: Given the same situation as before, you have a second choice. Instead of buying the option to close the position out at a profit, you may simply hold it until expiration. As long as the stock does not recover in market value, the entire $400 premium becomes profit. In this case, though, you also expose yourself to ongoing risk that the stock's value will rise and your call will be exercised.

Market Value of Underlying Stock Falls In this case, the option will also fall in value. This provides you with an advantage as a call seller. Remember, you are paid a premium at the time you sell the call. You want to close out your position at a later date, or wait for the call to expire worthless. You can do either in this case. Because time works for the seller, it would take a considerable change in the stock's market value to change your profitable position in the sold option.

Example: You sell a call and receive a premium of 5 ($500). The stock's market value later falls far below the striking price of the option and, in your opinion, a recovery is not likely. As long as the market value of the stock is at or below the striking price at expiration, the option will not be exercised. By allowing the option to expire in this situation, you receive the entire $500 as profit.

Example: Given the same circumstances as before, let's assume that you are not certain whether the stock will recover. This stock has a history of volatile fluctuations in value, and there are more than three months to go until expiration. At present the call's value is $200 and, given the risks of exercise in the event the stock's price rebounds, you decide to sell and take your profit now. By closing the position and paying $200, you realize a net profit of $300 in this transaction.

Remember three key points as a call seller. First, the transaction takes place in reverse order, with the sale occurring before the purchase. Second, when you sell a call, you are paid a premium; in comparison, a call buyer pays the premium at the point of purchase. And third, what is good news for the buyer is bad news for the seller, and vice versa. A call seller wants the stock's market value to fall, not rise. A rise in market value means the call's value rises as well, so that the call will be worth more than it was when the seller sold it. Understanding how call selling works is helped by a review of similar transactions in other markets:

- ✔ An art dealer sells limited-edition prints, but has only one example of each print to show to customers. After a sale has been made, the dealer orders and pays for prints needed to deliver to the purchaser. The art dealer has completed a sale in advance of making the purchase.
- ✔ A car dealer sets the price of a car with special features and sells it to a customer. Only after the sale has been contracted does the dealer place the order with the factory. A delivery date is part of the contract. If the dealer does not deliver the car by that date, the buyer has the right to cancel the deal. In this case, the car dealer sold the car before paying the factory to build it.
- ✔ A contractor sells hundreds of tract homes by showing models to potential buyers before the homes have been built. Buyers pick out empty lots for the homes of their choice and enter into contracts. The contractor then uses funds supplied by buyers and lenders to pay for materials and labor to build the homes.

short position
the status assumed by investors when they enter a sale order in advance of entering a buy order. (The short position is closed by later entering a buy order, or through expiration.)

long position
the status assumed by investors when they enter a buy order in advance of entering a sell order. (The long position is closed by later entering a sell order, or through expiration.)

When you sell a call option, you are a short seller, and that places you into what is called a *short position*. The sale is the opening transaction, and it can be closed in either of two ways. One way is to enter a buy order, and that closes out the position. Alternatively, you can wait until expiration, at which point the option ceases to exist and the position closes automatically. In comparison, the better-known "buy first, sell later" approach is called a *long position*. The long position is also closed in one of two ways. Either the buyer enters a sell order, closing the position, and receives some premium to help offset the call's original cost, or the option expires worthless, so that the buyer loses the entire premium value.

Investment Standards for Call Selling

The standards for investing as a call seller are vastly different than those for call buying. It remains true that you need to be familiar with the market, procedures, and terminology of the options market; however, the risk levels are substantially different for selling than they are for buying, so a different investment standard is applied to sellers.

As a call buyer, you have a limited risk. You stand to lose only the amount of the premium that you pay. However, sellers grant the right to buyers to buy 100 shares at a fixed price per share; in theory, their risk is unlimited. As a practical matter, risks for sellers are limited in two ways. First, the time element naturally limits the degree to which a stock will rise in value. Second, each stock is somewhat limited in market value by the nature of its market and competition. Stocks have been known to take phenomenal leaps, though, so such events can and do take place.

Example: You sell a call and receive a premium of 7 ($700). The striking price is 35 ($35 per share). Two months later, an announcement is made that the company has been sold to another corporation for $60 per share. Your option is soon exercised, and you are required to deliver 100 shares of that stock at $35 per share. The difference between the striking price and current market value is $2,500. You received a premium of $700 for selling the call, and the net difference (your loss) is $1,800.

From the point of view of the broker who has to approve of a client's call selling, standards have to be set higher for sellers than for buyers. Risk is different and in many respects greater, so a more sophisticated and experienced investor is more suited to selling. For the buyer, the question of affordability relates only to the level of the premium being paid. For the seller, the question is whether you can afford to be at risk for potentially higher losses, which would be realized if the stock's market value rose dramatically before expiration.

The risk applies when you sell calls without also owning the stock. If you already own 100 shares of stock, exercise causes a loss, but, with the stock already in hand, risk is virtually nonexistent. You can deliver the 100 shares without losing, because you already own them. As long as you bought those shares below the striking price of the stock, you cannot have a loss in the event of exercise. Of course, you do lose the unrealized profit you would have earned if you had not sold the call. But every action you take or fail to take in the market includes the potential for profits you could have earned by doing something else.

Example: Given the same circumstances as in the previous example, let's now assume that you already own 100 shares of the stock; let's also assume that you acquired that stock for $32 per share. The call has a striking price of 35, so you know that if the call is exercised, you will keep the premium and earn an additional $300 on your original investment. When the announcement is made that the company has been sold for $60 per share and the call is exercised, you are required to deliver your 100 shares at the striking price of $35 per share. It is true that you lose the *potential* gain that you would have made if you had not sold the option. However, by owning the 100 shares, you have escaped the risk of needing to come up with the difference between striking price and market value. You received a premium of $700 when you sold the call. In practice, you have gained $1,000 in the transaction—$700 in premium for selling the call plus $300 in gain on the value of the stock (you acquired it at $32 per share and delivered it at $35 per share).

Such potential gains missed are not really losses at all, and in some cases are looked upon as being advantageous to the call seller. Some stock investors sell calls against stock positions as a means of making a profit. They know that their stock will be called eventually upon exercise of a call, but they have designed their strategy so that they will earn a profit in any outcome. As long as the original purchase price is lower than the striking price of the call, the investor will make a profit upon exercise.

THE PUT OPTION

A put is the opposite of a call. It is a contract granting the right to *sell* 100 shares of stock at a fixed price per share and by a specified expiration date in the future. As a put buyer, you acquire the right to sell 100 shares of stock; and as a put seller, you grant that right to the buyer. (See Figure 1.2.)

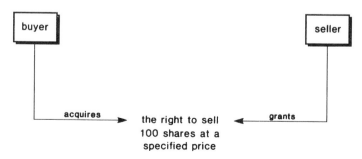

FIGURE 1.2 The put option.

Buying Puts

As a buyer of a put, you expect the underlying stock's value to fall. A put is the opposite of a call, so it acts in the opposite manner as the stock's market value changes. If the stock's market value falls, the put's value rises; and if the stock's market value rises, then the put's value falls. There are three possible outcomes when you buy puts.

Market Value of the Stock Rises In this case, the put's value falls in response. You can sell the put for a price below the price you paid and take a loss; or you can hold onto the put, hoping that the stock's market value will fall before the expiration date.

Example: You bought a put two months ago, paying a premium of 2 ($200). You expected the stock's market price to fall, in which case the value of the put would have risen. Instead, the stock's market value rose, so that the put's value fell. It is now worth only $25 with two weeks until expiration. You have a choice: Sell the put and take a $175 loss, or hold onto the put, hoping the stock will fall before the expiration date. If you hold the put until expiration, it will be worthless.

This example demonstrates the need to assess risks. For example, with the put currently worth only $25—nearly nothing—there is very little value remaining, so you might judge it too late to cut your losses in this case. Considering that there is only $25 at stake, it might be worth the long shot of holding the put until expiration. If the stock's price does fall between now and then, you stand the chance of recovering your investment, and perhaps even a profit.

Smart Investor Tip Option traders constantly calculate risk and reward, and often make decisions based not upon how they hoped prices would change, but upon how an unexpected change has affected their position.

Market Value of the Stock Does Not Change If the stock does not move in value enough to alter the value of the put, then the put's value will still fall due to the passage of time. The put, like the call, is a wasting asset; so the more time that passes and the closer the expiration date becomes, the less value will remain in the put. In this situation, you can sell the put and accept a loss, or hold onto it in the hope that the stock's market price will fall before the put's expiration.

Example: You bought a put three months ago and paid a premium of 4 ($400). You had expected the stock's market value to fall, in which case the put's value would have risen. Expiration comes up later this month. Unfortunately, the stock's market value is about the same as it was when you bought the put, which now is worth only $100. Your choices: Sell the put for $100 and accept the $300 loss; or hold onto the put on the chance that the stock's value will fall before expiration.

The choice comes down to a matter of timing and an awareness of how much price change is required. In this example, the stock would have to fall at least four points below the put's striking price just to create a break-even outcome (before trading costs). Of course, if you have more time, your choice is easier because you can defer your decision. You can afford to adopt a wait-and-see attitude with a long time to go, because the value falls out of the option slowly at first, and then more rapidly as expiration approaches.

Market Value of the Stock Falls In this case, the put's value will rise. You have three alternatives in this case: (1) You may hold the put in the hope that the stock's market value will decline even more, increasing your profit. (2) You may sell the put and take your profit now. (3) You may exercise the put and sell 100 shares of the underlying stock at the striking price. That price will be above current market value, so you will profit from exercise by selling at the higher striking price.

Example: You bought a put last month and paid a premium of $50. Meanwhile, the stock's market value has fallen $7 per share below the striking price, so your put has a current value of $750. You have three choices: The first possibility is to sell the put and take a $700 profit on your $50 investment. Second, you may hold onto the put in the hope that the stock will continue to fall, which would translate to more profit for you (plus the risk of a price rebound, meaning your current profit could evaporate). Or, third, you may exercise the put and sell 100 shares at the striking price, which is $7 per share above current market value.

Example: You own 100 shares of stock that you bought last year for $38 per share. You are worried about the threat of a falling market; however, you would also like to hold onto your stock as a long-term investment. To protect yourself against the possibility of a price decline in your stock, you recently bought a put, paying a premium of $1/2$ ($50). This guarantees you the right to sell 100 shares for $40 per share. Recently, the price of your stock fell to $33 per share. The value of the put increased to $750, offsetting your loss in the stock.

You can make a choice given this example. You can sell the option and realize a profit of $700, which offsets the loss in the stock. This is appealing because you can take a profit in the option, but you continue to own the stock—so if the stock's price rebounds, you will benefit twice.

A second alternative is to exercise the option and sell the 100 shares at $40 per share (the striking price of the option), which is $7 per share above current market value (but only $2 per share above the price you paid originally for the stock). This choice could be appealing if you believe that circumstances have changed and that it was a mistake to buy the stock as a long-term investment. By getting out now with a profit instead of a loss, you recover your full investment even though the stock's market value has fallen.

A third choice is to hold off taking any immediate action, at least for the moment. The put acts as a form of insurance on your investment in the stock, protecting you against further price declines. That's because, at this juncture, for every drop in the stock's price the option's value will offset that drop point for point. If the stock's value increases, the option's value will decline dollar for dollar. So the two positions offset one another. As long as you take action before the put's expiration, your risk is virtually eliminated.

Smart Investor Tip At times, inaction is the smartest choice. Depending on the circumstances, you could be better off patiently waiting out price movements until the day before expiration.

Selling Puts

While some investors buy puts believing the stock's market value will fall, or to protect their stock position, other investors sell puts. As a put seller, you grant someone else the right to sell 100 shares of stock to you at a fixed price. If the put is exercised, you will be required to buy 100 shares of the stock at the striking price, which would be above the market value of the stock. For taking this risk, you are paid a premium when you sell the put. Like the call seller, put sellers do not control the outcomes of their positions as much as buyers do, since it is the buyer who has the right to exercise at any time.

Example: Last month, you sold a put with a striking price of 50 ($50 per share). The premium was $2^{1}/_{2}$ ($250), which was paid to you at the time of the sale. Since then, the stock's market value has remained in a narrow range between $48 and $53 per share. Currently, the price is at $51. You do not expect the stock's price to fall below the striking price of 50. As long as the market value of the underlying stock remains at or above that level, the put will not be exercised. (The buyer will not exercise, meaning that you will not be required to buy 100 shares of stock.) If your opinion turns out to be correct, you will make a profit on selling the put.

Your risk in this example is that the stock's market price could decline below $50 per share before expiration, meaning that upon exercise you would be required to buy 100 shares at $50 per share. To avoid that risk, you have the right to cancel the position by buying the put at current market value. The closer you are to expiration (and as long as the stock's market value is above the striking price), the lower the market value of the put— and the greater your profit (up to the amount of premium you received).

The risk in selling puts is less than the risk associated with selling calls. Remember, the call seller has an unlimited risk, at least in theory, because there is no limit to how high a stock's market price may rise. For the put seller, the maximum risk is the price per share, down to zero. Of course, a company's book value per share will limit the real risk exposure. For example, if a company has a book value of $35 per share and its stock is selling at $50 per share, the real risk is only $15 per share. That does not mean that the stock cannot fall below book value, but it is unlikely.

Put selling also makes sense if you believe that the striking price represents a fair price for the stock. In the worst case, you will be required to buy 100 shares at a price above current market value. If you are right, though, and the striking price is a fair price, then the stock's market value will eventually rebound to that price or above. In addition, to calculate the real "loss" on buying overpriced stock has to be discounted for the premium you received.

Example: You sold a put with a striking price of 50 and received a premium of $2\frac{1}{2}$ ($250). Immediately before expiration, the stock's market value fell to $44 per share, and the value of the put was 6 ($600). The buyer will probably exercise the put before expiration in this case, requiring you to pay for 100 shares of stock at $50 per share. You have two choices. You can avoid exercise by buying the put and closing the position; this will give you a loss of $350 on the transaction, but avoids picking up 100 shares of stock at $600 above market value. The second alternative is simply to wait for exercise in the belief that $50 per share is a fair price. If the put is exercised, your real cost is only $47.50 per share, because you also received $250 for selling the put. So in fact your real basis is only $3.50 per share higher than current market value, before calculating trading costs.

Selling puts is a vastly different strategy than buying puts, because it places you on the opposite side of the transaction. The risk profile is different as well. If the put you sell is exercised, then you end up with overpriced stock. So you need to establish a logical standard for yourself if you will sell puts. Never sell a put unless you would be willing to acquire 100 shares of the underlying stock, at the striking price.

One advantage for put sellers is that time works for you and against the buyer. As expiration approaches, the put loses value. However, if movement in the underlying stock is opposite the movement you expected, you could end up taking a loss or having to buy 100 shares of stock for each put you sell. Sudden and unexpected changes in the stock's market value can occur at any time. The more inclined a stock is to volatile price movement, the greater your risk as a seller. You might also notice as you observe the pricing of options that, due to higher risks, options on volatile stocks tend to hold higher premium value than those on more predictable, lower-volatility issues.

Smart Investor Tip   Option price behavior is directly affected by the underlying stock and its attributes. So volatile (higher-risk) stocks demand higher option premiums and tend to experience faster, more severe price changes.

As a put seller, your risk is also limited to how far a stock is likely to fall, the absolute worst case being zero. The risk of exercise is not absolute, either. A put buyer will exercise only if the gap between market value and striking price justifies the action. For example, let's say a stock is two points below its striking price, but the put buyer paid 3 for the put. Exercise would produce a loss of a dollar per share, so that particular buyer will not exercise. At the point of exercise by any buyer, the option exchange assigns the exercise to a put seller. Remember, the exchange facilitates the market by acting as seller to all buyers, and as buyer to all sellers. So when a put is exercised, you have a random chance of its being assigned to you. If your gap between market price and striking price is significant, the chances of being assigned an exercise at or before expiration are increasingly high.

Investment Standards for Buying and Selling Puts

Every investor has to decide whether a particular investment strategy is appropriate, given the individual circumstances, willingness to assume risk, and personal goals. This decision is not a simple one, and there are no easy formulas to help you make the decision. However, it is critical for anyone involved with options to understand exactly what works and does not work, given the need to define what you expect from the market, and what risks complement those goals.

Example: You own 100 shares of stock that slowly but steadily grows in value over the years, and that pays dividends consistently. You also own 100 shares of stock that tends to bounce up and down in value over a wide range, and for which price movement is impossible to predict. Given these differences, it might make sense to buy a put on the second issue as a means of insuring against the possibility of a price drop in the near future. But the other 100 shares are more stable, so buying puts on those shares might not make as much sense.

As you can see, the decision to buy or sell options depends not only on the current price and time to expiration, but also upon the attributes of the stock *and* upon your own long-term goals and tolerance for risk. Consider applying the following rules for buying or selling puts, remembering that rules should remain flexible because things change, and because different situations may also require dissimilar approaches.

1. Buy puts with money you have available for speculation. Never buy puts with money you cannot afford to have at risk.

2. Buy puts only if you understand the risks involved, with enough time until expiration so that there is a reasonable opportunity for the stock's market value to fall.

3. Sell puts only if you are willing to buy 100 shares of the underlying stock at the striking price.

4. Trade in puts only if you are able to keep an eye on the market on a regular basis, so that you will be able to take fast action if and when sudden price movements occur.

5. Plan ahead. Before you trade in puts, establish what actions you will take in all scenarios—if the stock's price rises, if it falls, or if it remains within a narrow range during a specified time period. Set firm standards for what you would consider an acceptable profit *and* for the maximum loss you are willing to take.

The last rule is perhaps the most important. In the options market, self-discipline is an absolute requirement. You need to know in advance when you have to take specific actions, such as closing positions and taking profits or losses. Only by knowing ahead of time how to react can you ensure that your strategies make sense. When faced with indecision, the temptation to hold off—even in violation of your own preset rules—is a strong impulse. You will need to resist it, make decisions on your own thought-out formula, and remain on track in order to succeed in the options market.

Smart Investor Tip Self-discipline—the ability to follow your own rules—may be the most important attribute if you want to succeed in options.

THE UNDERLYING STOCK

Option values change in direct proportion to the changing market value of the underlying stock. Every option is married to the stock of a specific company and cannot be interchanged with others. How you fare in your option positions depends on how that stock's value changes in the immediate future.

This is a pivotal point to remember for options investors. The selection of the option cannot be made in isolation, without also looking closely at the fundamental and technical attributes of the underlying stock. Whether you treat options only as a form of side bet or as important aspects associated with buying and selling stocks, the judgment you apply in selection has to take into account the option *and* the underlying stock. Criteria for the selection of worthwhile stocks are at the center of smart stock market investing. The need for careful, thorough, and ongoing analysis cannot be emphasized too much. You will succeed in trading options by being aware of the attributes of the underlying stock—financial strength, price stability or volatility, the quality of a corporation's management, dividend and profit history, and more. These are the important fundamental considerations for buyers of stock, and they are equally important to options traders.

Of equal importance are the technical indicators as well, the nonfinancial points watched by investors. The price of the stock is entirely separate from the company's fundamentals, especially in the short term. And by their nature, options are short-term instruments, and technical indicators of the underlying stock reveal the perception of value in the market. This is just as important as the financial strength of the company, and contrary indicators— strong technical signs but weak fundamentals—have to be studied carefully.

This phenomenon is common in the stock market. For example, many of the newly formed online sales companies developed in the late 1990s experienced spectacular price movement without ever showing a net profit. This is an example of a stock having strong technical indicators—

the perception of value—along with poor fundamentals, such as a record of net losses over the entire history of the company.

Smart Investor Tip In the stock market, the perception of value is far more important to stock prices than actual fundamental value. This is especially true in the short term, which by definition means the entire options market.

The importance of the fundamentals cannot be ignored in terms of sound stock and option selection. However, it is important also to recognize that short-term price changes are what really define the difference between profit and loss in the options market. Both fundamental and technical indicators have to be followed.

Selection of stock, by itself, is a complex topic involving variables and degrees of judgment that every investor has to sort through individually. A healthy dose of intuition also plays an important role in the complexity of stock selection. The analysis of stocks is made more complex when options are included in the study. Even limiting an analysis to price movement is not an easy task. As shown in Table 1.1, you will consider price movement in the underlying stock as either positive or negative, depending on whether you are an option buyer or a seller, and on whether you are planning to use calls or puts.

Example: Two months ago, you bought a call and paid a premium of 3 ($300). The striking price was 40 ($40

TABLE 1.1 Price Movement in the Underlying Security		
	Increase in Price	*Decrease in Price*
Call buyer	Positive	Negative
Call seller	Negative	Positive
Put buyer	Negative	Positive
Put seller	Positive	Negative

per share). At that time, the underlying stock's price was at $40 per share. In this condition—when the option's striking price is identical to the current market value of the stock—the option is said to be *at the money*. If the market value per share of stock increases so that the per-share value is above the call's striking price, then the call is said to be *in the money*. When the price of the stock decreases so that the per-share value is below the option's striking price, then the call is said to be *out of the money*.

These definitions are the opposite for puts. When the stock's price rises above the put's striking price, then the put is out of the money; and when the stock's market price falls below the put's striking price, then the put is in the money.

Figure 1.3 shows the price ranges that are in the money, at the money, and out of the money in comparison with the striking price of a call. Remember that the definitions of these ranges are reversed in the case of a put.

at the money
the status of an option when the underlying stock's value is identical to the option's striking price.

in the money
the status of a call option when the underlying stock's market value is higher than the option's striking price, or of a put option when the underlying stock's market value is lower than the option's striking price.

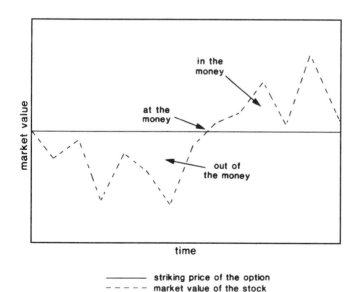

FIGURE 1.3 Market value of the underlying stock in relation to striking price of a call.

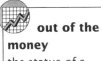

out of the money
the status of a call option when the underlying stock's market value is lower than the option's striking price, or of a put option when the underlying stock's market value is higher than the option's striking price.

The approximate dollar-for-dollar price movement of an option's value occurs whenever an option is in the money. At those times, the tendency is for option values to mirror stock price changes dollar for dollar. Of course, this is not always the case because as expiration nears, the time factor will also affect the option premium.

When the option is out of the money, changes in value relate primarily to the time element, and very little to the stock's price changes. Some price movement in option premium will be seen with out-of-the-money stock price changes, but it is far more significant when the option is in the money.

Example: You bought a put last month with a striking price of 30 ($30 per share) and paid 2 ($200). At that time, the stock's market value was $34 per share, so the option was $4 out of the money. More recently, the stock's price fell to $31 per share; however, the put's premium value rose only $1\frac{1}{2}$ points. Because the put remains out of the money, its premium value cannot be expected to change in the same degree as the stock's market value.

In the preceding example, a significant change would occur if the stock's price continued to fall below the striking price. Once in the money, the put can be expected to rise one dollar for each dollar that the stock's price falls—again, subject to some variation due to the continuing factor of time until expiration.

Example: You bought a call with a striking price of 45 ($45 per share) and paid a premium of 3 ($300). At the time of purchase, the stock's price was $44 per share, so that the call was one dollar out of the money. About two weeks later, the stock's price rises to $45. The call then is at the money. However, you observe that the call's value has not changed at all, but remains at 3. The next day, the stock's market value rises half a point, and the call's market value also rises the same degree, to $3\frac{1}{2}$. The following week, the stock rises 7 points, and again, the call's value follows suit and rises 7 points, to $10\frac{1}{2}$ ($1,050). If you were to sell the option at this point, you would earn a $750 profit. Note that when the option is in the money, price movement corresponds to the price movement in the underlying stock.

The value of options that are in the money is inescapably related to the underlying stock's current market value. But in the stock market, value depends on two additional factors. First is the stock's *volatility*, the tendency to trade within a narrow range (low volatility) or a broader range (high volatility); the degree of volatility will be experienced in both the stock and the option. Second is the time remaining until expiration. Besides these two elements that affect price, value changes often are accompanied by changes in *volume*—the level of activity in trading in the stock, the option, or both, or in the market as a whole. The level of trading volume in the underlying stock tends to affect the volume of trading in options written on the stock.

volatility
a measure of the degree of change in a stock's market value, measured over a 12-month period and stated as a percentage. (To measure volatility, subtract the lowest 12-month price from the highest 12-month price, and divide the answer by the 12-month lowest price.)

How to Pick a Stock

The question of selecting stocks is more involved and complex than the method of picking an option. For options, the selection has to do with risk assessment, current value, time until expiration, and your own risk tolerance level; in addition, numerous strategies you may employ will affect the ultimate decision. But option selection is formulated predictably. In comparison, stock selection involves no precise formula that works in every case. Price movement in a stock is itself unknown, whereas the reaction of option premium value is completely predictable, based on the way the stock's price changes.

volume
the level of trading activity in a stock, an option, or the market as a whole.

The selection of a stock is the critical decision point that determines whether you will succeed with options. This observation applies for buying or selling stock, and also applies when you never intend to own the stock at all, but only want to deal with options themselves. It is a mistake to pick options based only on current value and time, hoping to succeed without also thinking about the particulars of the stock—volatility, relation to striking price of the option, and much more. Of course, to some degree, the features of the option can be used to calculate likely outcomes, but that is only a part of the whole picture. Because option value is tied to stock price and volatility, you also need to develop a dependable method for evaluation of the underlying stock.

Some investors pick stocks strictly on the basis of *fundamental analysis.* This includes a study of financial statements, dividends paid to stockholders, management, position within the specific industry, debt and capital financing, product or service, and other types of information that are strictly financial in nature.

The importance of the fundamentals cannot be emphasized too much, as they relate to a company's long-term growth prospects, consistent ability to produce profits, and tendency for market strength over a long period of time. However, it should also be remembered that the fundamentals are historical and have little to do with short-term price changes in the company's stock. The financial strength of the company is important for selection of long-term stocks, but price movement is affected more by perception of value and less by financial strength. These indicators are classified under the umbrella of *technical analysis.* This is the study of price trends in stocks.

Both fundamental and technical approaches have something to offer, and you can use elements of both to study and identify stocks for option trading. The distinctions should be kept in mind, however, including both advantages and disadvantages of each method.

Investors also make use of subscription services to identify stocks and to find well-priced options. These are available through the mail and online as well. A popular and widely used service of this kind is Value Line, which constantly studies major stock issues and their fundamental and technical indicators, and ranks them into comparative recommendation levels for both safety and timeliness. Value Line also provides an option analysis service.

fundamental analysis
a study of financial information and attributes of a company's management and competitive position, as a means for selecting stocks.

technical analysis
a study of trends and patterns of price movement in stocks, including price per share, the shape of price movements on charts, high and low ranges, and trends in pricing over time.

Smart Investor Tip   For a detailed look at Value Line and its services, check its web site at www.valueline.com.

Another service offering competitive market analysis is provided by the Standard & Poor's Corporation. These two—Value Line and Standard & Poor's—are worth study and comparison if you believe you need a subscription service to help gather fundamental and technical analysis.

Smart Investor Tip   Take a look at the services offered by S&P at its web site: www.standardandpoors.com.

No stock or option should ever be picked without a thorough investigation—not only of the issue itself, but also of the various methods used for the analysis of the stock or option. Never depend solely on the advice of a broker, a friend, or anyone else as to which investment strategies should be used or which stocks or options to deal in. Perform your own research, drawing from as many sources as you need to make a well-informed decision. Develop your own combinations of information to identify and quantify risk, understand the comparative nature of one stock vis-à-vis another, and better comprehend how the market at large affects specific stocks.

Why is it a bad idea to depend on advice from experts and professionals? The answer is simple: Brokers are in the business of making money on commissions, and they earn commissions only when investors buy or sell. They are not compensated for giving advice, although a great effort has been put into trying to convince the investing public that advice is what investors are paying for. This illusion is disappearing as online information becomes increasingly available, most of it free. The growth of highly discounted transaction services—fees for executing trades without advice—makes the point as well. If you can get useful information by yourself and without paying a broker, then it makes sense to shop for economical brokerage services. By their nature, options are best suited for people who want to make their own decisions and who are able to act quickly in a fast-changing market. The nature of the options market makes brokerage services impractical and unnecessary.

Another problem in the brokerage business is that brokerage firms often take positions in stocks themselves, so that individual brokers are told when to encourage clients to purchase shares—not because they represent a worthwhile investment for a particular customer, but because the brokerage firm wants to sell the shares it has purchased. Such an environment is unhealthy for investors who believe they are getting individualized services.

The true picture was disclosed by a 1966 study conducted by the Columbia University Business School. Although this took place many years ago, it confirmed that a broker's advice was not always good for the customer. The study involved an analysis of more than 8,000 stock evaluations made by brokerage houses. The study concluded that brokers often are pressured to give their customers overly optimistic advice on securities sold by client companies through the brokerage. While this was known for many years in general, the Columbia University study was the first extensive analysis of its kind that proved the existence of the problem.

So every investor still faces the question: How do I pick a stock? The answer is to read and conduct your own research. Ask brokers their opinions on issues of interest to you, rather than allowing the broker to tell you what to buy. Read industry reports and use updated subscription services rather than reacting to rumors, and read the financial press regularly. Become familiar with the various methods of study, both fundamental and technical; learn how to develop a series of analytical tools that enable you to pick good stock investments consistently.

Intrinsic Value and Time Value

Once you are comfortable with the methods of stock selection, you will be ready to use that knowledge in the selection of options. Remember that options themselves change in value based on the underlying stock. Because option value is inescapably tied to stock value and market conditions, it is fair to say that options really do not have fundamental value other than that which grows from the fundamental value of the underlying stock. Every *listed option*—ones tied to listed stock securities—and its pricing structure are most easily comprehended by a study of its value, and that value has two distinct parts.

The first of the two segments of value is called *intrinsic value*, which is that part of an option's premium equal to the number of points in the money. Intrinsic value will be three points for a call three points higher than the striking price, or for a put three points lower than the striking price.

Any value above intrinsic value is known as *time value*. This is going to decline predictably as expiration date nears. With many months to go, time value can represent a substantial portion of an option's value, and all of it if the option is at the money or out of the money. But as expiration approaches, time value evaporates at a quickening pace, so that no time value remains at the very end. Time value also tends to fall away when the option is farther out of the money. In other words, an option that is two points out of the money will tend to have more time value than another option with the same distance from expiration, but 15 points out of the money. Option valuation can be summed up in the statement:

> *The relative degree of intrinsic value and time value is determined by the distance between striking price and current market value of the stock, adjusted by the time remaining until expiration of the option.*

Example: A call is valued currently at 3 ($300) and has a striking price of 45 ($45 per share). The underlying stock's market value also is $45 per share. Because the option is at the money, it contains no intrinsic value. The entire premium represents time value alone. You know that

listed option
an option traded on a public exchange and listed in the published reports in the financial press.

intrinsic value
that portion of an option's current value equal to the number of points that it is in the money. ("Points" equals the number of dollars of value per share, so 35 points equals $35 per share.)

time value
that portion of an option's current value above intrinsic value.

by expiration the time value will disappear completely; so it will be necessary for the stock to increase in value at least three points before expiration in order for you to break even (before transaction costs), and to exceed that level if the option is to increase in value by expiration. This does not mean that it will be necessary to gain all of those points; it applies only if you hold the option until expiration.

A comparison between option premium and market value of the underlying stock is presented in Table 1.2. This reveals the direct relationship between intrinsic value using a call as an example, market value of the underlying stock, and time value of the option. If the option were a put, intrinsic value would be represented by the degree to which the stock's market value was below striking price.

Another helpful illustration is found in Figure 1.4. This summarizes how movement in the underlying stock

		Option Premium (Striking Price of $45)		
Month	Stock Price	Total Value	Intrinsic Value[1]	Time Value[2]
1	$45	$3	$0	$3
2	47	5	2	3
3	46	4	1	3
4	46	3	1	2
5	47	4	2	2
6	44	2	0	2
7	46	2	1	1
8	45	1	0	1
9	46	1	1	0

TABLE 1.2   The Declining Time Value of an Option

[1]Intrinsic value reflects the price difference between the stock's current market value and the option's striking price.
[2]Time value is greatest when the expiration date is furthest away and declines as expiration approaches.

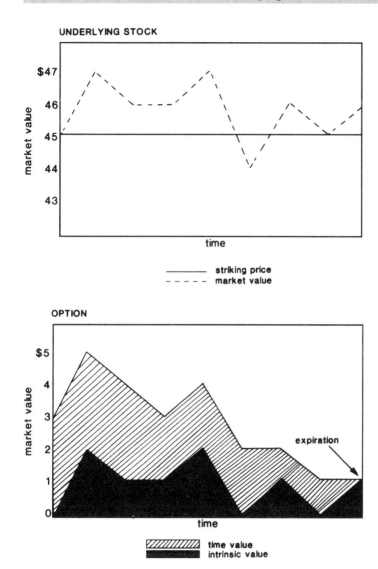

FIGURE 1.4 Time and intrinsic values of underlying stock and options.

(top graph) is identical to the option's intrinsic value (bottom graph). The underlying stock and intrinsic value share the same pattern (darker portion) when the call used in this example is in the money. Note how time value moves independently, affected by time more than by price movement in the underlying stock. From this, you can see how time value dissolves predictably over the life of the option.

The total amount of option premium can be expected to vary greatly between two different stocks at the same price level and with the same option features due to other influences. These include the perception of value by other investors, the stock's price history, the company's financial and technical indicators, the industry of the company, volatility, interest in the options among buyers and sellers, and dozens of more subtle influences. For example, two different stocks are associated with options at striking prices of 55 and identical expiration dates, and both stocks currently have market value of $58 per share. But the option premium for one is 5 and for the other 7.

The variable is always in time value, by definition. That is where market factors, primarily perception of value, come into play. There is a perception, in other words, that the option with greater time value has greater prospects for change in value than the one with lesser time value. While the way that option time value and intrinsic value change as expiration nears is predictable, the actual level of time value itself is subject to different market conditions for each stock. News, rumors, and gossip about a company or its industry affect time value, whether that information is true or false. A stock with higher-than-average volume and greater-than-average volatility might also have options with greater-than-average time value, indicating higher interest among investors.

The potential for price movement in the underlying stock and the perception of near-term value are the primary attributes affecting short-term price changes. Greater interest in a stock will invariably affect option premium as well, leading to inflated time value premium. Option buyers will be willing to pay more for the option when they perceive that there is greater potential for price movement (upward movement for calls and downward movement for puts). When a stock is less interesting to the market, demonstrating lackluster price change and volume, then time value will also be much lower. The opportunity level for buyers is matched by the risk level for sellers in the option market; so a seller who faces a higher degree of volatility in stock prices and related option premium will expect to receive more premium for selling the option, in compensation for those higher risks.

Making sound judgments about an option's time value is one very important way to find bargains in the options market, whether you are acting as buyer or seller. Buyers look for attractively underpriced purchases, and sellers look for attractively overpriced ones. For example, an option with many months until expiration might have exceptionally low time value today, but it is close to the money. This reflects an overall market attitude that the stock is not likely to increase in value enough to justify higher time value. As a buyer, you might believe that the option is underpriced at its current level. The opposite is true for sellers. Suppose that an option with a striking price close to current market value of the stock has an unusually high time value premium and a relatively short time to go until expiration. As a seller, you might see this as an opportunity, knowing that the time value will disappear rapidly. By selling that option, time works for you as the time value falls away quickly. Such opportunities are rare and fleeting, but they can be found.

You can recognize time value easily by comparing the stock's current value to the option's premium. For example, a stock currently is priced at $47 per share; an option has a premium value of 3 and a striking price of 45. To break down the total premium between intrinsic and time value, subtract striking price from current market value (if the option is out of the money, then there is no intrinsic value).

Stock Price

Current market value of the stock	$47
Less: Striking price of the option	−45
Intrinsic value	2

Option Premium

Total premium	3
Less: Intrinsic value	−2
Time value	1

In the next chapter, several important features of options—striking price, expiration date, and exercise—are more fully explored, especially in light of how these features affect your personal options strategy.

Chapter 2

Opening, Closing, and Tracking the Option

I was brought up to believe that the only thing worth doing was to add to the sum of accurate information in the world.
—Margaret Mead, *New York Times*, August 9, 1964

Every option is characterized by four specific attributes, collectively called the *terms* of the option. These are striking price, expiration month, type of option (call or put), and the underlying security. They are also alternatively referred to as *standardized terms*.

These are the four essential pieces you need in order to see the whole picture, to know which option is being discussed, and to distinguish it from all other options. In evaluating risk and potential gain, every buyer and seller needs to have these four essential pieces of information. Of course, because point of view between buyer and seller is going to be opposite (as it often will be between investors involved with calls versus those involved with puts), an advantageous situation to one person may well be disadvantageous to another. That is the nature of investing in options: You can take a position on one side or the other for any particular option, depending on where you believe the advantage lies.

To review the four terms briefly:

terms the attributes that describe an option, including the striking price, expiration month, type of option (call or put), and the underlying security.

standardized terms same as **terms**.

1. *Striking price.* The striking price is the fixed price at which the option can be exercised. It is the pivotal piece of information that determines the relative value of options based on their proximity to that set price; it is the price per share to be paid or received in the event of exercise. The striking price normally is divisible by 5 points. The exceptions: Some very low-priced shares may be sold in increments divisible by $2\frac{1}{2}$ and other issues end up with fractional values after a stock split. High-priced stocks may be associated with options selling at intervals divisible by 10 points. The striking price remains unchanged during the entire life of each option, no matter how much change occurs in the market value of the underlying stock.

For the buyer, striking price identifies the price at which 100 shares of stock can be bought (with a call) or sold (with a put). For a seller, striking price is the opposite: It is the price at which 100 shares of stock must be sold (with a call) or bought (with a put) in the event that the buyer decides to exercise.

2. *Expiration month.* Every option exists for only a limited number of months. That is a problem or an opportunity, depending on whether you are acting as a buyer or as a seller, and depending on the specific strategies you employ. Every option eventually either is canceled through a closing transaction, is exercised, or expires, but it never just goes on forever. Because the option is not tangible, the number of potential active options is unlimited except by market demand. A company issues only so many shares of stock, so buyers and sellers need to adjust prices according to supply and demand. This is not the case with options, which have no specific limitations such as numbers issued.

Options active at any given time are limited by the risks involved. An option far out of the money will naturally draw little interest, and those with impending expiration will similarly lose market interest as their time value evaporates. Buyers need to believe there is enough time for a profit to materialize, and that the market price is close enough to the striking price that a profit is realistic; or, if in the money, that it is not so expensive that risks are too great. The same considerations that create disadvantages for buyers represent opportunities for sellers. Pending expiration reduces the likelihood of out-of-the-money options being exercised, and distance between market price of the stock and striking price of the call means the seller's profits are more likely to be realized than are the hopes of the buyer.

3. *Type of option.* The distinction between calls and puts is essential to success in the options market; even so, some first-time investors are confused in trying to understand how and why calls and puts are different and must be considered as opposites. Identical strategies cannot be used for calls and puts, for reasons beyond the obvious fact that they are opposites. Calls are by definition the right to buy 100 shares, whereas puts are the right to sell 100 shares. But comprehending the essential opposite nature of the two contracts is not enough.

It might seem at first glance that, given the behavior of calls and puts when in the money or out of the money, it would make no difference whether you buy a put or sell a call. As long as expiration and striking price are identical, what is the difference? In practice, however, significant distinctions do make these two ideas vastly different in terms of risk profile. When you buy a put, your risk is limited to the amount you pay (premium). When you sell a call, your risk can be far greater because the stock may rise many points, requiring the call seller to deliver 100 shares at a price far below current market value. Each specific strategy has to be reviewed in terms not only of likely price movement given a set of market price changes in the underlying stock, but also how one's position is affected by exposure to varying degrees of risk. Some of the more exotic strategies involving the use of calls and puts at the same time or buying and selling of the same option with different striking prices are examples of advanced strategic approaches, which will be explored in detail in later chapters.

4. *Underlying security.* Every option is identified with a specific company's stock, and this cannot be changed. Listed options are not offered on all stocks traded, nor are they available on every stock exchange. (Some options trade on only one exchange, while others trade on several.) Options can exist only when a specific underlying stock has been identified, since it is the stock's market value that determines the option's related premium value. All options traded on a specific underlying stock are referred to as a single *class* of options. Thus, a single stock might be associ-

class

all options traded on a single underlying security, including different striking prices and expiration dates.

ated with a wide variety of calls and puts with different striking prices and expiration months, but they all belong to the same class. In comparison, all of those options with the same combination of terms—identical striking price, expiration month, type (call or put), and underlying stock—are considered a single *series* of options.

A NOTE ON THE EXPIRATION CYCLE

Expiration dates for options of a single underlying stock occur on a predictable *cycle*. Every stock with listed options can be identified by the cycle to which it belongs, and these remain unchanged. There are three cycles:

✔ January, April, July, and October (JAJO)
✔ February, May, August, and November (FMAN)
✔ March, June, September, and December (MJSD)

In addition to these fixed expiration cycle dates, active options are available for expiration in the upcoming month and perhaps in the month following that, regardless of expiration cycle. For example, let's suppose that a particular stock has options expiring in the cycle month of April. In February, you may be able to trade in short-term options expiring in March even though that is not a part of the normal cyclical expiration.

Smart Investor Tip   Some options traders use the short-term options as good speculative tools. Because they come and go more rapidly than the cyclical options, they often are overlooked as opportunities. For example, they can be used to temporarily protect longer-term short option positions.

An option's expiration takes place on the third Saturday of the expiration month. An order to close an open position has to be placed and executed no later than the *last trading day* before expiration day, and before the indicated *expiration time* for the option. As a general rule, this means that the trade has to be executed before the close of business on the Friday immediately before the Saturday of expiration; a specific cutoff time

series
a group of options sharing identical terms.

cycle
the pattern of expiration dates of options for a particular underlying stock. The three cycles occur in four-month intervals and are described by month abbreviations. They are (1) January, April, July, and October, or JAJO; (2) February, May, August, and November, or FMAN; and (3) March, June, September, and December, or MJSD.

last trading day
the Friday preceding the third Saturday of the expiration month of an option.

could be missed on an exceptionally busy Friday, so you need to ensure that your brokerage is going to be able to execute your trade under the rules.

The last-minute order that you place can be one of three types of transactions. It can be an order to buy a short position option to close it; an order to sell a long position option to close it; or an exercise order to buy or to sell 100 shares of stock for each option involved.

Example: You bought a call scheduled to expire in the month of July. Its expiration occurs on the third Saturday in that month. You need to place a sell order for the call or an order to exercise the call before expiration time on the preceding day (Friday), which is the last trading day prior to expiration. If you fail to place your order by that time, the option will expire worthless and you will receive no benefit.

With the crucial deadline in mind and the unknown potential for a busy Friday at your brokerage house—the trade can occur on the floor or over the Internet—you need to place that order with adequate time for execution. You can place the order far in advance with instructions to execute it by the end of business on Friday. If the brokerage accepts that order, then you will be protected if the brokerage fails to execute—as long as you placed the order well in advance of the deadline.

OPENING AND CLOSING OPTION TRADES

Every option trade you make must specify the four terms: striking price, expiration month, call or put, and underlying stock. If any of these terms changes, it represents an entirely different option.

There are two ways to open a position in an option: by buying and by selling. And there are three ways to close an option: by cancellation (selling a previously bought option or buying a previously sold option), by exercise, and by expiration.

Whenever you are holding an option, the status is called an *open position*. When you buy, it is described as an *opening purchase transaction*. And if you start out by selling an option, that is called an *opening sale transaction*.

expiration time
the latest possible time to place an order for cancellation or exercise of an option, which may vary depending on the brokerage firm executing the order and on the option itself.

open position
the status of a transaction when a purchase (a long position) or a sale (a short position) has been made, and before cancellation, exercise, or expiration.

opening purchase transaction
an initial transaction to buy, also known as the action of "going long."

opening sale transaction
an initial transaction to sell, also known as the action of "going short."

closing sale transaction
a transaction to close a long position, executed by selling an option previously bought, closing it out.

closing purchase transaction
a transaction to close a short position, executed by buying an option previously sold, canceling it out.

Example: You bought a call two months ago. When you entered your order, that was an opening purchase transaction. That status remains the same as long as you take no further action. The position will be closed when you enter a *closing sale transaction* to sell the call; or you may exercise the option. If you do not take either of these actions, the option will expire.

Example: You sold a call last month, placing yourself in a short position. As long as you take no further action, the position remains open. You can choose to wait out the expiration period, or you may execute a *closing purchase transaction* and cancel the option before expiration.

DEFINING POSSIBLE OUTCOMES OF CLOSING OPTIONS

Every option will be canceled by an offsetting closing transaction, by exercise, or by expiration. The results of each affect buyer and sellers in different ways.

Results for the Buyer

1. If you cancel your open long position with a closing sale transaction, you will receive payment. If the closing price is higher than the original purchase amount, you realize a profit; if lower, you suffer a loss.

2. If you exercise the option, you will receive 100 shares (if a call) or sell 100 shares (if a put) at the striking price. You will exercise only when that action is advantageous based on current market value of the underlying stock. To justify exercise, market value should be higher than the striking price (of a call) or lower than the striking price (of a put).

3. If you allow the option to expire, the entire amount of premium you paid at the time of purchase will be a complete loss.

Results for the Seller

1. If you cancel your open short position with a closing purchase transaction, you pay the premium, which is due on the business day following your order. If the price you pay to close is lower than the amount you received when you opened the position, you realize a profit; if it is higher, you suffer a loss.

2. If your option is exercised by the buyer, you are required to deliver 100 shares of the underlying stock at the specified striking price (of a call) or to purchase 100 shares of stock at the specified striking price (of a put).

3. If the option expires worthless, you earn a profit. Your open position is canceled through expiration, and the premium you received at the time that you sold the option is yours to keep.

These outcomes are summarized in Figure 2.1. Notice that buyers and sellers have opposite results for each outcome upon close. The investor who opened the position through buying receives payment upon sale; and the investor who opened the position through selling makes payment upon a later purchase. The buyer elects to exercise, whereas the seller has no choice as to the decision or timing of exercise. If the option expires

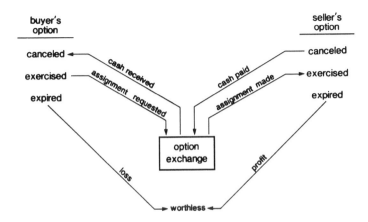

FIGURE 2.1 Outcomes of closing the position.

worthless, the buyer suffers a total loss, and the seller realizes a total profit.

Smart Investor Tip   Analysis of the possible outcomes is essential to identifying opportunities in the options market. Risk and opportunity evaluation is the key. Successful options traders need to be shrewd analysts.

EXERCISING THE OPTION

Option transactions occur through the exchange on which an option has been listed. While several different exchanges handle options trading, and electronic trading is becoming widespread on the Internet (especially in options), there is but one registered clearing agency for all listed option trades in the United States. The Options Clearing Corporation (OCC) has the broad responsibility for *orderly settlement* of all option contracts, which takes place through contact between brokerage houses and customers working with the exchange. Orderly settlement means, generally, that buyer and seller both trade in confidence knowing that they will be able to execute their orders when they want, finding a ready market and not having to worry about uncertainty. It also means that all terms of the contract are ironclad; exercise price, expiration date, and availability of shares upon exercise are all a part of the orderly settlement.

When a customer notifies a broker and places an order for execution of an option trade, the OCC ensures that the terms of the contract will be honored. Under this system, buyer and seller do not need to depend on the goodwill of one another; the transaction goes through the OCC, which relies on member brokerage firms to enforce *assignment*. Remember that buyers and sellers are not matched together one-on-one. A disparate number of open "buy" and "sell" options are likely to exist at any given time, so that exercise will be meted out either at random or first in, first out (FIFO) to options that are in the money—thus the term "assignment." Since buyers and sellers are not matched to one another as in other types of transactions, how does a seller know whether a specific option will be exercised? There is no way to

orderly settlement
the smooth process of buying and selling, in full confidence that the terms and conditions of options contracts will be honored in a timely manner.

assignment
the act of exercise against a seller, done on a random basis or in accordance with orderly procedures developed by the Options Clearing Corporation and brokerage firms.

know. If your sold option is in the money, exercise could occur at any time. It might not happen at all, or it might take place on the last trading day.

When exercise occurs long before expiration date, that exercise is assigned to any of the sellers with open positions in that option. This takes place either on a random basis or on the basis of first in, first out (the earliest sellers are the first ones exercised). Upon exercise, 100 shares *must* be delivered. The idea of *delivery* is in relation to the movement of 100 shares of stock from the seller of the option to the exercising buyer. The buyer makes payment and receives registration of the shares, and the seller receives payment and relinquishes ownership of the shares.

Smart Investor Tip The seller usually can avoid exercise through a series of steps—picking out-of-the-money options, taking short-term profits, and exchanging short-term options for longer-term ones.

delivery
the movement of stock ownership from one owner to another. (In the case of exercised options, shares are registered to the new owner upon receipt of payment.)

What happens if the seller does not deliver shares as demanded by the terms of the option contract? Remember that the OCC "facilitates" the market and enforces assignment. The buyer is given timely possession of 100 shares of stock, even when the seller is unwilling or unable to comply. The broker will deal with the seller by attaching other assets, as well as suspending the seller's trading privileges or taking other actions as necessary. The buyer would have no awareness of these problems in the event this occurs, because the problem is between the violating seller and the system of broker, exchange, and the OCC. So orderly settlement ensures that everyone trading in options in good faith experiences a smooth, dependable system in which terms of the option contract are honored automatically and without fail.

When a buyer decides to exercise an option, 100 shares are either purchased from ("called from") or sold to ("put to") the seller. When you have sold a call, exercise means your 100 shares could be called away and transferred to the buyer; and when you sell a put, exercise means that 100 shares of stock can be put to you upon exercise, meaning you are required to buy. The entire process of calling and putting shares of stock upon exercise is

conversion
the process of
moving assigned
stock from the
seller of a call
option or to the
seller of a put
option.

**called
away**
the result of hav-
ing stock
assigned. (Upon
exercise, 100
shares of the
seller's stock are
called away at
the striking
price.)

**early
exercise**
the act of exercis-
ing an option
prior to expira-
tion date.

broadly referred to as *conversion*. Stock is assigned at the time of exercise, a necessity because the number of buyers and sellers in a particular option will rarely, if ever, match. The assignment of a call option's exercise, by definition, means that 100 shares of stock are *called away*.

Is exercise always a negative to the seller? At first glance, it would appear that being exercised is undesirable, and it often is seen that way; many sellers take steps to minimize the risk of exercise, or to avoid it altogether. However, the question really depends on the seller's intentions at the time he or she entered the short position. For example, a seller might recognize that being exercised at a specific price is desirable, and will be willing to take exercise with the benefit of also keeping the premium as a profit.

Smart Investor Tip   Some sellers enter into a short position in the hope that exercise will occur, recognizing that (for call sellers) the combination of capital gain on the stock and option premium would represent a worthwhile profit.

It is logical that most sellers will close out their short positions or pick options the least likely to be exercised. Sellers have to be aware that exercise is one possible outcome and that it can occur at any time that the option is in the money. The majority of exercise actions are most likely to occur at or near expiration, so the risk of *early exercise* is minimal, although it can and does occur.

Exercise is not always generated by a buyer's action, either. The Options Clearing Corporation (OCC) can order an *automatic exercise* policy acting through the exchange. Remember, the exchange acts as buyer to every seller, and as seller to every buyer. Exercise orders will be assigned as they are made by owners of option contracts. But if, at the point of expiration, there are more open short positions than exercising long positions, those open short positions that are in the money will be exercised by the OCC.

The decision to avoid exercise is made based on current market value as well as the time remaining until expiration. Many option sellers spend a great deal of time and effort avoiding exercise and also trying to avoid taking losses in open option positions. A skilled options trader can achieve this by exchanging one option for another, and by timing actions to maximize deteriorating time value while still avoiding exercise. As long as options remain out of the money, there is no practical risk of exercise. But once that option goes in the money, sellers have to decide whether to risk exercise or cancel the position with an offsetting transaction.

Example: You bought 100 shares of stock several months ago for $57 per share, investing $5,700 plus transaction fees. The stock's market value is now $62 per share. At this time, you sell a call with a striking price of 60 ($60 per share), and are paid a premium of 7 ($700). You are willing to assume this short position. Your reasoning: If the call is exercised, your profit will be $1,000 before transaction fees. That would consist of 3 points ($3) per share of profit in the stock plus the $700 you were paid for selling the option.

Striking price	$60
Less: Your cost per share	−57
Stock profit	$ 3
Option premium	7
Total profit per share	$10

> **automatic exercise**
> action taken by the Options Clearing Corporation at the time of expiration, when an in-the-money option has not been otherwise exercised or canceled.

This example shows that it is possible for an investor to sell a call in the money, hoping for exercise. The key is in the profit made combining high option premium with a profit on the stock. The premium on the option effectively discounts your basis in the stock, so that exercise creates a nice profit.

Example: You recently sold a put and received a premium of 3 ($300). The striking price is 35. At the time of your transaction, the stock's market value was $33 per share. Even though the put is 2 points in the money, you are not concerned. If the put is exercised, you will be required to buy 100 shares at $35, 2 points higher than current market value. Three factors should be kept in mind in this situation: First, you received $300 for selling the put, so in the event of exercise your real basis would still be 1 point below current market value. Second, whenever you sell a put, it should include a belief on your part that the striking price represents a fair price for the stock. And third, if the stock's value rises above the striking price, the put will be out of the money and no exercise will occur.

Example: You have owned 100 shares of stock for many years, which you purchased originally for $48 per share. Current market value is $59 per share. You want to sell a call against the stock. Recognizing that current market value is $11 per share above your basis, you are willing to risk part of your profit in exchange for getting a call premium. You sell a call with a striking price of 55, which is 4 points in the money. You receive a premium of 6 ($600). In the event of exercise, you will gain $700 on the stock plus the option premium of $600, for a total profit of $1,300. The $600 premium includes 4 points of intrinsic value plus 2 points of time value. As a seller, time is on your side; so unless the option is exercised, time value will evaporate between purchase date and expiration date.

The decision to act or to wait depends on the amount of time value involved, and on the proximity of striking price to market value of the stock. As a general rule, the greater the time until expiration, the higher the time value will be; and the closer the striking price is to market value of the stock, the more important the time value becomes, both to buyer and to seller. For the buyer, time value is a cost, so the higher the amount paid for time value, the greater the risk. For the seller, the opposite is true. Buyers pay the time value, which can also be considered the amount above intrinsic value—the difference between the stock's *current market value* and the option's striking price—knowing that the time value will disappear by expiration. The seller picks options to sell with the same thing in mind, but recognizing that more time value means more potential profit.

current market value
the market value of stock at any given time.

Example: You have decided to buy a call with a striking price of 30. The underlying stock's current market value is $32 per share and the option premium is 5 ($500). Your premium includes 2 points of intrinsic value and 3 points of time value. If the stock's market value does not increase enough by expiration to offset your cost, then you will not be able to earn a profit. One of two things needs to happen in this situation: Either the stock's current market value needs to rise quickly so that your call premium will be greater than the 5 you paid, enabling you to sell the call at a profit, or the stock's market value has to rise enough points by expiration to offset time value (3 points) just to break even.

The previous example shows how option buyers need to evaluate risk. In this example, time value represents three-fifths of the total premium. If expiration comes up quickly, the stock will need to increase significantly in a short period of time to produce a profit. In thinking about whether it makes sense to buy such a call, some alternatives might also be considered, especially if you believe that the stock will rise in value. These include:

✔ Buy 100 shares of the stock. If you believe it has potential to increase in value, owning the shares without the built-in deadline of expiration makes ownership more desirable.

✔ Sell a put instead of buying a call. Put sellers have limited exposure compared to call sellers; and if the stock's market price rises, the entire premium will represent profit. Compared to buying a call, the selling of a put often is an overlooked strategy that could make a lot of sense.

A third opportunity could present itself in taking the opposite approach to buying. Given the previous example, in which significant increase in value would be required to make a profit, it might be an opportunity to sell a call instead of buying one—as long as you remember the relatively higher risks that are involved.

Example: Given the same circumstances as those in the previous example, you decide to *sell* a call instead of buying one. Instead of paying the $500 premium, you receive $500 as a seller. Of this, $300 represents time value, which now is an advantage rather than a problem. The looming expiration presents an advantage as well. The pending expiration places pressure for time value to evaporate, meaning greater profits for you as a seller. As long as the stock's current market value does not increase more than 3 points between now and expiration, the transaction will be profitable.

By the time of expiration, all of the time value will have disappeared from the premium value, and all remaining premium will represent intrinsic value only. This condition is known as *parity*.

parity
the condition of an option at expiration, when the total premium consists of intrinsic value and no time value.

USING THE DAILY OPTIONS LISTINGS

When you invest in shares of stock, a good deal of emphasis is placed on research and tracking *before* the investment has been made. Once you own the stock, you can afford to let matters take their own course; in other words, a well-selected stock will continue to grow, yield dividend income, and hold its price. With options, however, you need to be able to keep an eye on a quickly changing market on a daily basis. Both buyers and sellers have to watch the stock's price movement as well as reaction in the pricing of the option, so that they can take advantage of pricing opportunities when they appear. Quick action often is required because opportunities may appear and then disappear very suddenly. Open positions on both sides of the transaction have to be monitored continuously.

Online trading is a natural for options traders. The ability to monitor a changing market on the basis of only a 20-minute delay is a significant advantage over telephone calls to a broker, and for an extra charge you can get real-time quotations (or as close as possible to real time) online. The Internet is also likely to be far more responsive than a broker, who may be on another line, with another client, or away from the desk when you call. For an options trader, even a few minutes of inaccessibility can have the consequence of a lost opportunity.

In the past, options traders depended on alert brokers, hoping to be able to telephone them if price changes made decisions necessary. Some placed stop-limit orders, a cumbersome and limiting method for managing an options portfolio. And in the worst of all cases, some investors used to wait until the day after to review options listings in the newspaper. None of these antiquated methods are adequate for the modern options trader, who should be able to find a dependable online source for rapid options quotations.

Smart Investor Tip You can find brokerage sites that offer free daily options quotes by performing online searches. Two sites that have especially accessible quotation services are DLJ*direct* at www.dljdirect.com and E*Trade at www.e.trade.com.

Options traders have a great resource with the Internet. Before online access, the problem was chronic—the lack of fast, reliable, consistent, and *updated* information about rapidly changing option pricing. Not only should options investors work on their own through discount service brokers and without expensive and unneeded broker advice; they also need to be online to maximize their market advantage. Option pricing can change from minute to minute in many situations, and you need to be able to keep an eye on the market.

Whether you use an automated system or published options listings, you also need to learn how to read options listings. A typical daily options listing is summarized in Figure 2.2. The details of what this shows are:

> *First column:* The underlying stock and the current market value of the stock. In this example, Motorola closed at $37 per share.
>
> *Second column:* This shows the striking price for each available option. As a general rule, stocks valued at $100 or less will have options available at 5-point intervals, and stocks with market value above $100 at 10-point intervals.

		CALLS			PUTS		
		JAN	APR	JUL	JAN	APR	JUL
Motorola	25	12	14	17 1/2	1/16	—	—
37	30	7 1/2	8 3/8	9	—	1/8	—
37	35	2 5/8	5 1/8	7	3/8	2	3 1/2
37	40	1/8	1 1/2	—	3 1/4	5	—
37	45	—	—	—	8 1/2	11	14 1/8

FIGURE 2.2 Example of daily options listing.

> *Third, fourth, and fifth columns:* These report current premium levels for calls.
>
> *Sixth, seventh, and eighth columns:* These report current premium levels for puts.

In this example, Motorola is on the January, April, July, October (JAJO) cycle, so the January, April, and July monthly expiration dates are reported. Since options exist for only up to nine months or so, the furthest reported month in the cycle is not shown in this reporting format. In this illustration, no October calls or puts are shown; they will appear only after expiration of the January options. In some other reporting formats, it is possible that more options are reported.

Note that the illustration shows options in the eighth-of-a-point traditional format. This format applies to the majority of option and other listings as of publication of this edition; however, all exchanges in the United States are undergoing a conversion to decimalization, the reporting of all values in dollars and cents. The project is scheduled to be tested and completed before the year 2003.

The following table shows how fractional and decimal values are reported for stocks:

Fractional Value	*Decimal Value*
$15\frac{3}{8}$	15.375 (rounded to 15.38)
$22\frac{5}{16}$	22.3125 (rounded to 22.31)
$48\frac{3}{4}$	48.75

In the case of options, reported values are in hundredths of dollars rather than in dollars and cents, so decimalization does not apply in the same way. For example, an option premium of $\frac{1}{2}$ is equal to $50, and an option premium of $7\frac{1}{2}$ is equal to $775.

MAKING AN EVALUATION

As an options investor, you will need to make several judgment calls concerning both option and underlying stock, including how you should react to:

✔ Recent volatility and volume in the stock.

✔ Time until expiration of the option in light of current stock pricing.

✔ Relative levels of intrinsic value and time value.

✔ Current premium level and its effect on your profitability in the option.

Example: You are interested in buying calls on a particular stock. You recognize that some stocks undergo patterns of price movement that are desirable for particular option strategies. The subject stock currently is valued at $47 per share. You eliminate calls with striking prices of 35 and 40 as being too expensive; and the 55 striking price is 8 points in the money. Considering the element of time, you narrow down your practical choices to calls with striking prices of 45 or 50.

In this example, the 45 call is 2 points out of the money and the 50 call is 3 points in the money. The in-the-money call will move dollar for dollar with price movement in the stock and, because it contains $3 of intrinsic value, its value is far higher than that of the 45 call. Considering time until expiration along with these pricing concerns, you will be able to identify those options whose pricing and time make the most sense to you.

When time until expiration is short, the buyer has to consider the risk of buying any option. With little or no time value remaining, it will be necessary for the stock's price to change enough in a short period of time to produce a profit for the option investor. The decision is further complicated by the transaction cost on both sides of the transaction. You have to consider the degree of point change you need to produce a profit, allowing for the cost of the opening and closing orders, all within the time between opening transaction date and expiration.

These points make up the evaluation of options that every buyer and seller needs to go through. The same process of evaluation should be applied to puts, with varying levels of risk involved. In order to profit from investing in puts, buyers are hoping for an adequate downward price movement to offset time value and to surpass the premium cost at the time of purchase—

all before expiration. For put buyers, the desirable direction of price movement is downward.

For sellers of either calls or puts, the point of view about time is entirely different. Time is on the side of the seller. Sellers hope that time value evaporates rapidly and before price movement occurs in the stock toward the in-the-money position, which would increase intrinsic value. Motive and strategy for sellers are the reverse of those for buyers.

OPENING AND CLOSING STOCK TRADES

Many options investors are first attracted to the market because they already have invested in common stocks. In fact, a significant number of options investors use options in conjunction with stocks that they already own and trade. As you will see in coming chapters, speculation in short-term price movement is only one of many reasons for buying or selling options.

With the inescapable connection between stocks and options, you will be most likely to succeed in option trades when you have mastery over the methods of picking stocks. One of the most common criticisms of option trading is that it is too risky and speculative; in fact, skilled stock pickers tend to also do well in option trading.

Smart Investor Tip   Some investors make distinctions between stocks and options as though they were unrelated. The truth is, skilled options traders have first mastered the ability to pick the right stocks.

With that in mind, it makes sense to place a lot of emphasis on proper study and analysis of stocks. A detailed study of the methods involved in selecting and evaluating stocks is not the subject of this book. Every options investor should be comfortable with the rules, terminology, and risks of stock trading, and needs to have some experience with stocks before embarking on a serious options program. It is fair to say that a good knowledge of stock buying and selling will aid in proper understanding of options; the two are so closely related that they cannot really be considered separately.

Following is a summary of how stocks are listed in the financial pages, and what each segment means. This is a brief review of information that every stock trader should already know. The daily listing of a stock includes on a single line a great amount of detail used to judge the relative health and history of a stock's price and yield. A typical stock exchange listing looks like the following example (although this example shows fractional-style values, the exchanges are currently undergoing a transition to decimalization; in the near future, all listings will report values in dollars and cents):

37¼ 22½ Ronbar 1 3.0 6 234 33½ 33 33¼ –¼

The first two columns summarize the trading range for the past two months. During the past year, this stock traded between the high of 37¼ and the low of 22½. This trading range not only reveals where the stock's current price is in relation to its historical trading range; it also helps you to spot varying degrees of volatility in a stock. As a general rule, the broader the trading range, the greater the stock's volatility.

The fictitious stock is called Ronbar; listings provide full or abbreviated names for each company. The "1" in the next column tells you that Ronbar's regular dividend is $1 per share per year. If paid quarterly (the normal schedule), each share receives 25 cents in quarterly dividend. The next column shows dividend yield; in this case, it is 3.0%. That is calculated by dividing the dividend per share by the ending price per share (in this case, 33¼ as shown in the second-to-last column).

The next column shows "6." This is the price/earnings ratio, or the P/E ratio. More about this is presented in Chapter 6; for now, a brief explanation only: The P/E ratio is a factor resulting from dividing the current market price per share of the stock by the earnings per share of common stock. The P/E is used for comparative evaluation of stability and potential price appreciation.

Following this is a column containing the value 234. This is the volume of trading for the day. Since it represents equivalent round lots of stock traded, it means that 23,400 shares were traded in the stock.

The remaining columns deal with trading prices for

the day. First is the day's high, in this case 33½. Next is the day's lowest trading price, 33. The next column shows the closing price per share for the day, which was 33¼. Finally, the last column shows the net change in the stock's price. In this example, the stock was down ¼ from its previous day's level, or 25 cents per share.

Smart Investor Tip   It's a mistake to look only at the closing price and day-to-day price movement. Price is only one feature to a stock's financial health and market popularity. In fact, price by itself is relatively uninteresting once you see what else the daily listing contains.

Beyond the study of price per share and related material, stock market investors use much more—the various formulas and comparisons of fundamental and technical analysis. Our purpose here is to review the basics. Even if you are familiar with the abbreviated codes used in the stock market, a review is always worthwhile. In the options market, an additional series of codes and abbreviations has to be mastered.

UNDERSTANDING OPTION ABBREVIATIONS

Option values are expressed in abbreviated form, both in listings and in communications between brokers and customers. The value of an option contract has traditionally been expressed in fractional values, just like stocks, and, when the transition to decimalization has been completed, option trading will also be communicated in dollars and cents. Table 2.1 presents a brief view of fractions and decimal (dollar value) equivalents. Options usually trade in fractional values as low as ¹⁄₁₆ point, or $6.25 in decimal equivalent.

The abbreviated expressions in the options market go far beyond current premium. Both expiration month and striking price are expressed in shorthand form as well. For example, an October option with a striking price of 35 ($35 per share) is referred to as an Oct 35 option. And a January option with a 50 striking price is called a Jan 50. Like the premium value, striking price is expressed without dollar signs.

	TABLE 2.1	**Fractional Values**	
Fraction	Dollar Value	Fraction	Dollar Value
$1/16$	$ 6.25	$9/16$	$ 56.25
$1/8$	12.50	$5/8$	62.50
$3/16$	18.75	$11/16$	68.75
$1/4$	25.00	$3/4$	75.00
$5/16$	31.25	$13/16$	81.25
$3/8$	37.50	$7/8$	87.50
$7/16$	43.75	$15/16$	93.75
$1/2$	50.00	1	100.00

The complete option description must include all four terms plus value: underlying stock, expiration month, striking price, type of option (call or put), and current premium. A sample of this follows. Here, all of the required elements are expressed. The terms, remember, must all be present to distinguish one option from another. In this example, the single expression gives you the underlying stock, expiration month, striking price, type of option, and current premium:

Motorola Oct 35 Call at 3

When you call a broker on the telephone or sign onto a web site and place a trade, an additional coding system is used to specify the expiration month and striking price, and to distinguish calls from puts. This helps to avoid misunderstandings and to classify options properly. A large number of options can exist on a single stock, so the coding system used for trading purposes is very helpful and efficient. After trading options actively, you might memorize these codes; however, it also helps to make a chart and keep it handy for quick reference. Figure 2.3 summarizes the symbols used for buying and selling options. You will need these for typing in correct option designations online or, if you trade by telephone, for communication with a broker.

The expiration month is always expressed first (after the stock symbol), followed immediately by the striking price. Note that striking prices of 5, 105, and 205 have

expiration month symbols		
MONTH	**CALLS**	**PUTS**
January	A	M
February	B	N
March	C	O
April	D	P
May	E	Q
June	F	R
July	G	S
August	H	T
September	I	U
October	J	V
November	K	W
December	L	X

striking price symbols			
STRIKING	**PRICE**		**SYMBOL**
5	105	205	A
10	110	210	B
15	115	215	C
20	120	220	D
25	125	225	E
30	130	230	F
35	135	235	G
40	140	240	H
45	145	245	I
50	150	250	J
55	155	255	K
60	160	260	L
65	165	265	M
70	170	270	N
75	175	275	O
80	180	280	P
85	185	285	Q
90	190	290	R
95	195	295	S
100	200	300	T
7½	–	–	U
12½	–	–	V
17½	–	–	W
22½	–	–	X

FIGURE 2.3 Option trading symbols.

identical symbols. This works because the market value of the underlying stock quickly determines which range of pricing applies.

Example: You want to trade in calls with October expiration and 35 striking price. The symbols to use are "J" for striking price (October is the 10th month and "J" is the 10th letter) and "G" for the striking price. In this case, a call would have the designation JG. (A put would be coded as VG.)

As mentioned, the complete option quote starts with the abbreviated symbol for the underlying stock. Every listed stock on every stock exchange has a unique abbreviation that distinguishes it from all other listed stocks. Motorola, for example, is abbreviated MOT. So a Motorola option code consists of five letters. First is the stock code, followed by a period, and followed by the two-letter code indicating month and striking price. Distinction between call and put is part of the month code. A Motorola October call with a striking price of 35 is designated as:

MOT.JG

A put for the same striking price and month is designated as:

MOT.VG

Smart Investor Tip   If you know the name of the company but not its abbreviated symbol, most online sites offering free quotations also offer cross-reference services. One example is found at www.quote.com/quotecom; from this page, go to "symbol search" and type in the company name. This is also a free service.

SETTING STANDARDS

Before entering into any option trade, it is important to set standards for yourself. While this is good advice for all forms of investing, it is especially crucial to succeeding with options—if only because they exist for just a short period of time, so that you need to be decisive. The questions that come up for options standards should include:

✔ Should the position be closed or allowed to expire?

✔ On what basis should that decision be made? Should you set a minimum acceptable profit level you will take and a maximum loss you are willing to tolerate?

✔ What types of options should you buy, and for what purposes?

✔ How much money should you invest in options and keep at risk?

✔ What portion of your total portfolio should be dedicated to options?

✔ What specific risks are you willing and able to accept?

Setting standards helps you to decide what levels and types of risks are appropriate in your circumstances. This requirement applies at every phase of the investment process. Without having goals and investment standards, you would have no means for measuring your success (nor even for defining what constitutes success) or for gauging to what degree your strategies worked. Without these basic definitions, you would have no investment plan whatsoever. Identification of risk is crucial to all forms of options investing.

Smart Investor Tip   It is easy to see only the opportunities in specific option strategies. Remember that every opportunity is accompanied by a parallel risk; the degree of risk and of opportunity are related directly to one another.

Example: You purchased a call that expires in seven months. You paid 3 and have accepted the risk that the underlying stock's market value might not go in the money sufficiently to yield a profit. The risk of loss is limited to your investment of $300. However, you are willing to accept that risk in exchange for the opportunity for profit during the coming seven months.

The prospect that an option position will result in a profit needs to be a part of your goal. For that to occur, any position you open has to have a reasonable chance of being profitable. For example, it does not make sense for a buyer to expect to make a profit on time value alone; time value rarely increases.

As a buyer of a call, it is important to set what-if types of standards. For example, if you buy a call for 3, you have $300 at risk. When will you close out the position? You might set the standard that you will sell if and when the option's premium value gets to 5 or above; and that you will bail out if it falls to 1½ or below. This creates a profit of 67% or a loss of 50%. The same is true for sellers; no matter what side of the transaction you are on, you need to know how and when you will close out the position.

One of the greatest problems for option buyers is the

greed factor. If you have a poorly defined goal or no specific goal whatsoever, then you have no way to know whether to take action in response to changes in premium value.

Example: You own 100 shares of stock currently valued at $46 per share. You sell a call with a striking price of 45 and receive a premium of $400. You realize that if the call is exercised, your stock will be called away at $45 per share. The risk in this position is that the stock's market value might rise substantially above that level, and you will miss out on any profit from that rise. However, you are willing to accept that risk in exchange for the $400 premium.

In this example, you have set a standard. It states that you are willing to let your stock go at $45 per share in exchange for the option premium. You will accept exercise even if the stock's market value is far higher than $45 per share. You could set additional standards as well. For example, you could decide that if the option's premium value falls by 2 points, you will buy it and close the position, taking a $200 profit. This frees up the stock; in addition, you could later sell another call and repeat the transaction.
　　Consider what could happen if you do not set a standard. A pattern could develop in which you program yourself so that you can never win. This is a common problem for option buyers; rather than operating from well-defined standards and goals, some people cannot act decisively and take profits or cut losses when they should. This is a pattern worth avoiding.

Example: You bought a put two weeks ago, believing that the underlying stock's market value would fall. You paid a premium of 2. Originally, you hoped to double your money. If the stock fell below the striking price so that it was in the money, only a 2-point drop would be required to achieve this goal. As of last week, the stock's market value was 3 points below the striking price and the put was worth 5. You could have sold it and taken a profit of $300. But you hesitated, modifying your point of view in the belief that the stock might continue to fall, which would create even more profit in your put. Three days ago, the stock rebounded 2 points and the put was worth only 3. Yesterday, the stock again fell, down 4 points. The put was worth 7. You knew you should sell

and take your profit at that point, but again you specu-
lated that the stock might fall even farther. Today, the
stock rebounded several points and the put now is worth
1, half the price you paid.

Smart Investor Tip   The option trader's worst enemy is
indecision. Those who stick to their plan are likely to profit;
those without a plan have no idea when or how to decide.

This scenario is not at all uncommon. Many paper
profits are lost because investors overlook the necessity of
setting standards—rules for their own trading conduct—
or they fail to follow them once they have been set. When
a decision point arrives, you need to act without hesitation
and with confidence. With the option market changing
constantly and rapidly, time will continue passing, and will
not pause because investors cannot make up their minds.
You are better off losing future, unrealized profit potential
than you are losing money today. If you are willing to take
greater risks and pass up short-term profits, you also need
to be willing to experience more losses than are experienced by those who set and follow specific rules.

Smart Investor Tip   You are better off taking a certain
profit today than waiting for the possibility of higher profits later.

You can set and enforce your own standards by using
a *stop order*. This order is placed with your broker with the
provision that it is to be executed only if a specified price
has been reached. The stop order does not ensure that the
transaction will be completed at the specified price; that is
only the point at which the order gets placed. It could take
place above (for a buy order) if the trend is upward, or below (for a sell order) if the trend is downward. Once the
threshold price has been reached or passed, the order con-
verts to a *market order*, meaning an order to buy at the lowest available price or to sell at the highest available price.
The market order is the most common type of order. For
options buyers, the stop order can serve as a valuable tool
for preventing losses that otherwise could arise from hesitation. The order can be put into effect as a way of ensuring that you follow your own standards.

stop order
an order from an
investor to a
broker to buy at
or above a speci-
fied price, or to
sell at or below a
specified price
level. (Once that
level has been
met or passed,
the order
becomes a mar-
ket order.)

**market
order**
an order from an
investor to a
broker to buy or
sell at the best
available price.

Example: You bought a call last week for 6, in the belief that the stock's market value would rise. However, you are aware of the risk that the stock's market value could fall, meaning you would suffer an immediate loss of value in your call. So you place a stop order for 4. If the option's value falls to 4 points or below, a sale will be executed automatically and as soon as possible. This does not mean you are guaranteed to sell for 4; if the option's value falls rapidly, then the premium value could be lower than 4 at the time the order is executed.

Example: You buy a call for 4 and place a stop order at 3. Once the premium value falls to 3 or below, a sale will be executed automatically and as soon as possible. The actual price could be 3 or lower, depending on how rapidly the premium value of your option is declining.

You can also place an order specifying an exact price. This ensures that a transaction will take place only if that price is available. The problem here is that the specified price could be surpassed rapidly and might never be available again, so your order would not be executed at all. This type of order is called a *stop-limit order*. This is an instruction to the broker to execute a trade at a specified price, or within a specified price range. For example, you could specify that you want to sell an option after it has fallen to 4 or below, but not below 2.

Stop-limit orders are useful for both buy and sell transactions, and can be used to help you enforce your standards when you cannot keep an eye on the market from minute to minute. *A word of caution:* A specific exchange might not allow the use of stop orders for options trading, and the rules of one exchange do not always apply to another. Before devising a strategy including the use of specialized ordering, check with your broker and make sure that such orders are allowed on the exchange where the option is listed.

It is fair to say that the use of these devices makes it easier to enforce standards. But whether you use stop orders or not, you still need to set the standard before investing your money. Know when to close a position, whether you are ahead or behind, based entirely on the formula you develop *in advance*. Many investors try the options market; some succeed, whereas others fail. The

 stop-limit order

an order from an investor to a broker to buy or sell at a specified price (or within a specified range).

majority of those who fail did not establish standards ahead of time, so they had no way to know when they should close their open positions.

All investing contains an element of gambling. Proper research, understanding the attributes of a particular investment, knowing the risks, being aware of the importance of timing, and setting standards all add up to increased chances for success. The lack of these features virtually ensures failure.

Smart Investor Tip   Options investors need to know when to take profits. Of equal importance, they have to recognize when to wait patiently, and when to bail out. Like poker players, smart options traders know when to hold and when to fold.

CALCULATING THE RATE OF RETURN FOR SELLERS

rate of return
the yield from investing, calculated by dividing net cash profit upon sale by the amount spent at purchase.

Investors guide themselves and judge their success by their *rate of return*. In a single transaction involving one buy and one sell, rate of return is easily calculated. Simply divide the net profit (after trading fees) by the total purchase amount (including trading fees), and the resulting percentage is the rate of return. When you sell options, though, the rate of return is more complicated. The sale precedes the purchase, so rate of return is not as straightforward as it is in the more traditional investment.

Rate of return is normally applied in situations where a specific amount of money is placed into an investment, left there for a period of time, and then recovered through sale—in other words, the long position. Selling as a first step makes rate of return somewhat different. Option sellers have to consider the period that they are at risk—the time they are in a short position—as being equivalent to the long position, even though it really is not. However, this still provides a means for comparative analysis of a transaction, and you need to have a consistent method for measuring your success in the options market. Rates of return for sellers vary depending on four factors:

    1. Whether you own 100 shares of stock for each call sold.

2. The case when the option is exercised.

3. The decision to buy the option and close the position, rather than waiting for expiration.

4. Significant changes in the stock's market value during the period you have the open short position.

Rate of return can only be looked at in comparative form. In other words, comparing one short position outcome to another, given dissimilar holding periods, makes the comparison invalid. The calculation should be adjusted so that all short position outcomes are reviewed and compared on an *annualized basis*. Because different lengths of time can be involved in a short position—from a few hours up to several months—it is not realistic to compare calculated rates of return without making the adjustment. A 50% return in two months is far more significant than the same rate of return held for 10 months.

To annualize a rate of return, follow these steps:

1. Calculate the rate of return by dividing the net profit by the amount of purchase.

2. Divide the rate of return by the number of months the investment position was open.

3. Multiply the result by 12 (months in a year).

Example: You realize a net profit of 12% on an investment. The annualized rate of return will vary depending on the holding period:

1. *Three months:*
   Net profit = 12
   Holding period = 3
   12 ÷ 3 = 4
   4 × 12 = 48%

2. *Eight months:*
   Net profit = 12
   Holding period = 8
   12 ÷ 8 = 1.5
   1.5 × 12 = 18%

3. *Fifteen months:*
   Net profit = 12
   Holding period = 15

annualized basis
a method for comparing rates of return for holdings of varying periods, in which all returns are expressed as though investments had been held over a full year. (It involves dividing the holding period by the number of months the positions were open, and multiplying the result by 12.)

$$12 \div 15 = 0.8$$
$$0.8 \times 12 = 9.6\%$$

As these examples demonstrate, annualized rate of return differs dramatically depending on the period the position remains open. Annualizing applies for periods above one year, as in example number 3, as well as for shorter periods. A short period is properly extended though annualizing, just as a period beyond one year should be contracted to reflect rate of return as though the investment were held for exactly 12 months. By making all returns comparable, it becomes possible to study the outcomes realistically.

Annualized rate of return can be calculated using days instead of months. For options, this might be a more practical method, since many positions might be open only a matter of days. For simplicity in calculation, you might consider using a 360-day year and a 30-day month for calculating annualized rate of return. This is more easily calculated, and it will not change the outcome significantly. The other method, the exact days method, involves counting the number of days and using a 365-day multiplier.

Under the 360-day method, the rate of return is divided by the number of days held (a full month is always counted as 30 days), and the result is then multiplied by 360.

No matter which method you use, when you have a position open for a very brief period of time the annualized rate of return does not tell the whole story; such a comparison is unrealistic when an option position is open for only a few days. The annualized return can be hundreds of percentage points; but because the period at risk is minimal, it is not truly comparable to a longer-term holding period.

Example: You recently sold a call at 3 and, only two weeks later, closed the position by buying at 1. The profit, $200, is 4,800% on an annualized basis. This is impressive, but it is of little use in your comparative analysis. Not only is it untypical of the returns you earn from option trading; it also reflects an exceptionally brief period that you were at risk. For analytical purposes, this rate of return has to be ignored.

The nature of option investing makes annualized basis a useful tool for the study of typical transactions, but not for each and every individual transaction. Typically, options traders are involved in numerous transactions each year, often dozens per month. This activity might involve both long and short positions using several dissimilar strategies. One particular strategy might require a longer holding period to produce a satisfactory result, and another could involve a faster turnaround. Annualized basis is useful for tracking returns over a period of time, not only to compare percentage returns between transactions, but also to recognize the trend toward a more typical rate of return for a particular strategy.

Smart Investor Tip Annualized basis is helpful in judging the success of a series of transactions employing a particular strategy. It is less useful in looking at individual outcomes, especially those with very short holding periods.

One of the many factors that could distort short-term returns involves the use of funds in between transactions. For example, you might earn a large percentage return on one trade, and then leave the capital idle for several months; that certainly changes the outcome. In addition, short sale rates of return are not so much a study of return on capital invested as they are a calculation of return for exposing yourself to a specific risk and for a particular length of time. Remembering this distinction might help make the analysis more meaningful.

The study and comparison of rates of return should take into account the nature of the strategy involved; otherwise, the comparison has no real analytical value. The purpose in tracking option-related rates of return is not to assess your overall portfolio return, but to monitor your success in a particular strategy using options.

When you sell calls against stock you own, you need to adjust the comparative analysis to study the possible outcome based on two possible events. The first is called *return if exercised*. This is the rate of return you will earn if the call you have sold is exercised and 100 shares of stock are called away. It includes both the profit on your option and profit or loss on the stock, as well as any dividends you received during the period you owned the stock.

return if exercised
the estimated rate of return option sellers will earn in the event the buyer exercises the option. (The calculation includes profit or loss in the underlying stock, dividends earned, and premium received for selling the option.)

return if unchanged
the estimated rate of return option sellers will earn in the event the buyer does not exercise the option. (The calculation includes dividends earned on the underlying stock, and the premium received for selling the option.)

The second calculation is called *return if unchanged.* This is a calculation of the return to be realized if the stock is not called away, and the option is allowed to expire worthless (or it is closed out through a closing purchase transaction).

In both types of return, the calculations take into account all forms of income. The major difference between the two rates has to do with profit or loss on the underlying stock. These factors complicate the previous observation that comparisons should be made on an annualized basis. It is extremely difficult to account for each dividend payment, especially if the stock has been held over many years. In addition, how do you account for the return on stock held but not sold? There is a valid "return" involved in the paper profit, and the stock's market value affects option return directly, but this is not a legitimate return because the profit has not been realized.

Both of these analytical tools do not lend themselves to annualized return. That is a good tool for the study of relatively simple transactions involving only one source of income. The return if exercised and return if unchanged are far more valuable as a method for determining *in advance* the wisdom of a decision to sell a call before actually taking that step. By comparing these potential rates of return, you can determine which options are more likely to yield profits adequate to justify tying up 100 shares of stock with a short call position.

The actual steps involved in calculation should always be net of brokerage fees, both for sale and purchase. Remember that no attempt should be made to make comparisons on an annualized basis, however, because a complex transaction with differing types of profit generated over different lengths of time makes annualized return inappropriate. While the following examples use single-option contracts, in practice options traders often use multiple options and involve more than 100 shares of stock.

Example: You own 100 shares of stock that you purchased originally at $58 per share. Current market value is $63 per share. You sell a call with a striking price of 60 and receive a premium of 7. Between the date the option is sold and expiration, you also receive two dividend payments, totaling $68.

Return If Exercised

Striking price	$6,000
Less: Original cost of stock	−5,800
Profit on stock	$ 200
Dividends received	68
Call premium received	700
Total profit	$ 968

Return if exercised: $968 ÷ $5,800 = 16.69%

Return If Unchanged

Call premium received	$ 700
Dividends received	68
Total profit	$ 768

Return if unchanged: $768 ÷ $5,800 = 13.24%

Annualizing these returns is not recommended because the transactions involve three different time periods: stock holding period, dividend income, and short position in the call. In addition, the purpose here is not to compare results after the transaction has been completed, but to make a comparison in advance to determine whether the transaction would be worthwhile.

Another reason that annualizing would not make sense is that the two outcomes are not truly comparable. One assumes the required sale of 100 shares of stock and the other does not. So if the option is not exercised, you continue to own the stock with a paper (unrealized) profit. You are free to repeat the call sale again after expiration. But if the stock is called away, that is the end of the transaction. Too many factors make these returns incomparable.

Smart Investor Tip   The purpose in comparing returns on option selling is not to decide which outcome is more desirable, but to decide whether to enter into the transaction in the first place.

Once an option has been exercised, you have to deal with another problem. When you sell your 100 shares of stock through exercise, you receive a sum of cash that needs to be invested again. Depending on timing and market conditions, exercise could create problems for you that are not anticipated in the purely mathematical analysis of the option trade. Timing is all-important in the market, and it might not be a good time to place money in the market. In the example used previously, the 100 shares of stock had been purchased below the subject striking price, so that exercise produced a profit. You now have to pick a new stock to buy that you believe will increase in value, a difficult task if you think that stocks currently are overvalued.

This is one of the risks faced not only by options traders but by all investors. Whenever you sell stock, voluntarily or through exercise of an option, you then need to decide what to do with the resulting funds. Every options trader needs to calculate not only possible rates of return, but risks as well. You might determine that, given current market conditions, the timing is not appropriate for selling calls against 100 shares of stock. This is especially true if you do not want to have those shares called away. In addition to establishing minimum acceptable rates of return on all forms of trading, the timing of a decision should also affect you. Consider also whether you want to take profits before year-end with income tax consequences in mind. You might want to select options expiring after the beginning of the New Year if you need to defer profits this year.

Succeeding in options trading means entering open positions with complete awareness of all possible outcomes and their consequences or benefits. You need to know when it makes sense to close out a position with a closing transaction, whether to take profits or to avoid exercise; or just wait for expiration. You also need to be aware of market conditions and the timing of options trades, as well as the relative degree of risk to which you are exposed by entering into open options positions. Knowledge about potential profit is only part of a more complex picture. The more you study options and participate in the market, the more skill you develop in making an overall assessment and comparison.

Buying Calls

When written in Chinese, the word crisis *is composed of two characters.*
One represents danger and the other represents opportunity.
                                    —John F. Kennedy, speech, April 12, 1959

I f you embark upon a program of buying calls, you enter upon a highly speculative course. Since time
works against you, substantial change in the underlying stock is required in order to produce a profit. Remember, a call grants the *buyer* the right to purchase 100
shares of the underlying stock, at an established striking
price per share, and before a firm expiration date in the
near-term future. The buyer acquires that right in exchange for paying a premium. As a call buyer, you will
choose one of three alternatives: You can either sell the
call before it expires, exercise the call and purchase 100
shares of the underlying stock, or allow the call to expire
worthless.

As a call buyer, you are never obligated to buy 100
shares. In comparison, the seller *must* deliver 100 shares
to the buyer upon exercise of a call. The buyer has the
right to determine which of the three outcomes will occur. The decision depends on:

✔ Price movement of the underlying stock and the
resulting effect on the call's premium value.

✔ Your reasons for buying the call in the first place, and how related strategies are affected through ownership of the call.

✔ Your risk posture and willingness to wait for future price movement of both the stock and the call, as opposed to taking a profit or cutting a loss today (this is where setting and following standards comes into play).

UNDERSTANDING THE LIMITED LIFE OF THE CALL

You can become a call buyer simply for the potential profit you could earn within a limited period of time. That profit will be realized if the premium value increases, so that the call can be sold for more than it cost; or by exercising the call and buying 100 shares of stock below current market value. The call also can be used to offset losses in a short position held in the underlying stock. These uses of calls are explored in more detail later in this chapter.

Every investor experiences risk in many forms, but risks for buyers are not the same as those for sellers; in fact, they often are the exact opposite. Before becoming an options buyer, examine all of the risks and become familiar with potential losses as well as potential gains. Since the purchased option exists for a very limited time, you need to achieve your objective quickly. Time value evaporates with ever-increasing speed, and that is a significant factor that should affect your decision about *when* to close out your long position in the option. Because time value disappears by the point of expiration, the time factor should dictate which options you can afford to buy. More time value usually means both more time until expiration and more price movement you need to make a profit.

Smart Investor Tip   The passage of time works against you as a buyer, so the more time value in the option you buy, the more difficult it will be to make a profit.

Anyone who has purchased stock knows that time is a luxury. In fact, market wisdom dictates that the wise investor knows how to be patient. It takes time for stock

speculation
the use of money to assume risks for short-term profit, in the knowledge that substantial or total losses are one possible outcome. (Buying calls for leverage is one form of speculation. The buyer may earn a very large profit in a matter of days, or could lose the entire amount invested.)

prices to move, and to the inexperienced investor, nothing happens quickly enough. Stockholders who look for long-term growth settle for very small price increases each year, but collectively this adds up to a good return on the investment. The stockholder decides when or if to sell, and can time that decision based on personal requirements, stock price movement, and tax considerations. Call buyers, however, cannot afford to wait too long. To the stockholder, time means long-term profit. To the call buyer, time is the enemy.

A simple comparison between purchasing stock as a long-term investment and purchasing calls for short-term profit points out the difference between investment and *speculation*. Typically, speculators accept the risk of loss in exchange for the potential for profit, and they take their positions in short-term instruments such as options for the exposure to that potential. Because a relatively small amount of money can be used to tie up 100 shares of stock, call buying is one form of *leverage*, a popular strategy for making investment capital go further. Of course, the greater the degree of leverage, the greater the associated risk.

One of the most popular forms of leverage is borrowing money to invest. For example, if you purchase stocks on margin, you are using leverage; you can purchase more stock than you could by paying cash, so you borrow money from the brokerage firm. Another form of leverage is buying options. Because options are only rights and do not contain any tangible value, and because they exist for only a limited period of time, they are a form of side bet in the market. The call buyer is betting that a stock's market value will rise, and a call seller is betting that the market value will fall. Fast—and significant—profits or losses can be realized by call buyers, and knowing the extent of potential profit or loss is the key to success in this fast-moving strategy.

Knowing exactly what you are getting into, determining the best strategy, and full comprehension of risk add up to the definition of your own *suitability* for a particular investment or strategy. Suitability identifies what is appropriate, given your income, sophistication, understanding of markets and risks, and capital resources. All too often, investors understand the profit potential of a strategy, but not the full extent of risk.

leverage
the use of investment capital in a way that a relatively small amount of money enables the investor to control a relatively large value. (This is achieved through borrowing—for example, using borrowed money to purchase stocks or bonds—or through the purchase of options, which exist for only a short period of time but enable the option buyer to control 100 shares of stock. As a general rule, the use of leverage increases potential for profit as well as for loss.)

suitability
a standard by which a particular investment or market strategy is judged. (The investor's knowledge and experience with options represent important suitability standards. Strategies are appropriate only if the investor understands the market and can afford to take the risks involved.)

Example: An investor has no experience in the market, having never owned stock; he also does not understand how the market works. He has $1,000 available to invest today, and decides that he wants to earn a profit as quickly as possible. A friend told him that big profits can be made buying calls. He wants to buy three calls at 3 each, requiring $900 plus trading fees. He expects to double his money within one month.

This investor would not meet the minimum suitability standards for buying calls. He does not understand the market, know the risks, or comprehend the workings of options. He probably does not know anything about time value and the chance of the option going down in value. He is aware only of the profit potential, based solely on information he received from a friend. In this situation, the broker is responsible for recognizing that option buying would not be appropriate. One of the broker's duties is to ensure that investors know what they are doing and understand all of the risks. The broker should discourage this investor from buying calls and advise him to first read up on options to understand them fully. Given the circumstances, the broker's duty is to refuse to execute the transaction.

Call buyers who succeed develop a sense of timing in the market. However, that sense comes from experience and observation, and from seeing how a particular underlying stock moves over time. The price cycle for one stock could be unique, and there is no guarantee that past performance indicates future price movement. Still, some stocks reveal somewhat predictable short-term cyclical patterns, and the astute investor can time option trades based on the observation of these patterns. Timing is critical in both the timing of the transaction *and* the time remaining until the call's expiration. Risk levels are affected by time. The greater the time until expiration, the higher the time value will be—also meaning the more price movement that will be needed to produce the needed profit. So risk levels can vary by underlying stock in addition to option features, a fact that a novice is likely to miss completely.

Example: An investor with several years of experience in the stock market has never been involved with options. However, she has read about options extensively, has learned the terminology, and has studied the OCC prospectus. She has also learned how to read the financial press options listings. In tracking some hypothetical options positions over the past three months, she has begun to recognize some patterns in price changes. She owns a portfolio of diversified stocks and shares of a growth mutual fund, plus about $1,000 in cash. She wants to buy three calls at 3, costing $900 plus trading fees. She knows the potential for gain *and* loss.

This situation is far different that the one in the previous example. This investor understands the market; she can afford to place the $1,000 at risk; and she has studied the market to the extent that it is familiar to her. She knows that the potential for profit is accompanied by the potential for loss. Even though she has no experience with options trading, an initial foray into the options market is suitable, given her study of the market. Her decision will be an informed decision. A broker probably would accept her trade, although at this point more advanced strategies and risk positions would not be suitable.

Suitability refers not only to your ability to afford losses, but also to your understanding of the many forms of risk in the options market. If the investor in the second example worked with an experienced broker at the outset, it would also make sense to listen to that broker's advice about a proposed option position. Every would-be options investor should recognize that not every broker understands options, and the less knowledgeable ones might have a bias against that market. So an unexplained rejection of a proposed strategy could indicate the broker's lack of knowledge rather than an informed position. Make sure a broker knows *more* than you do about options before taking his or her advice.

JUDGING THE CALL

Most call buyers lose money, even with thorough understanding of the market and trading experience; this fact cannot be overlooked. In many situations, an underlying stock's value rises, but not enough to offset the declining time value in the option's premium. So if the stock rises, but not enough, then the call buyer will not be able to earn a profit.

Example: You recently bought a call for 4 with a striking price of 45, when it was at the money (the current market value of the underlying stock was identical to the call's striking price). By expiration, the stock had risen to $47 per share, but the call was worth only 2. Why? The entire $400 premium originally paid consisted of time value; it contained no intrinsic value. The time value was gone by expiration. The $200 value at closing represents the $2 of intrinsic value gained when the stock's price rose. In this case, the best action would be to sell the call and get half your money back. Another alternative is to allow the call to expire and lose the entire $400. Finally, you can exercise the call and buy shares below current market value.

It is a mistake to assume that a call's premium value will rise with the stock in every case, even when in the money. The time value declines as expiration nears, so a rise in the option's premium is seen only when intrinsic value rises to a greater extent. It is likely that even a rising stock price will not reflect dollar-for-dollar gains in the option until the time value has been used up.

Smart Investor Tip   The increase in premium value of an in-the-money option takes place only in intrinsic value. Time value has to be absorbed, too, and as expiration approaches, time value evaporates with increasing speed.

This means that if you buy a call with several dollars of time value, you cannot earn a profit unless the stock rises enough to (1) offset the time value premium, and (2) create enough growth above striking price. This double requirement is easy to overlook, but worth remembering.

Example: You bought a call two months ago and paid 1. At the time, the stock was 7 points out of the money. Now expiration date has arrived. The stock's market value has increased an impressive 6 points. The call is still 1 point out of the money, however, even though the underlying stock has increased 6 points. Thus the option is worthless because, with expiration pending, there is no intrinsic value.

Call buyers will lose money if they fail to calculate how much the underlying stock must increase in value. A mere increase of some kind is not enough if time value needs to be offset as well. For this reason, the call buyer needs to establish a bailout point, so that losses can be minimized when the situation appears hopeless. This is as important as knowing when to take profits. Today's momentary profit will disappear quickly if time value remains in the call, and the opportunity might not repeat itself.

Smart Investor Tip Knowing when to take a profit is only a part of the option trader's goal. It is equally important to know when to take a loss.

Example: You are the type of investor who believes in setting goals for yourself. So when you bought a call at 4, you promised yourself you would sell if the premium value fell to 2 or rose to 7. These standards would reduce the loss in the event that the transaction declines in value, while also providing a point at which the profit would be realized. You recognize that when it comes to options, time is the enemy and an opportunity might not return. Option buyers often do not get a second chance.

Goal-setting is important because *realized profits* can occur only when you actually close the position. For buyers, that means executing a closing sale or exercising; and for sellers, it requires an offsetting closing purchase. As an options trader, you need to set a standard and then stick to it. Otherwise, you can only watch the potential for realized profits come and go. Your *paper profits* (also known as unrealized profits) would end up as losses.

Most call buyers study four attributes: current premium value, the portion representing time value, time until expiration, and perception of the underlying stock (including the price proximity to striking price). For example, you might look through listings in the financial press seeking a call that can be bought at 2 or less that is in the money or close to it, with at least three months until expiration. Furthermore, you limit your search to options on a specific list of stocks you consider to be strong prospects for short-term price appreciation. This method encompasses all of the attributes, but it is

 realized profits
profits taken at the time a position is closed.

 paper profits (also called **unrealized profits**)
values existing only on paper but not taken at the time; paper profits (or paper losses) become realized only if a closing transaction is executed.

flawed. The lowest premiums do not necessarily represent the best values.

Bargain options are identified by all of the circumstances, but limiting the search to premiums of 2 or less might be unrealistic. For example, let's say the striking price of one call option is 40 and the stock is worth $35 on the market. In this case, at 5 points out of the money, you can expect a six-month option to be a low-priced bargain. Of course, with 5 points to go just to reach striking price, the stock will have to grow significantly by expiration.

The real bargain depends on the immediate circumstances. However, time to go until expiration, combined with the distance between current market value of the stock and striking price, together determine what is a bargain more than does the premium of the call.

Trading on time value is a very poor strategy, doomed from the start. It is possible for time value to increase, but that is rare. It is more likely that an out-of-the-money option will be unresponsive to price movement in the underlying stock, as long as the stock's price remains below striking price. So if striking price is 40 and the stock is trading between $34 and $39 per share, don't expect time value to grow as the stock's price rises. While price changes are taking place, time is passing; and that means a decline in the premium value.

Example: You bought a call with a striking price of 40 and paid a premium of 1. The call expires in seven months, which is a lot of time for the stock's price to move. The stock's market value is $34 per share, 6 points below striking price. In order for you to break even, the stock's price needs to rise 7 points (before considering trading costs), to $41 per share.

In this example, time passing works against you as a buyer. If you review only the relationship between the option's premium and time until expiration, it is easy to mislead yourself. It might seem reasonable that there is plenty of time to create a profit, but in fact if a large gap exists between the stock's market value and the striking price, then your expectations could be unrealistic.

If you buy a call and the stock experiences an unexpected jump in market value, it is possible that the time value will increase as well; but this will be temporary. The wider your out-of-the-money range, the slimmer your chances for realizing a profit. Remember that the real leverage value of options takes place when the option is in the money. Then the intrinsic value changes point-for-point with the stock price. As shown in Figure 3.1, whenever a stock is 5 points or more below the call's striking price, it is described as being *deep out* of the money. (For puts to be deep out of the money the number of points is the same, but the stock's market value would be 5 points or more *above* striking price.) If the stock's market value is 5 points or more above striking price of a call, it is said to be *deep in* the money.

These definitions are important to call buyers. A deep out-of-the-money option, because it requires significant price movement just to get to a breakeven point, is a long shot; and a deep in-the-money call is going to demand at least 5 points of premium just for intrinsic value, in addition to its time value. So the majority of calls bought are within the five-point range on either side of the striking price.

 deep out
condition when the underlying stock's current market value is 5 points or more below the striking price of the call or above the striking price of the put.

 deep in
condition when the underlying stock's current market value is 5 points or more above the striking price of the call or below the striking price of the put.

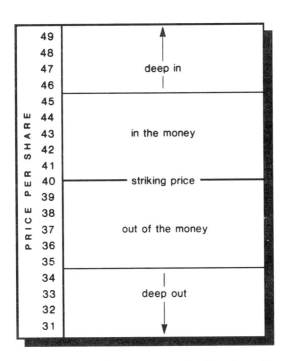

FIGURE 3.1 Deep in/deep out stock prices for calls.

CALL BUYING STRATEGIES

Most people think of buying call options as purely a speculative activity. If the stock's market value increases, you make a profit; if it falls, you lose. While there is an element of truth in this observation, it is far from the entire picture. As you saw in the previous section, it is not enough for the stock's price to rise. That does not ensure a profit, given the nature of time value. And while movement in the underlying stock's market value is essential to the call buyer, movement alone does not ensure that the option premium will move as well. It is only when the call is in the money that the premium values begin to change in important ways. Calls can also be used, though, for reasons beyond mere speculation.

Strategy 1: Calls for Leverage

Leverage, you recall, is using a small amount of capital to control a larger investment. While the term usually is applied to borrowing money to invest, it also perfectly describes call buying. For a few hundred dollars placed at risk, you control 100 shares of stock. By "control" we mean that the option buyer has the right to buy the 100 shares at any time prior to expiration, with the price frozen by contract. Leverage is a common and popular reason for buying calls. It enables you to establish the potential for profit with a limited amount of at-risk capital. This is why so many call buyers willingly assume the risks, even knowing that the odds of making money on the call itself are against them.

Example: You are familiar with a pharmaceutical company's management, profit history, and product line. The company has recently announced that it has received approval for the release of a new drug. The release date is three months away. However, the market has not yet responded to the news. You expect that the stock's market price will rise substantially once the market realizes the significance of the new drug. But you are not sure. By buying a call with six months until expiration, you expose yourself to a limited risk; but the opportunity for gain is also worth that risk, in your opinion. In this case, you have not risked the price of 100 shares, only the relatively small cost of the option.

Profits can take place rapidly in an option's value. In the example just given, if the price of the stock were to take off, you would have a choice: You could either sell the call at a profit or exercise it and pick up 100 shares at a fixed price below market value. That is a wise use of leverage, given the circumstances described.

Things can change quickly. This can be demonstrated by comparing the risks between the purchase of 100 shares of stock versus the purchase of a call that will expire in four months. (See Figure 3.2.) In this example, the stock was selling at $62 per share. You could invest $6,200 and buy 100 shares, or you could purchase a 60 call at 5 and invest only $500. The premium consists of 2 points of intrinsic value and 3 points of time value.

If you buy 100 shares, you are required to pay for the purchase within three business days. If you buy the call, you make payment the following day. The payment deadline for any transaction is called the *settlement date.*

As a call buyer, your plan may be to sell the call prior to expiration. Most call buyers are speculating on price movement in the underlying stock and do not intend to actually exercise the call; rather, their plan is to sell the call at a

 settlement date the date on which a buyer is required to pay for purchases, or on which a seller is entitled to receive payment. (For stocks, settlement date is three business days after the transaction. For options, settlement date is one business day from the date of the transaction.)

	STOCK (1)		CALL (2)	
	PROFIT OR LOSS	RATE OF RETURN	PROFIT OR LOSS	RATE OF RETURN
price increase of 5 points	$500	8.1%	$500	100%
price increase of 1 point	$100	1.6%	$100	20%
no price change	0	0	0	0
price decrease of 1 point	-$100	-1.6%	-$100	-20%
price decrease of 5 points	-$500	-8.1%	-$500	-100%

(1) purchased at $62 per share ($6200)
(2) striking price 60, premium 5 ($500)

FIGURE 3.2 Rate of return: buying stocks versus calls.

profit. In the example, a $500 investment gives you control over 100 shares of stock. That's leverage. You do not need to invest and place at risk $6,200 to gain that control. (The stock buyer, though, is entitled to receive dividends and does not have to work against the time deadline.) Without considering trading costs associated with buying and selling calls, what might happen in the immediate future?

If the stock were to rise 5 points in market value, the stockholder's $500 profit would represent an 8.1% return. Because the option premium will rise dollar for dollar (considering intrinsic value only) the call buyer realizes a 100% return in the same situation. (This could be modified by declining time value, if applicable. In other words, the rise of 5 points could be offset by a loss in some or all of the 3 points of time value premium.) Conceivably, if the 5-point gain occurred only at the point of expiration, it would translate to only a 2-point net gain:

Original cost	$500
Less: Evaporated time value	−300
Original intrinsic value	$200
Plus: Increased intrinsic value	500
Value at expiration	$700
Profit	$200

A point-for-point change in option premium value would be substantial. An in-the-money increase of 1 point yields 1.6% to the stockholder in this example, but a full 20% to the option buyer. If there were no price change between purchase and expiration, three-fifths of the option premium would evaporate due to the disappearance of time value. The call buyer risks losses in this situation even without a change in the stock's market value.

As a call buyer, you are under pressure of time for two reasons. First, the option will expire at a specified date in the future. Second, as expiration approaches, the rate of decline in time value increases, making it even more difficult for options traders to get to even or profit status as expiration nears. At that point, increase in market value of the underlying stock will not be sufficient. The increase must be adequate to offset time value *and* to yield a profit above striking price in excess of the premium price you paid.

It is possible to buy calls with little or no time value. To do so, you will have to select calls that are relatively close to expiration, so that only a short time remains for the stock's value to increase. The short time period increases risk in one respect; the lack of time value reduces risk in another respect.

Example: In the second week of May, the May 50 call is selling for 2, and the underlying stock is worth $51\frac{1}{2}$ ($1\frac{1}{2}$ points in the money). You buy one call. By the third Friday (the following week), you are hoping for an increase in the market value of the underlying stock. If the stock were to rise 1 point, the option would be minimally profitable. With only $\frac{1}{2}$ point time value, just a small amount of price movement is required to offset time value and produce in-the-money profits (before considering trading fees). Because time is short, your chances for realizing a profit are limited. But profits—if they do materialize—will be very close to a dollar-for-dollar movement with the stock, given the small amount of time value remaining. If the stock were to increase 3 points, you could double your money in a day or two. And, of course, were the stock to drop 2 points or more, the option would become worthless.

Smart Investor Tip Short-term call buyers hope for price movement, and they need only a few points. The risk, of course, is that price movement could go in the wrong direction.

The greater the time until expiration, the greater the time value premium—and the greater the increase you will require in the market value of the underlying stock just to maintain the call's value. For the buyer, the interaction between time and time value is the key. This is summarized in Figure 3.3.

Example: You buy a call at 5 when the stock's market value is at or near the striking price of 30. Your advantage is that you have eight months until expiration. For six

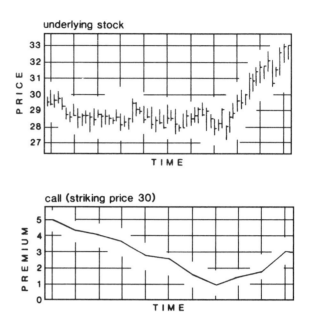

FIGURE 3.3 Diminishing time value of the call relative to the underlying stock.

months, the underlying stock's market value remains fairly close to the striking price, and the option's premium value—all or most of it time value—declines over the same period. Then the stock's market value increases to $33 per share. However, because most of the time value has disappeared, the call is worth only 3, the intrinsic value. You have lost $200.

Buying calls is one form of leverage—controlling 100 shares of stock for a relatively small investment of capital—and it offers the potential for substantial gain (or loss). But because time value is invariably a factor, the requirements for a successful experience are high. Even with the best timing and analysis of the option and the underlying stock, it is very difficult to earn profits consistently by buying calls.

Strategy 2: Limiting Risks

In one respect, the relatively small investment of capital required to buy a call reduces your risk. A stockholder stands to lose a lot more if and when the market value of the stock declines.

Example: You bought a call two months ago for a premium of 5. It expires later this month and is worth nearly nothing, since the stock's market value has fallen 12 points, well below striking price. You will lose your $500 investment or most of it, whereas a stockholder would have lost $1,200 in the same situation. You control the same number of shares for less exposure to risk, and for a smaller capital investment. Your loss is always limited to the amount of call premium paid. (This comparison is not entirely valid, however, in that the stockholder receives dividends, if paid, and has the luxury of being able to hold stock indefinitely. The stock's market value could rebound. The options trader cannot afford to wait, because expiration looms in the near future.)

The time factor impedes the value of risk limitation. You enjoy the benefits only as long as the option exists. The stockholder has more money at risk, but does not have to worry about expiration. It would make no sense to buy calls *only* to limit risks, rather than taking the risks of buying shares of stock. A call buyer has to believe that the stock will increase in value by expiration date. The point here is only that risks are limited in the event that the estimate of near-term price movement proves to be wrong.

Strategy 3: Planning Future Purchases

When you own a call, you fix the price of a future purchase of stock in the event you exercise that call prior to expiration. This use of calls goes far beyond pure speculation.

Example: The market had a large point drop recently, and one company you have been following experienced a drop in market value. You are convinced that market value will soon rebound. The stock had been trading in the $50 to $60 range, and you would like to buy 100 shares at the current depressed price of $39 per share. However, you do not have $3,900 available to invest at the moment. You will be able to raise this money within six months, but you expect that by then the stock's market value will have returned to its higher range. Not knowing exactly what will happen, you consider one alternative—to buy a call. To fix the price, you can buy calls while the market is low with the intention of exercising each call once you have the capital available. The 40 call currently is selling for 3, and you purchase one contract at that price. Six months later, the stock's market price has risen to $58 per share. The option is worth 18 just before expiration.

In this case, you would have two possible choices: Either you could sell the call at 18 and realize a profit of $1,500, or you could exercise the call and buy 100 shares of stock at $40 per share. If you seek long-term growth and believe the stock is a good value, you can use options to freeze the current price, with the idea of buying 100 shares later.

The advantage to this strategy is that your investment is limited. So if you are wrong and the stock continues to fall, you lose only the option premium. If you are right, you pick up 100 shares below market value upon exercise.

Some option speculators recognize that large drops in overall market value are temporary. There is a tendency for individual stock prices to follow the trend. So a large drop could represent a buying opportunity, especially in those stocks that fall more than the average. In this situation, many investors are afraid of further price drops, so they hold off and miss the opportunity. An options trader, however, can afford to speculate on the probability of a last rebound, and buy calls. When the market does bounce back, those calls gain value and can be sold at a profit.

Strategy 4: Insuring Profits

A final reason for buying calls is to protect a short position in the underlying stock. Calls can be used as a form of insurance. If you have sold short 100 shares of stock, you were hoping that the market value would fall so that you could close out the position by buying 100 shares at a lower market price. The risk, of course, is that the stock will instead rise in market value, creating a loss for the short seller.

Example: An investor sells short 100 shares of stock when market value is $58 per share. One month later, the stock's market value has fallen to $52 per share. The investor enters a closing purchase transaction—buys 100 shares—and realizes a profit of $600 before trading costs.

A short seller's risks are unlimited in the sense that a stock's market value could rise to any level. If the market value does rise above the initial sale price, each point represents a point of loss for the short seller. To protect against the potential loss in that event, a short seller can buy calls for insurance, which is known as a *hedge* strategy.

Example: An investor sells short 100 shares when market value is $58 per share. At the same time, the investor buys one call, with a striking price of 65, paying a premium of $^1\!/_2$, or $50. The risk is no longer unlimited. If market value rises above $65 per share, the call protects the investor; each dollar lost in the stock will be offset by a dollar gained in the call. Risk then is limited to 7 points (the difference between the short sale price of $58 and the call's striking price of 65).

In this example, a deep out-of-the-money call was fairly inexpensive, yet it provided valuable insurance for the short seller. The protection lasts only until expiration of the call, so if the short seller wants to continue to protect the position the insurance has to be replaced with another call. Short sellers reduce their potential loss through buying offsetting calls, but this also erodes a portion of their profits. Short sellers, like anyone else buying insurance, need to assess the cost of insurance versus the potential risk.

Example: A short seller pays a premium of 2 and buys a call that expires in eight months. Ordinarily, if the value of the stock decreases 2 points, the short seller might take the profit and close the position; however, with the added cost of the call, a 2-point drop represents a break-even point (before calculating the trading costs). The short seller needs more decrease in market value to create a profit.

 hedge
a strategy involving the use of one position to protect another. (For example, stock is purchased in the belief it will rise in value, and a put is purchased on the same stock to protect against the risk that market value will decline.)

Calls serve an important function when used by short sellers to limit risks. They use part of their potential profit for insurance, hoping that the short position will be profitable enough to justify the added expense.

Example: An investor sold short 100 shares of stock at $58 per share. At the same time, he bought a call with a striking price of 65 and paid a premium of 2. A few weeks later, the underlying stock's market price rose on rumors of a pending merger, to a price of $75 per share. The short seller is down $1,700 in the stock (shares were sold at $58, and currently are valued at $75). However, the call is worth 10 in intrinsic value plus whatever time value remains. To close the position, the investor can exercise the call and reduce the loss to $900—the sales price of the stock ($58) versus the striking price of the exercised call ($65 per share) plus the $200 paid for the call.

break-even price (also called the **break-even point**) the price of the underlying stock at which the option investor breaks even. (For call buyers, this price is the number of points above striking price equal to the call premium cost; for put buyers, this price is the number of points below striking price equal to the put premium cost.)

DEFINING PROFIT ZONES

Whatever strategy you employ in your investment portfolio, always be keenly aware of how much price movement is required to create a profit, the risks involved in the strategy required to achieve that profit, and the range of potential losses to which you expose yourself. Throughout the rest of this book, we will use illustrations to define the *break-even price* as well as *profit zone* and *loss zone* for each strategy. See Figure 3.4 for a sample. Note that prices per share are listed at the left in a column, and the various zones are divided according to price levels. (As with all examples, these zones are simplified for illustration purposes, and do not allow for the cost of trading. Be sure to add brokerage fees to the cost of all transactions in calculating your own break-even, profit, and loss zones.)

Example: You buy a call and pay a premium of 3 and with a striking price of 50. What must the stock's price become by point of expiration in order for you to break even (not considering trading costs)? What price must the stock achieve in order for a profit to be gained, assuming that only intrinsic value will remain at the time? And at what price will you suffer a loss?

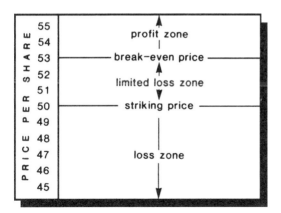

FIGURE 3.4 A call's profit and loss zones.

 profit zone
the price range of the underlying stock in which the option investor realizes a profit. (For the call buyer, the profit zone extends upward from the break-even price. For the put buyer, the profit zone extends downward from the break-even price.)

In this example, a loss occurs if the option expires out of the money, as is always the case. Because you paid a premium of 3, when the underlying stock's market value is 3 points or less above striking price the loss will be limited. (Striking price was 50, so if the stock reaches $52 per share there will be 2 points of intrinsic value at point of expiration, for example.) With limited intrinsic value between striking price and 53, there is not enough increase in market value to produce a profit. Once the stock reaches $53 per share, you are at breakeven, because you are 3 points in the money and you paid 3 for the option. When the stock rises above the $53 per share level, you enter the profit zone.

Defining break-even price and profit and loss zones helps you to develop a strategy with complete awareness of the range for potential profit or loss. It also helps to define the range of limited loss in cases such as option buying, so that risk can be quantified more easily. An example of a call purchase with defined profit zone and loss zone is shown in Figure 3.5. In this example, the investor bought one May 40 call for 2. In order to profit from this strategy, the stock's value must increase to a point greater than the striking price of the call plus 2 points (based on the assumption that all time value will have disappeared). So $42 per share is the break-even price. Even when buying a call scheduled to expire within a few months, you need to know in advance what risks you are taking, and how much price movement is needed to yield a profit.

 loss zone
the price range of the underlying stock in which the option investor loses. (A limited loss exists for option buyers, since the premium cost is the maximum loss that can be realized.)

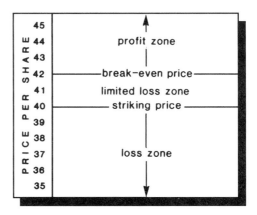

FIGURE 3.5 Example of call purchase with profit and loss zones.

Example: You have been tracking a stock with the idea of buying calls. Right now, you could buy a call with a striking price of 40 for a premium of 2. The stock's market value is $38 per share, 2 points out of the money. In deciding whether to buy this call, you understand that between the time of purchase and expiration, the stock will need to rise by no less than 4 points—2 points to get to the striking price plus another 2 points to cover your cost. If this does occur, the option will be worth exactly what you paid for it, and represents a break-even level (before trading costs). Because the entire premium consists of time value, the stock needs to surpass striking price and develop enough intrinsic value to cover your cost.

Example: Another stock you have been following has an option available for a premium of 1, and currently is at the money. Expiration is two months away, and the stock is only 1 point below breakeven (because of your premium cost). Considering these circumstances, this option has greater potential to become profitable.

In the first example, a break-even price is 4 points above current market value of the stock, and option premium is $200. In the second example, only 2 points of price movement are required to create a profit, and the option can be bought for half the price. The lower premium also means you are exposed to less potential loss in the event the stock does not rise.

You could make as much profit from a $100 invest-ment as from an equally viable $200 investment, as the previous examples demonstrate. The size of the initial premium cost cannot be used to judge potential profit, whereas premium amounts can be used to define poten-tial losses. Premium level can be deceptive, and a more thoughtful risk/reward analysis often is required to truly compare one option choice to another.

Smart Investor Tip   The option's premium level can-not be used reliably to judge the viability of a buy deci-sion. It can be used to define potential losses, however.

Before buying any option, you need to evaluate the attributes of the underlying stock in addition to the profit or loss potential of the option. The analysis of the under-lying stock should include, at a minimum, a study of market price, dividend rate, volatility, P/E ratio, earnings history, and numerous other fundamental and technical features that define a stock's safety and stability. There is no point to selecting an option that has price appeal when the underlying stock has undesirable qualities, such as price unpredictability, troubling financial prob-lems, weak position within a sector or industry, or incon-sistent earnings and dividend history. At the very least, you need to determine from recent history how respon-sive the stock's market price is likely to be to the general movement of the market. In a greater sense, options can-not be evaluated apart from their underlying stock. The real value and profit potential in your options strategy grows from first selecting likely stock candidates. It is the wise selection of a range of "good" stocks (by the defini-tion you use of what constitutes that value) that deter-mines viable option selection.

You may also evaluate the stock market as a whole before deciding whether the timing is right for buying calls. For example, do you believe that the market has been on an upward climb that may require a short-term correction? If so, it is possible that buying options, even on the best stock choices, could be ill-timed. A second question worth asking is how you define the "market." The Dow Jones Industrial Average comprises only 30 companies, whereas the S&P 500 is more representative. You might also judge the "market" in terms of changes in the New York Stock Exchange (NYSE) Composite Index. The best method for defining the market as a whole is to look at all of the popular indicators, and then develop a sense of overall price movement. A strong signal in one direction by a majority of the popular indexes is a good indicator for identifying overall market movement.

The problem with an opinion you develop about the market, no matter how well supported through analysis, is that in the end it is still only an opinion. No one truly knows how markets move, nor why they behave as they do. The process of buying and selling is based, invariably, on timing and opinion. See Chapter 6 for a more in-depth and expanded study and discussion of stock selection.

Beyond the point of stock and option analysis, you need to observe carefully the time factor, and how the passage of time affects option premium. Time value changes predictably, but in different degrees by stock and from one period to another. Your call expires within a short period, so you have only limited time to accumulate value. Changes in time value can be elusive and unpredictable in the degree and timing of their changes. The only certainty is that at expiration no time value will remain in the option premium.

In the next chapter, strategies for buying puts will be examined in depth.

Chapter 4

Buying Puts

The optimist proclaims that we live in the best of all possible worlds; and the pessimist fears this is true.

—James Branch Cabell, *The Silver Stallion*, 1926

You will recall that call buyers acquire the right to *buy* 100 shares of an underlying stock. In contrast, a put grants the buyer the opposite right: to *sell* 100 shares of an underlying stock. The premium paid to acquire a put grants the right to the buyer. Upon exercise of a put, the buyer sells 100 shares at the specified price, even if the stock's current market value has fallen below that level.

As a put buyer, you have a choice to make in the near future. You may sell the put before it expires; you may exercise the put and sell 100 shares of the underlying stock at the fixed striking price; or you may let the put expire worthless.

You are not obligated to sell 100 shares by virtue of owning the put. That decision is entirely up to you, and is a right but not an obligation. The put seller, however, would be obligated to buy 100 shares if the buyer does decide to exercise the put.

Smart Investor Tip The buyer of an option always has the right, but not the obligation, to exercise. The seller has no choice in the event of exercise.

As a put buyer, your decisions will depend on the same features that affect and motivate call buyers. These are:

✔ Price movement in the underlying stock and how that affects the put's premium value.

✔ Your motives for buying the put, and how today's market conditions meet or fail to meet that purpose.

✔ Your willingness to wait out a series of events between purchase date and expiration and see what develops, versus your desire for a sure profit in the short term.

THE LIMITED LIFE OF THE PUT

Puts can be bought purely on speculation. If you believe the underlying stock's market value will decline in the near future, you can take one of three actions in the market: sell short on shares of the stock, sell calls, or buy puts. When you buy a put, your desire is that the underlying stock's value will fall below the striking price; the more it falls, the higher your profit. Your belief and hope are opposite that of a call buyer. In that respect, many people view call buyers as optimists and put buyers as pessimists. It is more reasonable to define put buyers as investors who recognize the cyclical nature of prices in the market; when they believe that a stock is overvalued, put buying is sensible for two reasons: First, if the investor is correct, it may be a profitable decision. Second, put buying contains much lower risks than short selling or call selling.

Short Selling

Short selling of stock is a risky strategy. It involves opening a position by selling stock that is borrowed, not owned, in the belief that its market value will fall. At some point in the future, the short seller will close the position by buying those shares of stock, hopefully at a lower price. Short sellers borrow the stock from the brokerage firm and then sell it short. The brokerage firm requires a deposit equal to a portion of the stock's value as collateral at the time of the short sale. So short selling is not only risky; it also requires a commitment of capital. If the short seller is mistaken and the stock's market value rises, the brokerage firm will require that more collateral be placed on deposit; ultimately, the ill-timed short sale will be closed at a loss.

The short seller risks the entire amount of a stock's market value. Interest has to be paid on the borrowed stock's value, meaning that the price of the stock has to fall far enough to cover the interest *and* produce a profit. Risk is high because the stock's value could rise—in theory to any level. The short seller's only advantage over the put buyer is not having to be concerned with expiration. Of course, the longer the short seller keeps the position open, the higher the interest cost—not to mention the lost opportunity cost involved with keeping collateral on deposit with the brokerage firm. Even if that collateral is in the form of securities, the investor cannot remove it until the short position has been closed.

Call Selling

A second strategy employed when investors believe that a stock's market value is going to fall involves selling calls. At first glance, selling a call and buying a put seem to be the same strategy. If the stock's market value falls, either strategy produces the same profit. An important difference, though, is that the put buyer is not exposed to the high risks of the call seller when the stock's market price rises.

Remember that the seller has no say in the decision to exercise an option—that is up to the buyer. A call seller receives a premium at the time the call is sold, which mitigates the risk to a degree. The call seller can also eliminate the market risk if he or she owns 100 shares of the underlying stock at the time the call is sold. Upon exercise, those 100 shares can be delivered in satisfaction of the call. In effect, this covers the short position and allows the call seller the luxury of receiving the call premium. If the call is not exercised, the investor may then sell another call and continue that process indefinitely. Selling calls is a similar strategy to selling stock short, but the risks are much lower if the investor has covered the call with 100 shares of stock. Covered call selling—the lowest-risk use of options—is described in much more detail in the next chapter.

Buying Puts

The third strategy available to those who believe a stock's market price will fall is that of buying puts. The buyer's risk is limited to the premium paid to acquire the put. In that regard, put buyers face identical risks to those experienced by call buyers. But when compared to selling short 100 shares of stock, put buyers have far less risk *and* much less capital requirement. The put buyer does not have to deposit collateral or pay interest on borrowed stock, and does not face the same risks as the short seller; yet, the put buyer can make as much profit.

The only disadvantage is the expiration date that comes up in the short term. Time works against the put buyer, and time value premium evaporates with increasing speed as expiration approaches. If the stock's market value declines, but not enough to offset lost time value, you could experience a loss or only break even. The strategy requires price drops adequate to produce a profit. But still, your risk is limited to the price paid for the premium. Unlike short selling or call selling, put buying provides you with the right to exercise while limiting your overall risks.

Compare the various strategies you can employ using shares of stock or options, depending on what you believe will happen in the near-term future to the market value of the underlying stock:

	You Believe that the Market Will:	
Strategy Type	*Rise*	*Fall*
Stock strategy	Buy shares (long)	Sell shares (short)
Option strategy (long)	Buy calls	Buy puts
Option strategy (short)	Sell puts	Sell calls

Example: You have been watching a stock over the past few months. You believe it is overpriced today, and you expect market value to decline in the near term. Originally, you had planned to buy shares, but now you think the timing is wrong. Instead, you borrow 100 shares from your brokerage firm and sell them short. A few weeks later, the stock has fallen 8 points. You close the position by buying 100 shares. Your profit is $800, less trading costs and interest.

Example: You sold short a stock last month that was selling at $59 per share. At the time, you believed the stock was overpriced and that its market value was going to fall. However, a few days ago the company announced a tender offer for the company's stock at $75 per share. The stock jumped to $73 and trading was halted. If it reopens at $73 and you close your position, you will lose $1,400, the difference between your original sale price and current market value. If the tender offer is accepted and the stock continues to rise, you suffer in three ways. First, your market loss will become higher. Second, the brokerage firm will require more collateral. And third, your interest cost for the borrowed stock will continue as well.

Example: You believe that a particular stock is going to decline in value, so you sell a call, receiving a premium of 4. If you are right and the stock's market value falls, the value of the call will fall as well. Even if the stock remains at the same level, time value will decline, reducing the overall premium value of the call. In either case, you will be able to close the position and buy the call at a lower premium than you received (as long as the stock's market price does not rise substantially). Or you can wait for the call to expire worthless.

Example: You believe that a particular stock's market value will decline, but you do not want to sell short on the shares, recognizing that the risks and costs are too high. You also do not want to sell a call. You do not own 100 shares, and you recognize the high risks in selling calls; if the stock's market value goes up, you could lose a lot of money. That leaves you with a third choice, buying a put. You identify a put with several months until expiration, whose premium is 3. If you are right and the stock's market value falls, you could make a profit. But if you are wrong and market value remains the same or rises (or falls, but not enough to produce a profit), your maximum risk exposure is only $300.

You benefit from a stock's declining market value when you buy puts, and at the same time you avoid the cost and risk associated with short positions. Selling short or selling calls exposes you to significant market risks, often for potentially small profit potential. These strategies often do not justify the risk, whereas the limited risk of put buying makes more sense.

The limited loss is a positive feature to put buying. However, the put—like the call—exists for only a limited amount of time. To profit from the strategy, you need to have adequate downward price movement in the stock to offset time value and to exceed your initial premium cost. So as a put buyer, you trade limited risk for limited life.

Smart Investor Tip   As a put buyer, you eliminate risks associated with going short, and, in exchange, you accept the time restrictions associated with option long positions.

The potential benefit to a particular strategy is only half of the formula. The other half is the element of risk. For example, as a buyer, you need to know exactly how much price movement is needed to break even and to profit. Given time until expiration, is it realistic to expect that much price movement? There will be greater risks if your strategy requires a 6-point movement in two weeks, and relatively small risks if you need only 3 points of price movement over two months. Too many speculators buy puts with high time value, believing that in-the-money situations can produce fast profits with minimal price movement. That is true, of course, if the stock's price behaves as the speculator expects it to. But if it does not happen quickly enough, then time value begins to disappear and the requirement for a small price movement becomes a need for a much larger one.

Put buying is suitable for you only if you understand the risks and are familiar with the price history of the underlying stock, not to mention the other fundamental and technical aspects that make a particular stock a good prospect for your options strategy. You need to be willing to live with the potential loss of your entire premium. Without a doubt, buying puts is a risky strategy, and the smart put buyer knows this from the start.

Example: An investor has $600 available and believes that the market as a whole is overpriced. He expects it to fall in the near future. He buys two puts at 3 each. The market does fall as expected; but the underlying stock involved with the two puts remains unchanged, and the puts begin to lose their time value. At expiration they are worth only 1, and he sells, receiving only $200.

This investor's perception of the market was correct: prices fell. But put buyers cannot afford to depend on overall impressions. The strategy lost money because the particular stock did not behave in the same way as the market in general. The problem with broad market indicators is that there are so many, and none are completely reliable. Each stock has its own attributes and reacts differently in changing markets. Many issues tend to follow an upward or downward price movement in the larger market, and others do not react to markets as a whole. It is important to study the attributes of the individual stock.

In the example, it appears that the strategy was inappropriate for the investor. First of all, the entire amount of capital was invested in a high-risk strategy. Second, the whole thing was placed into puts on the same stock. It could be that this investor did not have enough capital to be involved in buying options in the first place; but by basing a decision on the entire market without considering the indicators for the specific company, the investor lost money. It is likely, too, that this investor did not understand the degree of price change that would be required to produce a profit. If you do not know how much risk a strategy involves, then it is not an appropriate strategy. More study and analysis are required.

Smart Investor Tip   When it comes to market risk, the unasked question can lead to unexpected losses. Whatever strategy you employ, you need to first explore and understand all of the risks involved.

It is not untypical for investors to concentrate on potential gain without also considering the potential loss, especially in the options market. In the previous example, one reason the investor lost was a failure to study the individual stock. One aspect not considered was the company's strength in a declining market, its ability to hold its price. This information might have been revealed with more focused analysis and a study of the stock's price history in previous markets. Options traders may lose not because their perception of the market is wrong, but because there was not enough time for their strategy to work—in other words, because the investor did not fully understand the implications of buying options.

Once you understand the risks and are convinced that you can afford the losses that could occur, you might conclude that it is appropriate to buy puts in some circumstances. Remember, though, that the evaluation has to involve not only the option—premium level, time value, and time until expiration—but also the attributes of the underlying stock.

Example: An experienced investor has a well-diversified investment portfolio. He owns shares in companies in different market sectors and also owns shares in two mutual funds, plus some real estate. He has been investing for several years and fully understands the risks in various markets, considering himself a long-term and conservative investor. He has always selected stocks using long-term price appreciation and stability in earnings as the primary selection criteria. Short-term price movement does not concern him. Outside of this portfolio, the investor has several hundred dollars available, which he uses for occasional speculation. He believes the market will fall in the short term, including shares of stock that he owns. He buys puts with this in mind. His theory: Any short-term losses in his permanent portfolio will be offset by gains in his put speculation. And if he is wrong, he can afford to lose the money he uses to speculate.

This investor understands the difference between long-term investment and short-term speculation. He has established a base in his portfolio, and thoroughly understands how the market works. He knows that long-term appreciation is a separate matter from short-term price fluctuation. He can afford some minor losses with capital set aside purely for speculation. Buying puts is an appropriate strategy given the investor's belief about the market, particularly since he understands that stocks in his portfolio are likely to fall along with the market. Not wanting to sell shares held for the long term, he uses his speculation funds to anticipate a temporary price drop.

The ability to afford losses, the investor's understanding of the market, and the proper selection of stocks on which to buy puts all add up to a greater chance of success.

JUDGING THE PUT

Time works against all option buyers. Not only will your option expire within a few month, but time value will decline even if the stock's price does not change. Buyers need to offset lost time value with price movement that creates intrinsic value in its place.

You can select low-priced puts—ones that are out of the money—but that means you require many points just to produce a profit. In other words, those puts are low-priced for a good reason. The likelihood of gain is lower than it is for higher-priced puts. When you buy in-the-money puts, you will experience a point-for-point change; but that can happen in either direction. (You will recall that for calls "in the money" means the stock's market value is higher than the striking price, but the opposite is true for puts.) For put buyers, a downward movement in the stock's market value is offset point for point with gains in the put's premium; but each upward movement in the stock's market value is also offset by a decline in the put's premium value.

Example: You bought a put and paid a premium of 5. At the time, the stock's market value was 4 points below the striking price. It was 4 points in the money. However, by expiration, the stock has risen $4^{1}/_2$ points and the option is worth only $^{1}/_2$ ($50). The time value has disappeared, and you sell on the last trading day before expiration, losing $450.

Example: You bought a put several months ago, paying a premium of $^{1}/_2$ ($50). At that time, the stock's market value was 5 points out of the money. By expiration, the stock's market value has declined $5^{1}/_2$ points, so that the put is $^{1}/_2$ point in the money. When you bought the put, it had no intrinsic value and only $^{1}/_2$ point of time value. At expiration, the time value is gone and there remains only $^{1}/_2$ point of intrinsic value. Overall, the premium value is the same; but no profit is possible because the stock's market value did not fall enough.

The problem is not limited to picking the right direction a stock's market value might change, although many novice options traders fall into the trap of believing that this is true. Rather, the *degree* of movement within a limited period of time must be adequate to produce profits that exceed premium cost and offset lost time value (and to cover trading costs on both sides).

Some speculators attempt to bargain hunt in the options market. The belief is that it is better to pick up a cheap option than to put more money into a high-priced one. This is not always the case; many cheap options are cheap because they have little worth. They are *not* good bargains, and this is widely recognized by the market overall. The question of quality has to be remembered at all times when choosing options and comparing prices. The idea of value is constantly being adjusted with regard to information about the underlying stock, but these adjustments are obscured by the double effect of (1) time to go until expiration and the effect on time value, and (2) distance between current market value of the stock and the striking price of the option. Obviously, when the market value of the stock is close to the striking price, this creates a situation in which profits (or losses) can materialize rapidly.

Smart Investor Tip   A bargain price might reflect a bargain, or it might reflect a lack of value in the option. Sometimes real bargains are found in higher-priced options.

Example: You bought a put last week when it was in the money, paying a premium of 6. You believed the stock was overpriced and was likely to fall. Two days after your purchase, the stock's market value fell 1 point. You sold the put and received $700. This represents a return on your investment of 16.7% in two days.

In this example, the investor turned the position around rapidly and walked away with a profit. So the bargain existed in this put because the investor was right. The return was substantial, which does not mean that it can be repeated consistently.

Remember, when you buy puts on speculation, you

are gambling that you are right about short-term price changes. You might be right about the general trend in a stock, but not have enough time for your prediction to become true before expiration. With this in mind, it is critical to set goals for yourself, knowing in advance when you will sell a put—based on profit goals as well as loss bailout points.

Example: You bought a put last month, paying a premium of 4. At that time, you decided to set a few goals for yourself. First, you decided that if the put's value fell by 2 points, you would sell and accept a loss of $200. Second, you promised yourself that if the put's value rose by 3 points, you would sell and take a profit. You decided you would be willing to accept either a 50% loss or a 75% gain. And failing either of these outcomes, you decided you would hold the put until just before expiration.

Setting goals is the only way to succeed if you plan to speculate by buying options. Too many speculators fall into a no-win trap because they program themselves to lose; they do not set standards, so they do not know when or how to make smart decisions.

Example: An investor bought a put last month and paid 5. His plan was to sell the put if its value went up 2 points. A week after his purchase, the stock's market value fell and the put's value went up to 8, an increase of 3 points. The investor did not sell, however, because he thought the stock's market value might continue to fall. If that happened and the put's value increased, he did not want to lose out on future profits. But the following week, the stock's value rebounded 4 points, and the put lost 4 points. The opportunity was lost.

This example demonstrates the absolute need for firm goals. This common trap shows that inexperienced option speculators do not recognize the need to take profits when they are there, or to cut losses soon enough—either decision based on a predetermined standard. When the put becomes more valuable, human nature tempts us by saying, "I could make even more money if I wait." When the put's value falls, the same voice says, "I can't sell now. I have to get back to where I started."

Ask yourself: If you listen to that voice, when do you sell? The answer, of course, is that you can never sell. Whether your option is more valuable or less valuable, the voice tells you to wait and see. Lost opportunities are unlikely to repeat themselves, given the time factor associated with options. The old stock market advice to "buy in a rising market" cannot be applied to options, because options expire. You need to take profits or cut losses at the right moment.

Example: You bought a put last month for 6, and resolved that you would sell if its value rose or fell by 2 points. Two weeks ago, the stock's market value rose 2 points and the put declined to your bailout level of 4. You hesitated, hoping for a recovery. Today, the stock has risen a total of 5 points since you bought the put, which is now worth 1.

In this example, at this point you have lost $500—$300 more than if you had followed your own standard and bailed out at 4 for only a $200 loss. Even if the subject stock does fall later on, time is working against you. The longer it takes for a turnaround in the price of the underlying stock, the more time value loss you need to overcome. The stock might fall a point or two over a three-month period, so that you merely trade time value for intrinsic value, with the net effect of zero; it is even likely that the overall premium value will decline if intrinsic value is not enough to offset the lost time value.

The problem of time value is the same problem experienced by call buyers. It does not matter whether price movement is required to go up (for call buyers) or down (for put buyers); time is the enemy, and price movement has to be adequate to offset time value as well as producing a profit through more intrinsic value. Those buyers who seek bargains several points away from the striking price often fail to recognize this reality. They need a substantial change in the stock's market value just to arrive at the price level where intrinsic value will begin to accumulate. The relationship between the underlying stock and time value premium is illustrated in Figure 4.1.

Example: You buy a put for 5 with a striking price of 30. Between purchase date and expiration, the underlying

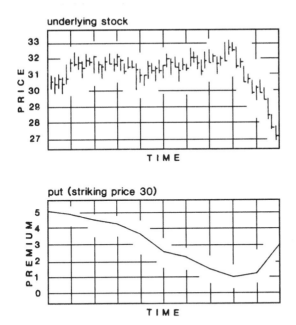

underlying stock

put (striking price 30)

FIGURE 4.1 Diminishing time value of the put relative to the underlying stock.

stock rises above striking price, but then falls to 27, which is 3 points in the money. At expiration, the put is worth 3, meaning you lose $200 upon sale. Time value has evaporated. Even though the stock is 3 points in the money, this is not enough to match or beat your investment of $500.

The farther out of the money, the cheaper the premium for the option—*and* the lower the potential to ever realize a profit. Inexperienced options traders fail to recognize that time value rarely increases, so deep out-of-the-money options are poor choices for buyers. The relationship between option premium and the gap between striking price and the stock's current market price demonstrates the problem. It is not coincidental; it is predictable. Likewise, the farther in the money the option, the more expensive it becomes. You are paying 1 point for each point in the money, plus time value.

If you buy an in-the-money put and the underlying stock increases in value, you lose 1 point for each dollar of increase in the stock's market value—as long as it re-

mains in the money (and, of course, for each dollar decline in the stock's market value, your put gains a point in
premium value). Once the stock's market value rises
above striking price, your put is out of the money, and the
premium value becomes less responsive to price movement in the underlying stock.

Smart Investor Tip   For option buyers, profits are realized primarily when the option is in the money. Out-of-
the-money options are poor candidates for appreciation,
because time value rarely increases.

Whether you prefer lower-premium puts that are out
of the money or higher-premium puts that are in the
money, always be keenly aware of the point gap between
the stock's current market value and striking price of the
put. The farther out of the money, the less likely it is that
your put will produce a profit.

To minimize your exposure to risk, limit your speculation to options within 5 points. In other words, if you
buy out-of-the-money puts, avoid those that are deep out
of the money. What might seem like a relatively small
price gap can become quite large when you consider that
all of the out-of-the-money premium is time value, and
that no intrinsic value can be accumulated until your put
goes in the money. Added to this problem is the time factor. As shown in Figure 4.2, you should avoid speculating
in puts that are either deep in the money or deep out of
the money. Deep in puts are going to be expensive—one
point for each dollar below striking price, plus time
value—and deep out puts are too far from striking price
to have any realistic chances for producing profits.

Set goals and stay with them. Consider the premium
value, the mix of time and intrinsic value, time until expiration, the underlying stock's price movement and history,
and the gap between current market value of the stock and
striking price of the option. Avoid the common mistake
made by novices: shopping for bargains based only on premium level, without considering the other factors. There is
an inescapable relationship between the stock's market price
and the put's premium value. Volatility and market perceptions about the stock will determine how your put per-

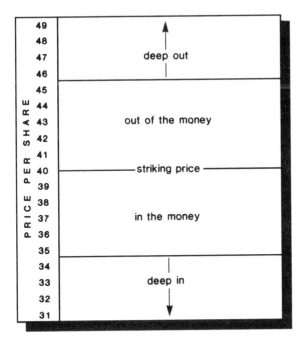

FIGURE 4.2 Deep in/deep out stock prices for puts.

forms—in other words, the stock's price movement is going to be the determining factor. So given the time element, a bargain based only on price often represents a poor choice.

PUT BUYING STRATEGIES

There are three reasons to buy puts. The first is purely speculative: the hope of realizing a profit in a short period of time, with relatively small risk exposure. This leveraged approach is appealing but contains higher risks along with the potential for short-term profits. The second reason to buy puts is as an alternative to short selling of stock. And third, you may buy puts to provide yourself with a form of insurance against price declines in a long position of stock.

Strategy 1: Gaining Leverage

Many put buyers recognize the value of leverage gained with the put. With a limited amount of capital, the potential for profits is greater for put buyers than through short selling, and with less risk. Here is how leverage works in the case of puts:

Example: A stock currently is valued at $60 per share. If you sell short 100 shares and the stock drops 5 points, you can close the position and take a profit of $500. However, rather than selling short, you could buy 12 puts at 5, for a total investment of $6,000. A 5-point drop in this case would produce a profit of $6,000, a 100% gain (assuming no change in time value). So by investing the same amount in puts, you could earn a 100% profit, compared to an 8.3% profit through short selling.

This example demonstrates the value in leverage, but the risk element for each strategy is not comparable. The short seller faces risks not experienced by the put buyer, and has to put up collateral and pay interest; in comparison, the put buyer has to fight against time. Risking $6,000 by buying puts is highly speculative and, while short selling is risky as well, the two strategies have vastly different attributes. The greater profit potential through leverage in buying puts is accompanied by equally higher risk of loss. However, even without a large sum of capital to speculate with, you can still use leverage to your advantage.

Example: Compare the outcomes between selling stock short and buying a put, as shown in Figure 4.3. The comparison is made between selling short at $62 per share versus buying an at-the-money put at 60. If you sell short and the stock drops 5 points, your profit is $500; however, your risk includes the potential loss in the event the stock's price were to rise. If you buy a put with a striking price of 60 and the stock drops 5 points, you also earn a profit of $500—assuming no change in time value premium for the sake of comparison. By purchasing a put, you escape the risk of increase in the stock's price, but in return you pay $500 for the put premium, and expose yourself to the risk of time value premium losses (if the underlying stock's price rises).

The short seller, like the put buyer, has a time problem. The short seller has to place collateral on deposit equal to a part of the borrowed stock's value, and pay interest on the

	STOCK (1)		PUT (2)	
	PROFIT OR LOSS	RATE OF RETURN	PROFIT OR LOSS	RATE OF RETURN
price decrease of 5 points	$500	8.1%	$500	100%
price decrease of 1 point	$100	1.6%	$100	20%
no price change	0	0	0	0
price increase of 1 point	-$100	-1.6%	-$100	- 20%
price increase of 5 points	-$500	-8.1%	-$500	-100%

(1) sold short at $62 per share ($6200)
(2) striking price 60, premium 5 ($500)

FIGURE 4.3 Rates of return: selling short versus buying puts.

borrowed amount. Thus, the more time the short position is left open, the higher the interest cost—and the more decline in the stock's value the short seller requires to make a profit. While the put buyer is concerned with diminishing time value and approaching expiration, the short seller pays interest, which erodes future profits, if they ever materialize, or which increases losses.

A decline of 5 points in the prior example produces an 8.1% profit for the short seller and a 100% profit for the put buyer. Compare the risks with this yield difference in mind. Short selling risks are unlimited in the sense that a stock's value could rise indefinitely. The put buyer's risk is limited to the $500 investment. A drop of $1 per share in the stock's value creates a 1.6% profit for the short seller, and a 20% profit for the put buyer.

Losses can be compared in the same way as one form of risk evaluation. When a short seller's stock rises in value, the loss could be substantial. It combines market losses with continuing interest expense and tied-up collateral (lost opportunity) loss. The put buyer's losses can never exceed the premium cost of the put. Most put buyers do not intend to exercise; the more likely action in event of an increase in the put's value due to a decline in the stock would be to sell the put and take the profit.

Strategy 2: Limiting Risks

It is possible to double your money in a very short period of time by speculating in puts. Leverage increases even a modest investment's overall potential (and risk). Risks increase through leverage due to the potential for loss. Like all forms of investing or speculating, greater opportunity also means greater risk.

Example: You recently bought a put for 4. However, expiration date is coming up soon and the stock's market value has risen above striking price. When the put expires, you face the prospect of losing the entire $400 premium. Time has worked against you. Knowing that the stock's market value might eventually fall below striking price, but not necessarily before expiration, you realize it is unlikely that you will be able to earn a profit.

In comparison to short selling, though, risks are lower for puts. A short seller in a loss position is required to pay the difference between short-sold price and current market value if the stock has risen in value, not to mention the interest cost. The limited risk of buying puts is a considerable advantage.

Example: An investor sold short 200 shares of stock with market value of $45 per share; he was required to borrow $9,000 worth of stock, put up a portion as collateral, and pay interest to the brokerage company. The stock later rose to $52 per share and the investor sold. His loss on the stock was $1,400. If the same investor had bought two puts instead (controlling 200 shares), the maximum loss would have been limited to the premiums paid for the two puts. The fear of further stock price increases that would concern the short seller would not be a problem for the put buyer.

The advantage enjoyed by the put buyer typifies the long position over the short position. Losses are invariably limited in the put buyer's situation. Although both strategies have identical goals, risks make the long and short positions much different. Some investors may prefer short selling over put buying because the expiration and deterioration of time value are not factors for the short seller. This overlooks the time problem for short selling, however, which comes from regular interest payments the short seller needs to make. The risks of the short position can be reduced through buying calls, as explained in Chapter 3. The risk that the stock's market price could rise is insured against because a call will rise dollar for dollar, offsetting losses in the stock. However, the viability of selling short in this condition has to be questioned, considering the overall cost—interest on the borrowed stock, tied-up collateral, and call premium. Collectively, a substantial profit has to be earned to justify this strategy. In comparison, alternative strategies of buying puts or selling calls begin to seem more reasonable.

Strategy 3: Hedging a Long Position

Put buying is not always merely speculative. A very conservative strategy involves buying one put for every 100 shares of the underlying stock owned, to protect yourself against the risk of falling prices. Just as calls can be used to insure against the risk of rising prices in a short sale position, puts can serve the same purpose, protecting against price declines when you are long in shares of stock. When a put is used in this manner, it is called a *married put*, since it is tied directly to the underlying stock.

The risk of declining market value is a constant concern for every investor. If you buy stock and its value falls, a common reaction is to sell in the fear that the decline will continue. In spite of advice to the contrary, many investors buy high and sell low. It is human nature. It requires a cooler head to calmly wait out a decline and rebound, which could takes months, even years. For protection against declines in value, some investors buy puts for insurance, which is known as a hedge strategy. In the event of a decline in the stock's value, the put can be exercised and the stock sold at the striking price; or the put can be sold at a profit to offset the lowered value in the

 married put
the status of a put used to hedge a long position. (Each put owned protects 100 shares of the underlying stock held in the portfolio. If the stock declines in value, the put's value will increase and offset the loss.)

put to seller
action of exercising a put and requiring the seller to purchase 100 shares of stock at the fixed striking price.

stock, a good idea if you believe the stock's price will rebound. When you exercise a put, that action is referred to as *put to seller*.

Example: You own 100 shares of stock which you purchased for $57 per share. This stock tends to be volatile, meaning its potential price range is broad. The potential for gain or loss is significant. To protect yourself against possible losses, you buy a put on the underlying stock. It costs 1 and has a striking price of 50. Two months later, the stock's market value falls to $36 per share and the put is near expiration. The put has a premium value of 14.

In this situation, you have a choice:

1. Sell the put and take the $1,300 profit. Your original cost was $58 per share (purchase price of $5,700 plus $100 for the put). Your net cost per share is $45 ($5,800 less $1,300 profit on the put). Your basis now is 9 points above current market value. By selling the put, you have the advantage of continuing to own the stock. If its market value rebounds to a level above $45 per share, you will realize a profit. Without the put, your basis would be 21 points above current market value. Selling the put mitigates a large portion of the loss.

2. Exercise the put and sell the stock for $50 per share. In this alternative, you sell at 8 points below your basis. You lose $100 paid for the put, plus 7 points in the stock.

Regardless of the choice taken in these circumstances, you end up with less loss by owning the married put than you would have just owning the stock. The put provides a degree of protection. It either cuts the loss by offsetting the stock's market value decline, or enables you to get rid of the depreciated stock at higher than market value. You have a loss either way, but not as much of a loss as you would have had without buying the put.

This example demonstrates how puts can be used to

protect a long position. It is also worth noting that puts are not available on all stocks; so this strategy is useful only if you happen to own shares of stock on which puts can be bought.

The put is used in this application to provide *down-side protection*, which reduces potential profits because you have to pay a premium to buy the insurance. If you intend to own shares of stock for the long term, puts will have to be replaced upon expiration, so that the cost is repetitive. However, long-term investors are not normally concerned with short-term price change, so the strategy might be employed only when you believe your shares currently are overpriced, given the rate of price change and current market conditions.

In the event the stock's market price rises, your potential losses are frozen at the level of the put's premium and no more. This occurs because as intrinsic value in the put declines, it is offset by a rise in the stock's market value. Whether you end up selling the put or exercising, downside protection establishes an acceptable level of loss in the form of paying for insurance to fix that loss at the striking price of the put, at least for the duration of the put's life. This strategy is appropriate even for long-term investors who expect instability in the market in the short term.

downside protection
a strategy involving the purchase of one put for every 100 shares of the underlying stock that you own. (This insures you against losses to some degree. For every in-the-money point the stock falls, the put will increase in value by 1 point. Before exercise, you may sell the put and take a profit offsetting stock losses, or exercise the put and sell the shares at the striking price.)

Example: You recently bought 100 shares of stock at $60 per share. At the same time, you bought a put with a striking price of 60, paying 3. Your total investment is $6,300. Before making your purchase, you analyzed the potential profit and loss and concluded that your losses would probably not exceed 4.8% ($300 paid for the put, divided by $6,300, the total invested). You also concluded that an increase in the stock's market value of 3 points or less would not represent a profit at all, due to the investment in the put. So profits will not begin to accumulate until the stock's market value exceeds $63 per share.

This strategy is especially appropriate when your stock's price movement is volatile. A decline in market value is protected by the put, and an increase is still profitable once the premium cost has been exceeded.

A summary of this strategy is shown in Figure 4.4. Note that regardless of the severity of decline in the stock's market value, the loss can never exceed 4.8% of the total amount invested (the cost of the put). That is because for every point of decline in the stock's market value, the put increases 1 point in intrinsic value. This would continue until the put expires.

DEFINING PROFIT ZONES

To decide whether buying puts is a reasonable strategy for you, always be aware of potential profits *and* losses, rather than concentrating on profits alone. Pay special attention to the gap between current market value and striking price, especially if you are buying out-of-the-money puts. Remember that the wider this gap, the more difficult it will be to earn a profit. Also remember that the shorter the time to expiration, the lower the time value (which is good) but the more pressure there is to achieve adequate

PRICE MOVEMENT, UNDERLYING STOCK	PROFIT OR LOSS STOCK (1)	PROFIT OR LOSS PUT (2)	NET PROFIT OR LOSS (3) AMOUNT	NET PROFIT OR LOSS (3) RATE
down 20 points	-$2,000	$1,700	-$ 300	- 4.8%
down 5 points	-$ 500	$ 200	-$ 300	- 4.8%
down 3 points	-$ 300	0	-$ 300	- 4.8%
no change	0	-$ 300	-$ 300	- 4.8%
up 3 points	$ 300	-$ 300	0	0
up 5 points	$ 500	-$ 300	$ 200	3.2%
up 20 points	$2,000	-$ 300	$1,700	27.0%

(1) stock purchased at $60 per share
(2) put striking price 60, premium 3
(3) return based on total cost of $6300

FIGURE 4.4 Downside protection: buying shares and buying puts.

price movement (which is bad). The selection of a put requires balance.

Comparing limited losses to potential profits when using puts for downside protection is one type of analysis that helps you pick value when comparing puts. And when looking for a well-priced speculative move, time to expiration coupled with the gap between current market value and striking price—which dictates the amount of time value premium—will help you to find real bargains in puts. Premium level is not a reasonable criterion for your selection.

The profit and loss zones for puts are the reverse of the zones for call buyers, because put owners expect a downward movement in the stock, whereas call buyers look for upward price movement. See Figure 4.5 for a summary of loss and profit zones and break-even point using the following example.

Example: You buy a put with a striking price of 50, paying 3. Your break-even price is $47 per share. If the underlying stock falls to that level, the option will have an intrinsic value of 3 points, equal to the price you paid for the put. If the price of the stock goes below $47 per share, the put will be profitable point for point with downward price movement in the stock. Your put can be sold for a limited loss when the underlying stock's market value is between $47 and $50 per share. And if the price of the

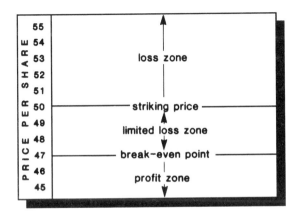

FIGURE 4.5 A put's profit and loss zones.

stock rises above $50 per share, the put will be worthless at expiration.

Before buying any put, determine the profit and loss zones and the break-even price (including the cost of trading on both sides of the transaction). For the amount of money you will be putting at risk, how much price movement will be required to produce a profit? How much time remains until expiration? Is the risk a reasonable one?

Another example of a put purchase with defined profit and loss zones is shown in Figure 4.6. In this example, the put was bought at 3 and has a May 40 expiration. The outcome of this transaction would be exactly opposite for the purchase of a call, given the same premium, expiration, and price of the underlying stock. You will profit if the stock falls below the striking price of 40 to a point greater than the premium level of the put.

Remember this guideline: Don't depend on time value to produce profits between purchase date and expiration, because that is highly unlikely to occur. If you do not have a price decline in the stock's price adequate to exceed the price you paid for the put, then you will have a loss. Like call purchasing, the passage of time works against you when you buy puts. The greater the gap between market price of the stock and striking price, the more time value premium you will have to overcome.

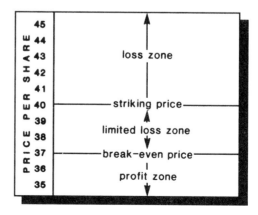

FIGURE 4.6   Example of put purchase with profit and loss zones.

The mistake made by many investors is failing to recognize what is required to produce a profit, and failing to analyze a situation to determine whether it makes sense. Such investors, having not gone through these basic steps, have not set investment standards for themselves. They might pick up options for very little premium cost, but in most instances it is still a waste of money. Remember these points in evaluating put buying:

✔ Your motive (leverage, reduction of risk, or downside protection).

✔ The premium level and amount of time value premium.

✔ Time remaining until expiration.

✔ Gap between the stock's current market value and the put's striking price.

✔ The number of points of movement in the underlying stock required before you can begin earning a profit.

✔ The characteristics of the underlying stock (see Chapter 6 for guidelines for selecting stocks appropriate for your option strategy).

Collectively, these guidelines define an investment strategy and work for you as tools for the evaluation of risks as well as for identification of profit potential. Option buyers have the opportunity to earn substantial short-term profits; they also face a correspondingly high risk level represented by time, the buyer's enemy.

On the opposite side of the option transaction is the seller. Unlike buyers, sellers have an *advantage* with pending expiration. Time is the seller's friend, and higher time value represents an opportunity rather than a risk. Because time value declines as expiration approaches, the seller benefits in the same degree as the buyer is penalized. The next chapter examines strategies and risks involved with selling calls.

$Chapter$

5

Selling Calls

───────────────

Wisdom consists of the anticipation of consequences.
  —Norman Cousins, *Saturday Review*, April 15, 1978

Most of us think about investing in a precise sequence. First, you buy a security; then, at a later date, you sell. If the sale price is higher than the purchase price, you earn a profit; if it is lower, you suffer a loss. However, when you are a call seller, this sequence is reversed.

If you buy a call and later sell it (see Chapter 3), the transaction conforms to the familiar pattern. In this chapter, you will see how you can first sell a call, and then buy it later. One outcome to taking a short position in calls is the same as for the more familiar long position: You can close by entering the opposite order (in the case of selling as a first step, a closing transaction requires that you buy). If the purchase price is lower than the original sale, then you earn a profit; if it is higher, you suffer a loss.

By starting out with an opening sale transaction, you are paid the premium at the time the order is placed. You will pay a purchase price later when you close the position or, if the option expires worthless, you never pay at all. In that case, the entire sale premium is yours to keep as profit. If this all sounds like a pretty good deal, you also need to remember that taking a short position is accompanied by inevitable risks as well. These risks are explained in this chapter and examined through examples. You will discover that some types of call selling are extremely high-risk and others are very low-risk and conservative.

Smart Investor Tip Sellers receive payment when they initiate the open transaction. That is compensation for accepting exposure to the risks.

Sellers enjoy some significant and important advantages over call buyers. In the previous two chapters, many examples demonstrated how time value works against the buyer; in fact, the time value premium makes it very difficult to earn a profit consistently as a buyer. Time value represents the majority of risk involved with call buying. Even when the underlying stock's market value moves in the desired direction, it might not happen soon enough or with enough point value to offset the time value premium. This buyer's disadvantage is the seller's advantage.

Because time value evaporates, buyers see time as the enemy. For sellers, though, time is a great ally. The more time value involved, the higher the potential profit; and the more that time value falls, the better. At the time that you enter the order for an opening sale transaction, you are better off if you have the maximum time value possible. With this in mind, longer-term options tend to be better bargains for sellers, although that also represents a longer risk exposure period. While buyers seek options with the lowest possible time value and with market value within reasonable proximity to striking price, sellers do the opposite. They seek calls with the highest possible time value, preferably as far out of the money as possible. You earn a profit as a call seller due to the decline in time value. That enables you to close out the position by buying the call for a lower premium than you received at the opening sale.

Smart Investor Tip Time is the option buyer's enemy, but the opposite is true for the seller. As as option seller, you make your profit as time value evaporates.

When you sell a call, you grant the buyer the right to buy 100 shares of the underlying stock at the striking price, at any time prior to expiration. That means that you assume the risk of being required to sell the buyer 100 shares, potentially at a striking price far below current market value. The decision to exercise is the buyer's, and that decision can be made at any time. Of course, as long as the call is out of the money, it will not be exercised. The majority of exercise decisions take place at or near closing.

Most investment strategies contain specific risk characteristics. These are identified clearly and should be fully understood by anyone undertaking that strategy. The risks tend to have unchanging attributes. For example, the risks of buying stocks are consistent from one moment to another. The experienced stock market investor understands this and accepts the risk. However, call selling has a unique distinction. It can be extremely risky or extremely conservative, depending on whether you also own 100 shares of the stock at the time you sell the call.

SELLING UNCOVERED CALLS

naked option
an option sold in an opening sale transaction when the seller (writer) does not own 100 shares of the underlying stock.

uncovered option
the same as a naked option— the sale of an option not covered, or protected, by the ownership of 100 shares of the underlying stock.

When call selling is reviewed in isolation, it is indeed a high-risk strategy. If you sell a call but you do not own 100 shares of the underlying stock, the option is classified as a *naked option* or *uncovered option*. You are exposing yourself to an unlimited risk. In fact, call selling in this situation could be one of the most risky strategies you could take, containing high potential for losses.

Remember that when you take a short position, the decision to exercise belongs to the buyer. You need to be able and willing to deliver 100 shares in the event that the call is exercised—no matter how high current market value has gone. If you do not already own 100 shares, you will be required upon exercise to buy 100 shares at current market value and deliver them at the striking price of the call. The difference in these prices could be significant.

Example: You sell a call for 5 with a striking price of 45 and expiration month of April. At the time, the underlying stock has a market value of $44 per share. You do not own 100 shares of the underlying stock. The day after your order is placed, your brokerage firm deposits $500 into your account (less fees). However, before expiration, the underlying stock's market price soars to $71 per share and your call is exercised. You will lose $2,100—the current market value of 100 shares ($7,100) less the striking price value ($4,500) less the $500 premium you received at the time you sold the call:

Current market value, 100 shares	$7,100
Less: Striking price	−4,500
Less: Call premium	− 500
Net loss	$2,100

When a call is exercised, you are required to deliver 100 shares of the underlying stock *at the striking price.* If you do not own 100 shares, this means you have to buy the shares at current market value, no matter how high that is. Because upward price movement, in theory at least, is unlimited, your risk in selling the call is unlimited as well.

Smart Investor Tip Selling uncovered calls is a high-risk idea, because in theory a stock's price could rise indefinitely. Every point rise is $100 more out of the call seller's pocket.

The risks of selling calls in this manner are extreme. With that in mind, a brokerage firm should allow you to sell calls only if you meet specific requirements. These include having enough equity in your portfolio to provide protection in the event of an unusually high loss. The brokerage firm will want to be able to sell other securities in your account to pay for losses if you cannot come up with the cash. You will need permission in advance from your brokerage firm before you will be allowed to sell calls. Each firm is required to ensure that you understand the risks involved, that you fully understand the options market, and that you have adequate equity and income to undertake those risks.

You will not be allowed to write an unlimited number of calls without also owning 100 shares of the underlying stock. The potential losses, both to you and to the brokerage firm, place natural limits on this activity. Everyone who wants to sell calls is required to sign a document acknowledging the risks and stating that they understand those risks. In part, this statement (from the Options Clearing Corporation, "Risk Disclosure Statement and Acknowledgments") includes the following:

Special Statement for Uncovered Option Writers

There are special risks associated with uncovered option writing which expose the investor to potentially significant loss. Therefore, this type of strategy may not be suitable for all customers approved for options transactions.

1. The potential loss of uncovered call writing is unlimited. The writer of an uncovered call is in an extremely risky position, and may incur large losses if the value of the underlying instrument increases above the exercise price.

2. As with writing uncovered calls, the risk of writing uncovered put options is substantial. The writer of an uncovered put option bears a risk of loss if the value of the underlying instrument declines below the exercise price. Such loss could be substantial if there is a significant decline in the value of the underlying instrument.

3. Uncovered option writing is thus suitable only for the knowledgeable investor who understands the risks, has the financial capacity and willingness to incur potentially substantial losses, and has sufficient liquid assets to meet applicable margin requirements. In this regard, if the value of the underlying instrument moves against an uncovered writer's options position, the investor's broker may request significant additional margin payments. If an investor does not make such margin payments, the broker may liquidate stock or options positions in the investor's account, with little or no prior notice in accordance with the investor's margin agreement.

You will be required to limit the scope of call writing when you do not also own associated shares of the underlying security. The requirement that your portfolio include stocks, cash, and other securities in order to sell calls is one form of *margin* requirement imposed by your broker. Such requirements apply not only to option transactions, but also to short selling of stock or, more commonly, to the purchase of securities using funds borrowed from the brokerage firm.

When you enter into an opening sale transaction, you are referred to as a *writer*. Call writers (sellers) hope that the value of the underlying stock will remain at or below the striking price of the call. If that occurs, then the call will expire worthless and the writer's profit will be the premium received. For the writer, the break-even price is the striking price plus the number of points received for selling the call.

Example: You sell a call for 5 with a striking price of 40. Your breakeven is $45 per share (before considering trading costs). Upon exercise, you would be required to deliver 100 shares at the striking price of 40; as long as the stock's current market value is at $45 per share or below, you will not have a loss, even upon exercise, since you received $500 in premium when you sold the call.

margin
an account with a brokerage firm containing a minimum level of cash and securities to provide collateral for short positions or for purchases for which payment has not yet been made.

writer
the individual who sells (writes) a call (or a put).

It is conceivable that you could write a call and make a profit even upon exercise. Given the previous example, if the call were exercised when the stock's market price was $42, you gain $300 before trading costs:

Current market value, 100 shares	$4,200
Less: Striking price	−4,000
Loss on the stock	$ 200
Premium received	500
Profit before trading costs	$ 300

Smart Investor Tip Exercise does not always mean a loss. The call premium discounts a minimal loss because it is yours to keep, even after exercise.

As a writer, you do not have to wait out expiration; you have another choice. You can close out your short position at any time by purchasing the call. Remember, as a writer, you initiate the position with a sale and close it with a purchase. There are four events that could cause you to close out a short position in your call:

1. The stock's value falls. As a result, time value and intrinsic value, if any, fall as well. The call's premium value is lower, so it is possible to close the position at a profit.

2. The stock's value remains unchanged, but the option's premium value falls due to loss of time value. The call's premium value falls and the position can be closed through purchase, at a profit.

3. The option's premium value remains unchanged because the underlying stock's market value rises. Declining time value is replaced with intrinsic value. The position can be closed at no profit or loss, to avoid exercise.

4. The underlying stock's market value rises enough so that exercise is likely. The position can be closed at a small loss to avoid exercise at a potentially greater level of loss.

Example: You sold a call two months ago for 3. The underlying stock's market value has remained below the striking price without much price movement. Time value has fallen and the option is now worth 1. You have a choice: You can buy the call and close the position, taking a profit of $200; or you can wait for expiration, hoping to keep the entire premium as a profit. This choice exposes you to risk between the decision point and expiration; in the event the stock's market price moves above striking price, intrinsic value could wipe out the profit and lead to exercise. Purchasing when the profit is available ensures the profit and avoids further exposure to risk. If the stock does rise, your break-even price is 3 points higher than striking price, since you were paid 3 for selling the call.

naked position
status for investors when they assume short positions in calls without also owning 100 shares of the underlying stock for each call written.

Whenever you sell a call and you do not also own 100 shares of stock, your risk is described as a *naked position*, which refers to the continuous exposure to risk from the moment of sale through to expiration. Remember, the buyer can exercise at any time, and that can happen whenever your naked call is in the money. Even though exercise is most likely at the time just before expiration, there is no guarantee that it will not happen before that time.

Example: You sold a naked call last week that had four months to go until expiration. You were not worried about exercise. However, as of today, the stock has risen above the striking price and your call is in the money. Your brokerage firm contacted you this morning and advised that your call was exercised. You are required to deliver 100 shares of the underlying stock at the striking price. Your call no longer exists.

In this example, you experienced a loss on the stock because you are required to purchase 100 shares at current market value and deliver them at the striking price. However, you may have an overall profit as long as the gap between current market value and striking price is less than the amount you received when you sold the call.

You can never predict early exercise, since buyer and seller are not matched one-to-one. The selection is random. The Options Clearing Corporation (OCC) acts as buyer to every seller, and as seller to every buyer. When a buyer decides to exercise a call, the order is assigned at random to a seller. You will not know that this has happened to you until your broker gets in touch to inform you of the exercise.

Smart Investor Tip Because exercise can happen at any time your call is in the money, you need to be aware of your exposure; even early exercise is a possibility. If you sell an in-the-money call, exercise could happen the same day.

In order for you to profit from selling calls, the underlying stock needs to act in one of two ways:

1. Its market value must remain at or below the striking price of the call, so that time value will evaporate over time. The option will expire worthless, or it can be closed with a purchase that is lower than the initial sales price.

2. The market value must remain at a stable enough price level so that the option can be purchased below initial sales price, even if it is in the money. The decline in time value still occurs, even when accompanied by intrinsic value.

The profit and loss zones for uncovered calls are summarized in Figure 5.1. Because you receive cash for selling a call, the break-even price is higher than the striking price. In this illustration, a call was sold for 5; hence, breakeven is 5 points higher than striking price. (This example does not take into account the transaction fees.)

Your brokerage firm will require that you deposit a percentage of the total potential liability at the time you write naked calls. The amount required could consist of cash or securities and will vary by broker. Because large losses can result in the event of a major change in market value, many brokerage firms restrict or even forbid naked call writing in options, or require exceptionally large deposits of cash or securities. When investors are unable to cover losses in their accounts, the brokerage firm has to make up the difference, and a sudden and large change in market value can require a large sum of money.

Example: You have advised your broker that you intend to write uncovered calls. Your portfolio currently is valued at $20,000 in securities and cash. Your broker restricts your uncovered call writing activity to a level that, in the broker's estimation, would not potentially exceed $20,000. However,

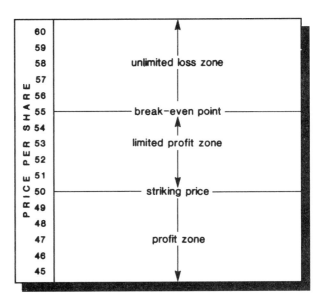

FIGURE 5.1   An uncovered call's profit and loss zones.

as market conditions change, your portfolio value could fall, in which case your broker could restrict your uncovered call activity or require the deposit of additional funds.

Example: You want to write puts in your portfolio as part of your investment strategy. (See Chapter 7.) Your portfolio value is $20,000. Again, your brokerage firm will place restrictions on uncovered put writing activity based on an estimation of potential losses. However, when you write puts, your liability is not as great; stocks can fall only so far, whereas they can rise indefinitely.

Writing uncovered puts involves limited losses, since the very worst outcome possible is a stock's decline to zero. (In reality, the maximum decline should be considered the decline to book value per share; book value often is overlooked in the market, but that level does provide a reasonable level for assessing liability. It is possible for market value to fall below book value, but that is not likely.) So uncovered puts are associated with a finite loss potential, whereas uncovered calls can lead to unknown levels of loss, especially if you write many uncovered calls at the same time.

Smart Investor Tip While a stock's market price could fall below book value, it is rare. Using book value as a likely low point to evaluate selling puts is a good plan.

Assessing Uncovered Call Writing Risks

All investors need to practice risk assessment as a primary means for determining what is appropriate. The examples in the preceding section demonstrate that risks are substantial for uncovered call writing. Later in this chapter and in future chapters, however, some alternatives are presented that demonstrate how writing calls is not always a high-risk venture.

For now, consider the risks involved with writing uncovered calls, especially in light of limitations that are placed on your activity by brokerage firms. These limitations are appropriate and necessary due to the risk of potential losses. A limited value in your portfolio at large will restrict the amount of uncovered call writing you will be allowed to activate. So the restrictions that are placed on this form of trading naturally limit your ability to participate in the high-risk end of this market.

The risks of uncovered call writing include the following:

1. The stock might rise in value; you will be required to buy the call to close your position and avoid further loss and exercise.

2. The stock might rise in value, leading to exercise, perhaps early exercise.

3. Although the stock might remain at or below striking price for a period of time, it could rise unexpectedly and suddenly, leading to exercise; you are at risk from the moment you sell the call all the way to expiration.

4. You lose opportunities to move your capital around in the market because your brokerage firm wants to limit your risk or loss as well as theirs, so your equity is committed as collateral for your open uncovered call positions.

5. If you do suffer unexpected large losses, your brokerage firm may sell other securities in your portfolio to pay for those losses. This may include securities whose sale is ill-timed; thus you lose long-term value in your portfolio.

6. Although you set standards for yourself, you might fail to take action when you should, so that today's profit disappears and you end up losing money upon exercise or having to buy the call at a loss to avoid exercise.

Smart Investor Tip It makes sense to know all of the risks involved with uncovered call selling. Not knowing can lead to some very expensive surprises.

SELLING COVERED CALLS

When you sell uncovered calls, potentially large losses result if you are required to deliver shares upon exercise, or to close out positions at a loss to avoid exercise. Imagine being able to sell calls without that risk—meaning that you would never be required to suffer large losses due to an unexpected rise in the stock's market value.

There is a way. By selling a call when you also own 100 shares of the underlying stock, you *cover* your position. If the option is called away, you can meet the obligation simply by delivering shares that you already own.

You enjoy several advantages through the *covered call*:

1. You are paid a premium for each call that you sell, and the cash is placed in your account at the time you sell. While this is also true of uncovered call writing, the same risks do not apply. You can afford exercise because you own 100 shares of stock. Upon exercise, you would not be required to buy shares at market price.

2. The true net price of your 100 shares of stock is reduced by the value of the option premium. It discounts your basis because you receive cash when you sell the call. This gives you flexibility and downside protection, and more versatility for selling calls with high time value.

3. Selling covered calls provides you with the freedom to accept moderate interim price declines, because the premium you receive reduces your basis in the stock. Simply owning the stock without the discount means that even small declines in the stock's market value represent paper losses.

 cover to protect oneself by owning 100 shares of the underlying stock for each call sold. (The risk in the short position in the call is covered by ownership of 100 shares.)

 covered call a call sold to create an open short position, when the seller also owns 100 shares of stock for each call sold.

The disadvantage to covered call selling is found in lost opportunity risk; but the opportunity may or may not materialize. If the stock's market value rises dramatically, your call will be exercised at the specified striking price. If you had not sold the call, you would benefit from higher market value in shares of stock. So covered call sellers trade the potential lost profits in the event of exercise for the certainty of premiums received today.

Smart Investor Tip The major risk associated with uncovered call writing is the possibility of lost income from rising stock prices. But that might not happen at all; when you sell a call, you accept the possible lost income in exchange for certainty.

Example: You own 100 shares of stock, which you bought last year at $50 per share. Current market value is $54 per share. You are willing to sell this stock at a profit. You write a November 55 call and receive a premium of 5. Now your real basis in the stock is $45 per share (original price of $50 per share, discounted 5 points by the option premium). If the stock's market value remains between the range of $45 and $55 between the date you sell the call and expiration, your investment will be profitable. In addition, the call would not be exercised within that price range, since striking price is 55. You can wait out expiration or buy the call at a profit. However, if the stock were to rise far above $55 per share and the call were exercised, you would not receive any gain above $55 per share. While exercise would still produce a profit of $1,000 ($500 stock profit plus $500 option premium), you would lose out on any profits above the striking price level.

One of three events can take place when you sell a covered call: an increase in the stock's price, a decrease in the stock's price, or no significant change. As long as you own 100 shares of the underlying stock, you continue to receive dividends even when you have sold the call. The value of writing calls should be compared to the value of buying and holding stock, as shown in Table 5.1.

Before you undertake any strategy, you need to assess the benefits or consequences in the event of all possible changes, including the potential for lost future profits that might or might not occur. To ensure a profit in the outcome of writing covered calls, it is wise to select those calls with striking prices above your original basis, or at least above original basis when discounted by the call premium you receive.

Example: You bought stock last year at $48 per share. If you sell a covered call with a striking price of 50 and receive a premium of 3, you have discounted your basis to $45 per share. Or, given the same original basis, you may

	TABLE 5.1 Comparing Strategies	
	Outcomes	
Event	Owning Stock and Writing Calls	Owning Stock Only
Stock goes up in value	Call is exercised; profits are limited to striking price and call premium.	Stock can be sold at a profit.
Stock remains at or below the striking price	Time value declines; the call can be closed out at a profit or allowed to expire worthless.	No profit or loss until sold.
Stock declines in value	Stock price is discounted by call premium; the call is closed or allowed to expire worthless.	Loss on the stock.
Dividends	Earned while stock is held.	Earned while stock is held.

be able to sell a call with a striking price of 45 and receive a premium of 8. That discounts your basis to $40 per share; in the event of exercise at the striking price of 45, you would net a profit of $500.

In comparing potential profits from various strategies, you might conclude that writing in-the-money calls makes sense in some circumstances. A decline in price reduces call premium dollar for dollar, with the added advantage of declining time value. If this occurs, you can close out the position at a profit, or simply wait for exercise. As a call seller, you are willing to *lock in* the price of the underlying stock in the event of exercise; this makes sense only if exercise will produce a profit to you, given the original purchase price of the shares, discounted by the call premium.

Assessing Covered Call Writing Risks

The seller of uncovered calls faces potentially large losses. As a covered call writer, your risks are reduced significantly. On the upside, the risk is limited to lost future profits that do not always take place. On the downside, the risk

lock in
to freeze the price of the underlying stock when the investor has sold a corresponding short call. (As long as the call position is open, the writer is locked into a striking price, regardless of current market value of the stock. In the event of exercise, the stock is delivered at that locked-in price.)

is the same as for simply owning shares: a decline in price represents a paper loss. The call writer discounts the basis, providing a degree of downside protection. When you write calls against stock using striking prices above your original basis, you virtually eliminate the upside market risk because upon exercise you have a built-in profit factor.

Smart Investor Tip   The call seller has fewer risks than others because call selling is a safe strategy. Even if the stock falls in value, writing calls provides downside protection.

Many investors are concerned with the lost opportunity risk associated with potential future profits in the stock. Once you sell a call, you commit yourself to selling 100 shares at the striking price, even if the stock's market value rises far above that price. Owning 100 shares covers the short position in the call; it also limits potential profit overall.

By properly structuring a covered call writing strategy, you can learn to manage the risk of losing potential future gains, in exchange for predictability and the certainty of current profits. The covered call writing strategy is going to produce profits consistently when applied correctly. So a very good return on your investment is possible through writing covered calls. You might lose the occasional spectacular profit when a stock's price rises suddenly; but for the most part, your rate of return will exceed what you could expect in your portfolio without writing covered calls. Some pitfalls to avoid in your covered call writing strategy:

1. *Setting up the call write so that, if exercised, you end up losing money in the underlying stock.* This is possible if you sell calls with striking prices *below* your original basis in the stock. This is an especially serious problem if the discounted basis (considering the option premium) is not adequate to cover the loss. For example, you buy stock at $34 per share and later sell a 30 call, receiving a premium of 3. In this example, exercise produces an overall net loss of $100—$400 lost on the stock, minus $300 received for selling the call.

2. *Getting locked into positions that you cannot afford to close out.* If you become involved in too high a level of

covered call writing, you will eventually find yourself in a position when you want to close out the call but you do not have the cash available to take advantage of the situation. You need to keep an adequate cash reserve so that you can act when the opportunity is there. Suppose, for example, you sold a call for 6 and since then the stock has been in the money; you think it will be exercised. However, the price dips and the call's premium value falls to 4. You would like to close the position at once, but you do not have $400 in your account; the opportunity is lost.

3. *Writing calls on the wrong stock.* When you begin comparing premium values, you might spot an unusually rich time value in a particular option. You might be tempted to buy 100 shares of the stock and sell a call at the same time, since the option premium will discount your basis in the stock. However, the stock is likely to be volatile, which accounts for the exceptionally high premium in the call; this means that the risks associated with owning that stock are greater than for more stable issues. You might profit on the option, but suffer a loss in the stock purchase. A moderate market correction could wipe out your profits.

CALCULATING RATE OF RETURN

If your purpose in owning stock is to hold it for many years, writing calls may not be an appropriate strategy—although in some instances this strategy can be used to enhance returns with only a moderate risk of exercise. The call writer's objective often is quite different from that of the long-term investor and, while the two objectives can coexist, it is more likely that you will use the covered call writing strategy on one portion of your portfolio while avoiding even moderate risks of exercise on another portion. You have three potential sources of income as a covered call writer:

✔ Call premium
✔ Capital gain on stock
✔ Dividends

Example: You bought 100 shares of stock and paid $32 per share. Several months later, the stock's market value had risen to $38 per share. You wrote a March 35 call and received 8. Your reasoning: Your original basis in the stock was $32, and selling the call discounts that basis to $24. If the call were exercised, you would be required to deliver the shares at $35, regardless of current market value of those shares. Your profit would be $1,100 if that occurred ($800 premium plus $300 profit on the stock), a return of 45.8%. The option premium at the time you sold contained 3 points of intrinsic value and 5 points of time value. If the stock's market value remained at the same level without exercise, that 5 points eventually would evaporate and the call could be closed through purchase at a lower premium. If the stock's market value rises far above the striking price, you would still be required to deliver shares at the striking price upon exercise; the potential future gain would be lost. By undertaking this strategy, you exchange the certainty of a 45.8% gain for the uncertainty of greater profits later, if they occur.

This example points out how a potential profit may be lost, a fact that covered call writers need to accept. Simply owning stock and not writing calls against it could produce profits in the event of a large run-up in price; but doing so also produces losses in the event of price decline, and selling calls provides downside protection in addition to the certainty of profit. Covered call writing does limit the potential profit you can earn, so that your profits are limited but certain.

What are the chances of a stock's price soaring? It does happen, but you cannot afford to depend on it. If you sell a call and limit your profits, have you really lost? Investors will have varying points of view about this question. Some will see missed potential future profits as losses if and when they occur; others will recognize the worth of the certainty of current profits.

A reasonable position may be to look at profits only if they are taken. In other words, potential future profits do not exist at the time you sell an option, and by the same argument, profits in open option positions are not profits unless you close the position. Covered call writers can earn consistent returns on their strategy, but they also have to accept the occasional lost profit from a stock's unexpected price change. As a covered call writer, you seek consistent returns and, in exchange, you willingly sacrifice the occasional unexpected profit in the stock.

Smart Investor Tip Take profits when they can be taken. You cannot count paper profits, because they could evaporate and never return.

By accepting this limitation associated with writing covered calls, you trade off the potential gain for the *discount* in the price of the stock. This downside protection is especially desirable when you remember that you also continue to receive dividends even though you have sold calls. You can earn better than average returns through covered call writing; it is possible for this strategy to produce greater overall profits than those to be realized from owning stock without writing calls.

A covered call writer needs to be aware of profit and loss zones that apply, as shown in Figure 5.2. A covered call's profit and loss zones are determined by the combination of two factors: option premium value and the underlying stock's current market value. If the stock falls below the break-even price (price paid for the stock, minus the

discount
to reduce the true price of the stock by the amount of premium received. (A benefit in selling covered calls, the discount provides downside protection and protects long positions.)

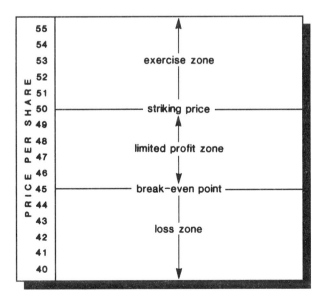

FIGURE 5.2 A covered call's profit and loss zones.

premium received for selling the call) there will be a loss. Of course, as a stock owner, you decide when and if to sell, so the loss is not realized. You have the luxury of being able to let the option expire worthless, and then wait for a rebound in the stock's price. The option premium discounts your basis, so by having sold the option, you lower the required rebound level.

The writer should also calculate the rate of return that will be realized given different outcomes. You need to apply one critical rule for yourself: Never sell a covered call unless you would be satisfied with the outcome in the event of exercise. Figure the *total return* before selling the call, and enter into the transaction only when you are confident that the numbers work for you.

Total return in the case of exercise includes stock appreciation, call premium, and dividend income. But if the option expires worthless, a different rate of return results; and if you close the option by buying it before expiration, a still different return results. Because the second and third outcomes do not include selling the stock, the rate of return can vary considerably. The return is calculated based on the original purchase of the stock.

 total return
the combined return including income from selling a call, capital gain from profit on selling the stock, and dividends earned and received. (Total return may be calculated in two ways: return if the option is exercised, and return if the option expires worthless.)

Example: You own 100 shares of stock that you bought at $40 per share. Current market value is $44 per share, and you have sold a July 45 call for 5. Between now and expiration, you will receive a total of $40 in dividend income.

Given this information, return upon exercise would consist of all three elements:

Stock appreciation	$400
Call premium	500
Dividends	40
Total return	$940
Yield	23.5%

If the call is not exercised but expires worthless, total return does not include appreciation from the underlying stock, since it would not be called away. (Current value compared to purchase price is a paper profit only and is not included in the rate of return.) In this case, return will be:

Call premium	$500
Dividend income	40
Total return	$540
Yield	13.2%

Although the yield in the second instance is lower, you still own the stock. After expiration of the option, you can sell another call, sell the stock, or continue to hold it for long-term appreciation.

TIMING THE DECISION

A first-time call writer might be surprised to experience immediate exercise. That can occur at any time that your call is in the money. It is more likely to occur close to expiration date, but you need to be prepared to give up 100 shares of stock at any time your option remains open. This is the contractual agreement you enter when you sell the call.

As shown in Figure 5.3, during the life of a call, the underlying stock might swing several points above or below striking price. If you own 100 shares and are thinking of selling a covered call, keep these points in mind:

1. When the striking price of the call is higher than the original price you paid for the stock, exercise is not a negative; it automatically triggers a triple profit—from appreciation of the stock, call premium, and dividend income.

Example: You bought stock at $38 per share and later sold a call with a striking price of 40, receiving 3. You are not concerned about exercise because it would mean a profit of $500—$200 in stock appreciation plus $300 from option premium.

2. If you sell a call for a striking price below your original cost of stock, be sure the premium you receive is greater than the loss you would experience in the stock in the event of exercise.

Example: You bought 100 shares of stock at $43 per share and sold a call with a striking price of 40. If exercised, your

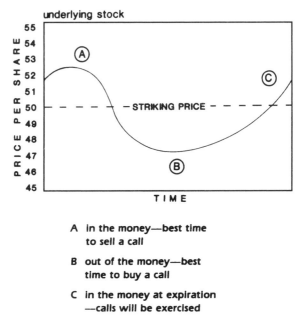

FIGURE 5.3 Timing of call transactions relative to price movement of underlying stock.

loss on the stock will be $300. Thus, if you receive an option premium of 3 or less, you lose money. This transaction makes sense only if the premium is high enough to offset losses on the stock.

Smart Investor Tip Be sure that the potential loss in the stock upon exercise is less than the call premium you receive. It makes no sense to program in a loss when you sell calls against stock.

3. In calculating potential yields, be sure to allow for trading costs on both stock and option, both for entering and leaving the positions.

Example: You bought 100 shares of stock at $53 and later sold a call with a striking price of 50, receiving a premium of 3. In the event of exercise, losses in the stock will be offset by the option premium. However, you will actually experience some loss in this example, because you have to allow for the cost of buying and selling the stock, as well as for buying and selling the call.

4. For the benefit of producing a consistent profit from writing calls, remember that you give up the potential for greater gains if and when the stock's current market value rises.

Example: You bought 100 shares of stock at $22 and later sold a call with a striking price of 25, receiving a premium of 4. In the event of exercise, profit will be $700—$300 in gain on the stock plus $400 for the option. However, the stock's market value recently rose to $34 and the call was exercised. You realize a 31.8% return—$700 on an investment of $2,200 (without counting dividends). But if you had not sold the call, your total profit would be $1,200, or 54.5% based on your original purchase of $2,200. This assumes, of course, that you sell the 100 shares when their value reaches $34 per share.

You cannot depend on sudden increases in a stock's market value. As a call writer, you acknowledge that this can occur, but you accept the certainty and consistency of gains from writing calls, and are willing give up the occasional bigger profit. The way you view such circumstances dictates whether you should write covered calls. If you would be overly concerned about the potential for big gains in the stock, then writing covered calls would not be appropriate for you.

Selection of the right covered call depends on your original purchase price, the value of the stock today, and the available calls and their premiums. Option premium depends on the characteristics of the underlying stock and on the degree of price difference between current market value of the stock and striking price of the option. In addition, time value premium depends on the time remaining until expiration. The more time, the higher the time value premium.

Example: You buy 100 shares of stock at $51 per share, and it then rises to $53. Rather than sell the stock, you choose to sell a call with a striking price of 50, and you are paid a premium of 7.

In this example, the premium is higher than average, with only 3 points of intrinsic value. The 4 points indicates the probability of a long time to go to expiration. Selling a call in this case provides several advantages to you:

1. If the stock's current market value falls below your purchase price, you can buy the option and close the position at a profit, or wait for it to expire worthless.

2. By selling the call, you discount your basis in the stock from $51 to $44 per share, providing yourself with 7 points of downside protection. In the event of a price decline in the stock's market value, this is a substantial degree of protection.

3. You continue to receive dividends as long as the option is not exercised.

You can also choose to sell a covered call that is deep in the money.

Example: You bought stock at $51 per share and it is now worth $53. You will receive a premium of at least 8 if you sell a call with a striking price of 45 (because there would be 8 points of intrinsic value). That also increases the chances of exercise substantially. For the 8 points in option premium, you would lose 6 points in the stock upon exercise. These outcomes would change if time value were also available. For example, a 45 call might have current premium of 11, with 3 points representing time value. Upon exercise, the additional 3 points would represent additional profit: $1,100 for selling the call, minus a loss of $600 on the stock, for a net profit of $500 upon exercise.

Smart Investor Tip   Selling deep in-the-money calls can produce high profits for call sellers, especially if they want to sell their stock anyway.

Such an outcome is not an unreasonable method for producing profits, but it occurs only if the call is exercised. In the event the stock's market value falls, the call premium is reduced one dollar for each dollar lost in the stock's market value. You can buy the call to close the position, with the profit discounting your basis in the stock.

Example: You bought shares of stock at $51 per share, and the stock is worth $53 at the time that you sell a 45 call. You received a premium of 11. The market value of the stock later falls 3 points, to $50 per share. The call is worth 7, representing a drop of 3 points of intrinsic value and 1 point of time value. You can close the position and buy the call for 7, realizing a $400 profit. You still own the stock and are free to sell covered calls again. For the moment, your $400 option profit reduces your basis in the stock from $51 per share down to $47 per share.

Always select options and time short sales with these considerations in mind:

- ✔ Your original price per share of the stock.
- ✔ The premium you will be paid for selling the call.
- ✔ The mix between intrinsic value and time value.
- ✔ The gap between current market value of the stock and striking price of the call.
- ✔ The time until expiration.
- ✔ Total return if the call is exercised, compared to total return if the option expires worthless.
- ✔ Your objective in owning the stock (long-term growth, for example), compared to your objective in selling the call (immediate income and downside protection, for example).

AVOIDING EXERCISE

Assuming that you sell a call on stock originally purchased as a long-term investment, you might want to take steps to avoid exercise. First, though, remember the overall guideline: Never sell a covered call unless you are willing to go through exercise and give up 100 shares of stock at the striking price. However, even with that in mind, you might be able to increase your profits from selling calls by avoiding exercise.

You can achieve this in several ways. The following examples are all based on a situation in which unexpected upward price movement occurs in the underlying stock, placing you in the position where exercise is likely.

Example: You sold a May 35 call on stock when the stock's market value was $34 per share. The stock's current market value is $41, and you would like to avoid exercise to take advantage of the higher market value of the stock.

The first method you can use to avoid exercise is simply to cancel the option by purchasing it. Although this creates a loss in the option, it is offset by a corresponding increase in the value of the stock. If time value has declined, this strategy makes sense—especially if the increased value of stock exceeds the loss in the option. A word of caution, however: The increased value in stock is a paper profit only, so to realize the profit in this case, you would need to sell the shares.

Example: You bought 100 shares of stock at $21 per share and later sold a June 25 call for 4. The stock's current market value is now at $30 per share and the call's premium is at 6. If you buy the call, you will lose $200; however, by avoiding exercise, you avoid having to sell the stock at $25 per share. You now own 100 shares at $30, and are free to sell an option with a higher striking price, if you want.

In this example, the outcome can be summarized in two ways. First, remember that by closing the call position at a loss, you still own the 100 shares of stock. That frees you to sell another call with a striking price of 30 or higher, which would create more option premium. (If you could sell a new option for 2 or more, that offsets your loss in the June 25 call.)

You can also analyze the transaction by comparing the exercise price of the option to the outcome of closing the option and selling shares at current market value. The flaw in this method is that it assumes a sale of stock, which is not necessarily going to occur; however, the comparison is valuable to determine whether avoiding exercise makes sense. A summary:

	Exercise	*Sale*
Basis in 100 shares of stock	−$2,100	−$2,100
Call premium received	400	400
Call premium paid	−	600
100 shares delivered at $25	2,500	
100 shares sold at $30		3,000
Net profit	$ 800	$ 700

This comparison shows that it would be more desirable by $100 to allow exercise of the call. That is a fair conclusion only if you would be willing to give up the 100 shares. It also excludes the advantages of keeping the stock and being able to sell another call after closing the original call position. In most cases, the purpose in avoiding exercise is to be able to continue trading options on that stock, preferably at a higher market value for the underlying stock.

Smart Investor Tip A careful comparison between choices is the only way to tell whether to accept exercise or to close out the whole position.

A second technique to avoid exercise involves exchanging one option for another, while making a profit or avoiding a loss in the exchange. Since the premium value for a new option will be greater if more time value is involved until expiration, you can trade on that time value. Such a strategy is likely to defer exercise even when the call is in the money, remembering that the majority of exercise actions take place close to expiration date. This technique is called a *roll forward*.

Example: The May 40 call that you wrote against 100 shares of stock is near expiration and is in the money. To avoid or delay exercise, you close the May 40 option by buying it, and you immediately sell an August 40 call that has the same striking price but a later expiration.

You still face the risk of exercise at any time; however, it is less likely with a call three months farther out. In addition, if you believe that expiration is inevitable, this strategy provides you with additional income. Because the

 roll forward
the replacement of one written call with another with the same striking price, but a later expiration date.

August 40 call has more time until expiration, it also has more time value premium. The roll forward can be used whether you own a single call or several. The more lots of 100 shares you own of the underlying stock, the greater your flexibility in rolling forward and adding to your option premium profits. Canceling a single call and rolling forward produces a marginal gain; however, if you cancel one call and replace it with two or more later-expiring calls, your gain will be greater. This strategy is called *incremental return*. Profits can increase as you increase the number of calls sold against stock.

Example: You own 300 shares of stock that you bought for $31 per share. You sold one call with a striking price of 35, and received a premium of 4. Now the stock is worth $39 per share and you would like to avoid exercise. You buy the original call and pay 8, accepting a loss of $400; and replace it by selling three calls with a later expiration for 4 each, receiving a total premium of 12. The net transaction yields you an extra $400 in cash: $1,200 for the three calls, minus $800 paid to close the original position.

In this example, you trade one exposure on 100 shares of stock for exposure on all 300 shares; but you avoid exercise as well. At the same time, you net out additional cash profits, which reduces your overall basis in the stock. This could make exercise more acceptable later on. Of course, you can continue to use rolling techniques to avoid exercise. The roll forward maintains the same striking price and buys you time. However, the plan does not always suit the circumstances. Another rolling method is called the *roll down*.

Example: You originally bought 100 shares of stock at $31 per share, and later sold a call with a striking price of 35, for a premium of 3. The stock has fallen in value and your call now is worth 1. You cancel (buy) the call and realize a profit of $200, and immediately sell a call with a striking price of 30, receiving a premium of 4.

In this case, the first call was sold 4 points above your original basis. The profit of $200 lowers that basis to $29 per share. The second call further reduces the basis by 4

incremental return
a technique for avoiding exercise while increasing profits with written calls. (When the value of the underlying stock rises, a single call is closed at a loss and replaced with two or more call writes with later expiration dates, producing cash and a profit in the exchange.)

roll down
the replacement of one written call with another that has a lower striking price.

more points, to $25. If the option is exercised (striking price is 30), the net profit will be $500.

The roll down is an effective way to offset losses in stock positions in a declining market. Profits in the call premium offset losses, reducing your basis in the stock. You face a different problem in a rising market. In that situation, you may use the *roll up*.

roll up
the replacement of one written call with another that has a higher striking price.

Example: You originally paid $31 per share for 100 shares of stock, and later sold a call with a striking price of 35. The stock's current market value has risen to $39 per share. You cancel (buy) the call and accept a loss, offsetting that loss by selling another call with a striking price of 40 and more time to go until expiration.

With this technique, the loss in the original call can be offset by replacement of the new call. This is true when there is more time to go until expiration. This technique depends on time value to make it profitable. Considering you will be picking up an extra 5 points in the stock's market value by avoiding exercise, you can afford a loss in the roll up as long as it does not exceed the 5-point difference.

Smart Investor Tip   Rolling techniques can help you to maximize option returns without going through exercise, most of the time. But the wise seller is always prepared to give up shares. That is the nature of selling options.

It is conceivable that the various rolling techniques can be used indefinitely to avoid exercise, while still producing profits. Figure 5.4 provides one example of how this could occur.

Example: You own 800 shares of stock that you bought at $30 per share; your basis is $24,000. You expect the value of the stock to rise, but you also want to write covered calls and increase profits while providing yourself with downside protection. So on March 15, you sell two June 30 contracts for 5 apiece, and receive payment of $1,000.

On June 11, the stock's market value is at $38 per share and you expect your calls to be exercised. To avoid exercise, you close the two calls by buying them, paying a

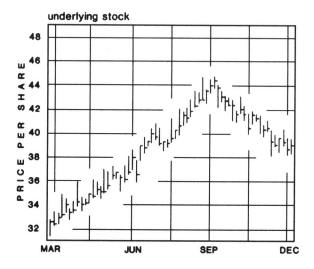

underlying stock

DATE	DESCRIPTION	RECEIVED	PAID
Mar 15	sell 2 Jun 30 calls at 5	$1000	
Jun 11	buy 2 Jun 30 calls at 8		$1600
	sell 5 Sep 35 calls at 6	$3000	
Sep 8	buy 5 Sep 35 calls at 9		$4500
	sell 8 Dec 40 calls at 6	$4800	
Dec 22	Dec 40 calls expire worthless	–	–
	totals	$8800	$6100
	profit	$2700	

FIGURE 5.4 Using the rolling technique to avoid exercise.

premium of 8 (total paid, $1,600). You replace these calls with five September 35 calls and receive 6 for each, getting a total of $3,000.

On September 8, the stock's market value has risen again, and now is valued at $44 per share. You want to avoid exercise again, so you cancel your open positions and pay a premium of 9 each, or $4,500 total. You sell eight December 40 calls in replacement at 6, for a total of $4,800.

By December 22, the day of expiration, the stock has fallen to $39 per share. Your eight outstanding calls expire worthless. Your total profit on this series of transactions is $2,700 for net call premium. In addition, you still own

800 shares of stock, now worth $39 per share, which is
$7,200 above your original basis.

For the volume of transactions, you might wonder if the
exposure to exercise was worth the $2,700 in profit, or
11.25%. It certainly was, considering that the strategy here
was dictated by rising stock prices. While you received a
profit, you avoided exercise while prices rose. The incremental return combining roll up and roll forward demonstrates how you can avoid exercise while still generating a
profit. You cannot depend on this pattern to continue or to
repeat, but strategies are to be devised based on the situation. It helped, too, that the example involves multiple lots
of stock, providing flexibility in writing calls.

This example is based on the premise that you
would have been happy to accept exercise at any point
along the way. Certainly, exercise would always have been
profitable, as striking prices were all above original basis.
If you were to sell the 800 shares at the ending market
value of $39 per share, total profit would have been sub-
stantial using covered calls:

Stock

Sell 800 shares at $39	$31,200
Less: Original cost	−24,000
Profit on stock	$ 7,200

Options

Sell 2 June contracts	$ 1,000
Buy 2 June contracts	−1,600
Sell 5 September contracts	3,000
Buy 5 September contracts	−4,500
Sell 8 December contracts	4,800
Profit on options	$ 2,700
Total profit	$ 9,900
Yield	41.25%

Whenever you roll forward, higher time value is a
benefit. Greater premium value is found in calls with the

same striking price but more time before expiration. The longer that time period, the higher your income and potential future income from selling the call. In exchange for the higher income, you agree to remain exposed to the risks for a longer period of time. You are locked into the striking price until you close the position, go through exercise, or wait out expiration.

Smart Investor Tip The key to profiting from rolling forward is in remembering that the longer the time until expiration, the more time value there will be in the call.

Your strategies to defer or avoid exercise combine two dissimilar goals: increasing your income while also holding onto the stock with value above striking price. This can be done with higher time value, in recognition of the probability that options will not be exercised until closer to expiration date.

Example: You own 200 shares of stock originally purchased at $40 per share. You are open on a short June 40 call, which you sold for 3. The stock currently is worth $45 per share, and you want to avoid being exercised at $40.

Table 5.2 shows current values of calls that are available on this stock. A review of this table provides you several alternatives for using rolling techniques:

> *Strategy 1: Rolling up and forward.* Sell one December 45 call at 5 while buying the June 40 call at 6. This produces a net profit of $200 ($500 for the December call less a $300 loss on the June call).

TABLE 5.2 Current Call Option Values			
Striking Price	Expiration Month		
	June	Sept.	Dec.
35	11	13	15
40	6	8	10
45	1	2	5

Strategy 2: Rolling with incremental return. Sell two September 45 calls, producing $400 in premium, resulting in $100 net income ($400 for the two September 45 calls, less the loss of $300 on the June 40 call).

Strategy 3: Rolling forward only. Sell one September 40 call at 8, resulting in net income of $500 ($800 for the September 40 call, less the $300 loss on the June call).

Note in these strategies that we refer to the *loss* on the June call. Because that call currently is valued at 6, it requires a cash outlay of $600 to close the position. You received $300 when you sold, so your net loss is $300.

The loss of $300 is acceptable in all of these strategies because either the striking price of 40 is replaced with one of 45, which is 5 points higher, or additional income is produced to offset that loss by replacing the call with one expiring later.

If the underlying stock is reasonably stable—for example, if its market value tends to stay within a 5-point range during a typical three-month period—it is possible to employ rolling techniques and avoid exercise indefinitely as long as no early exercise occurs. As stated before, however, you have to remember that when your short positions are in the money, exercise can occur at any time. Rolling techniques are especially useful when stocks break out of their short-term trading ranges and you want to take advantage of increased market value while also profiting from selling calls—all the while avoiding exercise.

To demonstrate how such a strategy can work, refer to Table 5.3. This shows a series of trades over a period of two and a half years, and is a summary of a series of trades taken from actual confirmation receipts. The investor owned 400 shares of stock. Sale and purchase prices show actual amounts of cash transacted allowing for brokerage fees, rounded to the nearest dollar. The total net profit of $2,628 involved $722 in brokerage charges, so that profits before those charges were $3,350.

The information in Table 5.3 shows each type of rolling trade and summarizes how an effective use of incremental return helps avoid exercise as the underlying stock's market value increases. This investor was willing to increase the number of short calls as long as all were

TABLE 5.3 Selling Calls with Rolling Techniques							
Calls Traded	Type	Sold		Bought		Profit	Notes
		Date	Amount	Date	Amount		
1	Jul 35	3/20	$ 328	4/30	$ 221	$ 107	
1	Oct 35	6/27	235	10/8	78	157	
1	Apr 35	1/15	247	4/14	434	−187	
1	Oct 35	4/14	604	6/24	228	376	1
1	Oct 35	7/31	353	9/12	971	−618	
2	Jan 45	9/12	915	12/16	172	743	2
2	Apr 45	12/16	379	2/24	184	195	
4	Jul 40	3/9	1357	5/26	385	972	3
4	Oct 40	6/5	1553	7/22	1036	517	
4	Jan 40	8/5	1504	9/15	138	366	
		Totals	$7475		$4847	$2628	

[1]A roll forward: The loss on the April 35 call was acceptable to avoid exercise, since the October 35 was profitable.

[2]A combination roll forward and roll up: The loss on the October 35 call was acceptable to avoid exercise at a low striking price. The number of calls was incrementally increased from one to two.

[3]A roll down combined with an incremental return: The number of calls changed from two to four, and the striking price of 45 was replaced with one for 40.

covered by shares of stock, to avoid exercise. When the stock's market value fell, the investor rolled down but did not write calls below the original striking price of 35.

Any form of covered call writing should be planned well ahead. Besides checking on the attributes of the call (proximity of striking price to current market value, amount of time and intrinsic value, time until expiration, and premium), it is equally important to analyze the underlying stock as well. There is no point in creating short-term profits through option writing if you do so on low-quality stock that does not have the potential for growth.

If you purchase shares primarily to write options—a common practice—chances are that you will pick issues more volatile than average, since these tend to be associated with higher-premium options. The strategy makes sense in one regard: You will have ample opportunity to take advantage of momentary price swings and their corrections by timing option trades. This works as long as you call the price movement correctly, which is easy in theory but much more difficult in practice. Volatile issues are attractive to option sellers because of their tendency to have higher time value; however, that also is a symptom of the stock's greater market volatility, thus lower safety as an investment.

Smart Investor Tip Stocks whose options offer greater time value do so for a reason. As a general rule, those stocks are higher-risk investments.

Whether you intend to write uncovered or covered calls, you will be less likely to succeed if you buy overpriced stocks that later fall below your basis. No call seller wants to be exercised at a level below one's basis in the stock. Check Figure 5.5. This shows the profit and loss zones for an uncovered call write. In this case, a single May 40 call was sold for 2. This strategy exposes the investor to unlimited risk. If the stock rises above the striking price and then exceeds the 2 points equal to the amount received in premium, losses rise point for point with the stock. Upon exercise, this investor will have to deliver 100 shares of stock at $40 per share, regardless of the current market value at that time.

The example of a covered call write shown in Figure 5.6 demonstrates that the loss zone exists only on the downside, so the strategy has a much different profile than

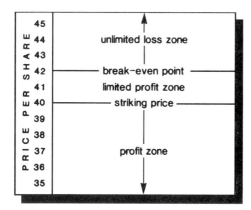

FIGURE 5.5 Example of uncovered call write with profit and loss zones.

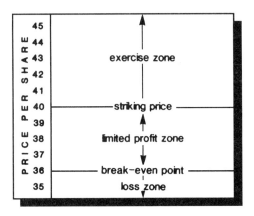

FIGURE 5.6 Example of covered call write with profit and loss zones.

the uncovered alternative. In this example, the investor owned 100 shares of stock that originally was purchased at $38 per share. The investor then sold a May 40 call for 2. This discounts the basis in stock by $2 per share, down to $36. As long as the stock's market value is at or below the striking price of 40, exercise will not occur. If the stock's market value rises above $40 per share, the call will be exercised and the 100 shares called away at $40 per share. In the event of exercise, profit would be $400—$200 in profit on the stock plus $200 for call premium. However, selling covered calls also locks in the striking price. In the event of a substantial price increase, profits are limited in accordance with the terms of the option contract.

Stock selection is of critical importance to the call writer. The next chapter examines methods for picking stocks with a call-writing strategy in mind.

Chapter

Choosing the Right Stock

Very few people are ambitious in the sense of having a specific image of what they want to achieve. Most people's sights are only toward the next run, the next increment of money.
—Judith Bardwick, *The Plateauing Trap*, 1988

Careful, well-researched selection is the key to solid, consistent investing success. This is true for all forms of investing and applies to all strategies. Investors whose stock portfolios are not performing as expected might be tempted to augment lackluster profits by becoming involved in options. Short-term income could close a gap by offsetting small losses, improve overall yields, and even bail out a paper loss position. However, short-term income is not ensured, and such investors have to face the fact that poorly selected stocks cannot be converted through options. Your best chances for success in the options market come from first selecting stocks wisely and from establishing rules for selection and strategy that suit your individual risk tolerance. A suitable options strategy has to be a sensible match for an individual stock, based on its volatility, your purpose in owning it, and its original basis versus current market value.

Only after setting an investment policy for yourself should you consider also using options. One of the more troubling problems in selling options, for example, comes up when you really do not want to sell shares of stock that you own. If you sell calls and the stock rises, you could be required to give up shares upon exercise. When your purpose in buying those shares was for appreciation, it makes no sense to have to sell when, in fact, the stock begins to appreciate. The relatively small profit from selling a call might not justify losing those shares.

A portfolio of well-chosen stocks should be considered as a long-term investment. It is true that such a portfolio can be used to produce short-term profits through options. As a general rule, stocks will hold their value over the long term whether or not you write options.

Smart Investor Tip   Value in your portfolio of stocks exists whether or not you sell options. You cannot expect to bail out poorly selected stocks by offsetting stock losses with option profits.

One common error made by options investors is buying stock specifically because current premium levels on options are attractive. Be aware of the *reasons* for higher-than-average time value. This indicates greater volatility in the stock, a likely higher-than-average risk factor for you as a stockholder. Pricing reflects the perception of the market at large, and exceptionally high risk arising from factors such as overpriced stock could be manifested by unusually high time value in option premiums. For example, a call writer might buy 100 shares of a particular stock just to write a call with high time value. This discounts the purchase price of the stock. If this step is undertaken without a corresponding evaluation of the stock, it invites problems.

Because of their attributes, some of the more volatile stocks also are associated with more interesting option premium levels and short-term price movement. Every investor should ensure that one's personal risk standards are given the highest priority in stock selection, and that those standards are used as a guiding force, and not just as a checklist for selection of stock.

While some option strategies can be highly profitable when a stock's price changes drastically, you also need to think about your investment in shares. For example, a significant price drop represents a loss, even when you do well in selling options. It does no good to trade short-term profits for a portfolio of poor-quality stocks—especially if your basis in those stocks was higher than current market value.

One of the great advantages in selling covered calls is that a minimum profit level is ensured as long as you also remember that the first step always should be proper selection of the stock.

Example: You bought 100 shares of stock at $38 per share. At the time, you analyzed the stock and believed it would be a safe investment with prospects for long-term price appreciation. You now are thinking of selling a covered call. One call expires in three months and has a striking price of 40 and a premium of 4. During the time between now and expiration, you also will earn $60 in dividends. Your calculations ensure an annualized profit of 48.4% (if the call expires worthless) or 69.6% (if the call is exercised at the point of expiration). These returns are reported on an annualized basis in order to ensure that they are comparable.

If the Call Expires

Call premium	$ 400
Dividend	60
Total profit	$ 460
Basis in stock	$3,800

Yield if the call expires: $460 ÷ $3,800 = 12.1%

Annualized return earned in three months:
$(12.1\% \div 3) \times 12 = 48.4\%$

If the Call Is Exercised

Call premium	$ 400
Dividend	60
Capital gain ($4,000 − $3,800)	200
Total profit	$ 660
Basis in stock	$3,800

Yield if the option is exercised:
$660 ÷ $3,800 = 17.4%

Annualized return earned in three months:
$(17.4\% \div 3) \times 12 = 69.6\%$

DEVELOPING A PRACTICAL APPROACH

Earning a consistently high yield from writing calls is not always possible, even for covered call writers. You could be able to sell a call today rich in time value, and profit from the combination of capital gains, dividends, and call premium. But the opportunity is not always going to be available, depending on a combination of factors:

1. The price of the underlying stock has to be at the right level in two respects. First, the relationship between current market value and your basis in the stock has to justify the exposure to exercise, to ensure that in the event of exercise, you will have a profit and not a loss. If this is not possible, then there is no justification in writing the call. Second, the current market value of the underlying stock also has to be correct in relation to the striking price of the call. Otherwise, the time value will not be high enough to justify the transaction.

Example: You bought 100 shares of stock at $43 per share and you want to write a call with a striking price of 45. If exercised, you would earn a $200 profit on the stock in addition to the call premium, plus any dividends earned. In the same circumstances, it would not make sense to sell a 40 call, because that ensures a $300 loss on stock in the event of exercise.

Smart Investor Tip   A fairly simple analysis reveals when an option strategy is likely to produce a profit or a loss. Do the math before you execute the transaction.

2. The volume of investor interest in the stock and related options has to be high enough to provide high enough time value to build in a profit.

Example: The stock you recently bought has had exceptionally high trading volume lately, because it is rumored that the company is negotiating a merger with a competitor. Call premiums on related options are unusually high in time value, which is the best possible situation for writing calls. Note, however, that if the rumors are true, the stock could rise suddenly so that more calls would be exercised. You could lose potential profits on your stock resulting from higher market value by writing calls now.

3. The time between the point of sale of a call and expiration should fit with your personal goals.

Example: You would like to sell your stock within four months and use the proceeds to pay off a loan that is coming due. You are confident that the stock's market value will hold up and you do not want to sell now because you would like to defer capital gains until next year. In the meantime, you would like to augment your short-term income by writing a call. Because you will need proceeds within four months, that goal limits the range of calls available to you to those expiring within the next four months. You should also note that your available option strategies are restricted. You cannot avoid exercise through rolling techniques because the stock has to be sold within four months.

These circumstances demonstrate that call writing is not always timely nor practical. The ideal situation involves long-term holdings that have appreciated in value well above original basis; that you would not mind selling at a profit; and that you can afford to hold indefinitely, even if primarily to use as cover for written calls. All of these observations assume as well that the stock continues to represent a worthwhile investment on its own merits. You might have to wait until price appreciation is sufficient to justify a program of call writing.

In considering various strategies you could employ as a call writer, one common mistake is to proceed as though today's conditions were permanent. Anyone who has observed the stock market should recognize the flaw in such thinking. For example, it might be possible to earn an annualized rate of 48% on a single transaction, but it will not necessarily be possible to repeat that result consistently. Markets change constantly, resulting in ever-changing stock price levels and option premiums. The ideal call write will be undertaken when the following conditions are present:

1. *The striking price of the option is higher than your original basis in the stock.* Thus, exercise would produce a profit both in the stock *and* in the option. If the striking price of the option is lower than your basis in the stock, the option premium should be higher than the difference, while also covering transaction fees in both stock and option. Lacking that, a covered call would result in a loss.

2. *The call is in the money.* This means it will contain a degree of intrinsic value, so stock movements will be paralleled with dollar-for-dollar price changes in option premium. While being in the money increases the chance of exercise, it also means you will receive higher option premium; there is also the likelihood that the premium will contain greater time value. In-the-money options may tend to hold time value better than out-of-the-money options—not always, but often. A decline in the underlying stock's value will produce immediate profits for writers due to decline in intrinsic value. The greater the time until expiration of the call, the more likely it will be that time value will be higher.

3. *There is enough time remaining until expiration that most of the premium consists of time value.* So even with minimal or no price movement in the stock, time value evaporates by expiration. Remember, the writer is compensated by being exposed to risk for a longer period, through higher time value. And to a degree, time value will exist whether the option is in the money or out. It is entirely possible to write an in-the-money option that remains in the money due to no change in the stock's market value, and to produce a profit strictly on the basis of declining time value.

4. *Expiration will occur in six months or less.* You might not want to be locked in to a striking price for too long, and the identification of six months as a cutoff is arbitrary. The point is, the longer the time until expiration, the higher the time value. But by the same argument, the longer that time, the longer your exposure to risk. Given changing market conditions, you need to decide how long a time is reasonable. The longer the period of time you need to forecast in the market, the less reliable your estimates will be.

5. *Premium is high enough to justify the risk.* You will be locked in until expiration unless you later close with an offsetting purchase. In that sense, you risk price increases in the underlying stock. A small premium does not justify an offsetting risk, whereas the risk could be acceptable if the premium level were higher. Every options trader needs to identify this relationship between risk and premium level in addition to the other factors used to determine validity of a short position.

Example: You own 100 shares of stock that you bought at $53 per share. Current market value is $57. You write a 55 call with five months to go until expiration that has a premium of 6. All of the ideal circumstances are present. Striking price is 2 points higher than your basis in the stock; the call is 2 points in the money, so that the option's premium value will be responsive to price changes in the stock; two-thirds of current option premium is time value; expiration takes place in less than six months; and the premium is $600, a rich level considering your basis in the stock. It is 11.3% of your original stock investment, an exceptional return ($600 ÷ $5,300).

In this example, you would earn a substantial return whether the option is exercised or expires worthless. If the stock's market value falls, the $600 call premium provides significant downside protection, discounting your basis to $47 per share. A worst-case analysis, then, would conclude that if the stock's market value fell to $47 per share and the option then expired worthless, the net result would be breakeven.

SELECTING STOCK FOR CALL WRITING

Some investors pick stocks based primarily on the potential yield to be gained from writing calls. This is a mistake. While a larger call premium discounts the stock's basis, it is not enough of a reason to buy shares. The best-yielding call premium most often is available on the highest-risk, most volatile stocks. So if you apply the sole criterion of premium yield to stock selection, you also assume the profile of much greater risks in your stock portfolio. Since there is a tendency among short-term investors to sell when profits are available, such a strategy often results in a portfolio of stocks with paper loss positions—all capital is committed in the purchase of overvalued stocks and investors then have to wait out a reversal in market value.

Example: You decide to buy stock based on the relationship between current call premium and the price of the stock. You have only $4,000 to invest, so you limit your review to stocks selling at $40 per share or less. For example, let's assume that your objective is to locate stocks on which call premium is at least 10% of current market value of the stock, with calls at the money or out of the money. You prepare a chart summarizing a few available stocks and options:

Current Value of Stocks	Call Premium
$36	$3
28	3½
25	1
39	4
27	1¾

You eliminate the first, third, and last choices because call premium is under 10%, and decide to buy the second stock on the list. It is selling at $28 per share and the call premium is 3½, a yield of 12.5%. This is the highest yield available from the list.

On the surface, this study and conclusion appears reasonable. The selection of the call premium discounts the stock's basis by 12.5%. However, there are a number of problems in this approach. Most significant is the fact that no distinction is made among the stocks other than call price and yield. The selected issue was not judged on its individual fundamental or technical merits. Also, by limiting the selection to stocks selling at $40 per share or lower, the range of potential choices is too restricted. It may be that with only $4,000 available, you would do better to select a stock on its own merits and wait until you are able to build up your portfolio.

The criteria for selection of a list of stocks and their associated options are twofold. First, the stocks should be prequalified by your fundamental tests. Only high-quality stocks that meet your investment criteria should be contemplated for purchase, without consideration for the current premium value of options. Second, once you have prequalified the stock, you should avoid committing yourself to writing calls when the potential yield does not justify that risk. Depending on what you expect to make from call writing, the appropriate yield levels may vary. It would be a trap to select stocks based only on potential call writing yield, since the higher-yielding options are likely to be found on the most volatile stocks.

The method in this case also failed to consider time until expiration. You receive higher premiums when expiration dates are farther away, in exchange for which you lock in your position for more time—meaning more change in the underlying stock's market value will be possible. Another flaw is that these calls were not judged in regard to the distance between striking price and current market value of the stock. The yield, by itself, is a misleading method for selecting options.

Smart Investor Tip Picking options based on yield alone is a popular, but flawed, method. It fails to recognize far more important considerations, such as the quality of the underlying stock.

The value of locking in 100 shares to a fixed striking price needs to be judged in relation to the number of months remaining until expiration. Otherwise, how can you fairly judge the value of that option? For example, a 10% yield might be attractive for calls with three to six months remaining until expiration, but far less attractive when the call will not expire for eight months. Yield is not a constant; it depends on time.

Covered call writing is a conservative strategy, assuming that you first understand how to pick high-quality stocks. First and foremost should be a stock's investment value, meaning that option potential should not be the primary factor in the selection of stocks in your portfolio. On the contrary, if you are led by the attractiveness of option premium levels, you are likely to pick highly volatile stocks. If you first analyze the stock for investment value, timeliness, and safety, the option value may then be brought into the picture as yet another means for selecting among otherwise viable investment candidates.

Benefiting from Price Appreciation

You will profit from covered call writing when the underlying stock's current market value is higher than the price you paid for the stock. In that case, you protect your position against a price decline and also lock in a profit in the event of exercise.

Example: You bought 100 shares of stock last year when the value was $27 per share. Today, the stock is worth $38.

In this case, you can afford to write calls in the money without risking an overall loss; or you can write out-of-the-money calls as long as time value is high enough. Remembering that your original cost was $27 per share, you have at least four choices in methods for writing covered calls:

1. *Write a call with a striking price of 25.* The premium will include 13 points of intrinsic value plus time value, which will be higher for longer-out calls. If the call is exercised you lose two points in the stock, but gain 13 points in the call, for an overall profit of $1,100. If the stock's market value falls before exercise, or when time value disappears, you can cancel with a purchase and profit on the option trade, which frees you up to write yet another call. Any decline in stock market value is offset by call profit in this case.

Example: You sold a call deep in the money. A few weeks later, the stock has dropped 6 points, and intrinsic value in the call has also fallen by the same amount. You can buy the call and take a profit of $600, which offsets the stock's market value decline. Any reduction in time value represents additional profit.

2. *Write a call with a striking price of 30.* In this case, intrinsic value is 8 points, and you can apply the same strategies as in choice number 1. However, because your position is not as deep in the money, chances for early exercise are reduced somewhat; in the event of exercise, you would keep the entire option premium, plus gaining $300 in profit on the stock.

Example: You sold a call with a striking price of 30. Two months later, 3 points of time value has evaporated while the stock's market price has not changed. You close the call by buying it, taking your $300 profit.

3. *Write a call with a striking price of 35.* With only 3 points in the money, chances for early exercise are low. Any decline in the stock's market value will be matched point for point by the call's intrinsic value, protecting your stock investment position. Because this call's striking price is close to current market value, there may be more time value than seen in the other alternatives.

Example: You sold a call with a striking price of 35. One month later, the stock has declined 1 point, but the call has lost 3 points overall, representing lost time value. You are able to buy the call to close it and take a profit of $300.

4. *Write a call with a striking price of 40 or 45.* Since both of these are out of the money, the entire premium represents time value. The premium level will be lower since there is no intrinsic value; but the strategy provides you with two distinct advantages. First, it will be easier for you to cancel this position at a profit because time value will decline even if the stock's market value rises. Second, if the option is eventually exercised, you will gain a profit in the option *and* in the stock.

Example: You sold a 40 call when the stock's market value was $38 per share. Your original basis was $27 per share. The call was exercised, and your overall profit includes all of the call premium plus $1,100 profit on the stock.

If you are holding stock with an appreciated market value over your basis, you face a dilemma that every stockholder has to resolve. If you sell and take a profit now, that is a sure thing, but you lose out in the event that further profits could also be earned by keeping those shares. You also face the risk of a decline in market value, meaning some of today's appreciated value will be lost. Long-term investors may be less concerned with short-term price changes; however, it remains valid that anyone would like to ensure a degree of safety in one's paper profits.

Covered call writing could represent the best way to maximize your profits while providing downside protection. As long as your call is in the money, every point lost in the stock is matched by lost points in the call; a paper loss in the stock can be replaced with profits in the call position. The time value premium is potentially all profit, since it will disappear even if the stock's market value goes up, an important point that too many options traders overlook (especially buyers). When your basis is far below striking price of the call, you lock in a capital gain in the event of exercise.

Smart Investor Tip Time value declines over time, even when the stock's market value goes up. This is a problem for buyers, but a great advantage for sellers.

Example: You bought 100 shares of stock several years ago at $28 per share. Today each share is worth $45. You sell a 45 call with four month to go until expiration. The premium was 4, all of which is time value. This discounts your original basis down to $24. If the stock were to fall 4 points or less, the call premium protects the paper profit based on current stock price. If the market value rises and the call is exercised, your shares would be called away at $45 per share.

In this example, two levels of downside protection are evident. First, the original basis is protected to the extent of the call premium; second, paper profits in the current market value have the same degree of downside protection. When stock has appreciated beyond its original cost, it makes sense to protect current value levels. Most investors would see a decline as a loss, even when the corrected stock price remains above original cost. Call writing solves that dilemma.

Selection Risks

Picking the best possible option is not as simple as it appears at first glance. Remember that the real value of any options is a factor of the value in the underlying stock. This includes the fundamental value of the company—its sales and profits, dividend history, competitive strength, and other dollars-and-cents comparisons; it also includes the technical aspects of the stock, which encompass overall market perception of future value, which is what current price levels summarize. For covered call writers, the best selection should always be based on the proper selection of stock. Once that is done, options should be chosen based on several factors:

1. *The current price of the stock versus your original basis.* This comparison certainly affects your decision about which options to write. If your stock's current market value is lower than your original cost, call writing is a problem. Premium level needs to be high enough so that, in the event of exercise, call profit offsets stock loss. If this

is not possible, then there is no good reason for writing a covered call. When the price is far higher than your cost, you have a wide range of flexibility in your choice, and you can even write deep in-the-money calls hoping for expiration and high profits.

2. *Your goals in writing calls.* If your stock has appreciated but you have no intention of selling it, writing calls might not be appropriate, even if you could use the short-term income. In this situation, you should restrict call writing to out-of-the-money calls, reducing the exposure to exercise. That means lower call premium, but less chance of having shares called away.

3. *The comparison between intrinsic value and time value.* This is always a crucial test for option selection. The higher the time value, the greater your potential profit. However, higher time value is accompanied by more time until expiration, meaning less chance for early exercise *and* longer exposure to the locked-in position. High time value might also be a symptom that the underlying stock is a higher risk than you thought, a question worth investigating.

4. *Time until expiration.* The longer the time, the more time value premium you will receive. Compare the number of months to the difference between available options. You might discover that for a relatively small difference in premium, you can cut three months off your exposure term. Shorter term also means that time value will decline more rapidly, a clear advantage to you as seller. You can succeed in covered call writing by dealing primarily in short-term contracts, profiting from rapidly disappearing time value.

5. *Premium level versus lock-in risks.* You might find that for many stocks, premium levels simply are too low to justify locking in your stock to a fixed striking price. Even with all other signals in place, you need to be able to justify the short position in terms of premium dollars you will receive as compensation for exposing yourself to the risk. You might need to wait until more favorable conditions arise.

AVERAGING YOUR COST

You can increase your advantage as a call writer using a strategy known as the *average up*. When the price of stock

 average up
a strategy involving the purchase of stock when its market value is increasing. (The average cost of shares bought in this manner is consistently lower than current market value, enabling covered call writers to sell calls in the money when the basis is below the striking price.)

has risen since your purchase date, this strategy allows you to sell calls in the money on stock you own, when the average basis in that stock is always lower than the average price you paid.

If you buy 100 shares and the market value increases, buying another 100 shares reduces your overall cost so that your basis is lower than current market value. The effect of averaging up is summarized by examples in Table 6.1.

How does averaging up help you as a call writer? When you are writing calls on several-hundred-share lots, you also need to be concerned about the consequences of falling stock prices. While that means you would profit from writing calls, it also means your stock loses value. For example, if you are thinking about buying 600 shares of stock, there are two approaches you can take: You can buy 600 shares at today's price, or you can buy only 100 shares now and wait to see how market values change, buying additional lots in the future. This means you will pay higher transaction costs, but it could also protect your stock's overall market value. By averaging your investment basis, you spread your risk. In effect, you use time as a form of diversification.

Example: You buy 600 shares of stock on January 10 at $26 per share. Market value later falls to $20, so you have a paper loss of $3,600. Later, the price rises to $32, so that you have a paper profit of $3,600.

Example: You buy 100 shares on the 10th of each month, beginning in January. The price of the stock changes over six months so that by June 10 your average basis is $29.50.

TABLE 6.1 Averaging Up			
Date	Shares Purchased	Price per Share	Average Price
January 10	100	$26	$26
February 10	100	28	27
March 10	100	30	28
April 10	100	30	$28^1/_2$
May 10	100	31	29
June 10	100	32	$29^1/_2$

The second example, as illustrated in Table 6.1, enables you to reduce your risk. The average price is always lower than current market value as long as the stock's price continues moving in an upward trend. A critic of this method will point out that buying 600 shares at the beginning would have produced greater profits. But how do you know in advance that the stock will rise? Averaging up is a smart alternative to placing all of your capital at risk in one move. The benefits to this approach are shown in Figure 6.1.

By acquiring 600 shares over time, you can also write six calls. Because your average basis at the end of the period is $29.50 and current market value is $32 per share, you can sell calls with striking price of 30 and win in two ways:

✔ When the average price of stock is lower than striking price of the call, you will gain a profit in the event of exercise.

✔ When the call is in the money, movement in the stock's price is matched by movement in the call's intrinsic value.

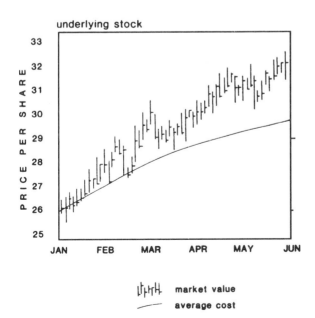

FIGURE 6.1 Example of averaging up.

average down

a strategy involving the purchase of stock when its market value is decreasing. (The average cost of shares bought in this manner is consistently higher than current market value, so a portion of the paper loss on declining stock value is absorbed, enabling covered call writers to sell calls and profit even when the stock's market value has declined.)

What happens, though, if the stock's market value falls? You also reduce your risks in writing calls if you *average down* over time. An example of this strategy is summarized in Table 6.2.

One risk in buying stocks is that if market value falls, you cannot afford to sell calls later. Striking prices with any worthwhile premium value will be below your basis in the stock. If basis is higher than current market value, you will lose money in the event of exercise. As a general rule, you should never sell covered calls if exercise would produce an overall loss.

Smart Investor Tip   When the stock's market value declines, selling covered calls is unlikely to produce profits. Never write calls when exercise would produce a net loss.

If you sell calls with higher striking prices when your stock has lost value, premium will be so minimal that the strategy is not worth it. The solution may be to buy stock through averaging down.

Example: You buy 600 shares of stock on July 10 when the price is $32 per share. The price rises 8 points and you have a profit of $4,800. The stock later falls to $24 per share, resulting in a paper loss of $4,800.

Example: You buy 100 shares of stock each month, beginning on July 10, when market value is $32 per share. By December, after periodic price movement, the current market value has fallen to $24 per share. Average cost per share is $29.

TABLE 6.2 Averaging Down			
Date	Shares Purchased	Price per Share	Average Price
July 10	100	$32	$32
August 10	100	31	$31^1/_2$
September 10	100	30	31
October 10	100	30	$30^3/_4$
November 10	100	27	30
December 10	100	24	29

Your average cost is always higher than current market value in this illustration using the average down technique, but not as high as it would have been if you had bought 600 shares in the beginning. The dramatic difference made through averaging down is summarized in Figure 6.2.

By owning 600 shares, you can write up to six covered calls. In the first example, you are at a disadvantage. Your basis is $32 per share, and current market value is 8 points lower. You would need to write deep out-of-the-money calls, for which premium will be minimal. It will be nearly impossible to justify this strategy, given the circumstances. For example, to lock in all 600 shares at a striking price of 30 would not be worthwhile. Upon exercise, you would lose 2 points per share of stock; yet it is unlikely that you would gain enough in call premium to justify taking the short position.

In the second example, average basis is $29 per share. By writing calls with striking price of 30, you would have 1 point of capital gain on the total of 600 shares in the event of exercise. This is a significant difference in comparison to the first example. It demonstrates how averaging down can be beneficial to call writers in the unfortunate event that the stock's market value falls.

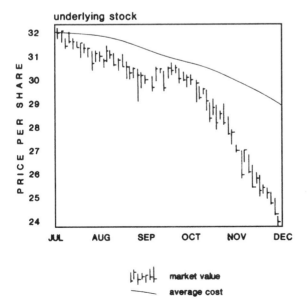

FIGURE 6.2 Example of averaging down.

Both averaging techniques are important tools that help you to mitigate the effects of quickly changing stock prices. In a fast-moving market, price changes represent a problem to the call writer, since locked-in positions can not be sold without exposing yourself to greater risks in the short call position. Both techniques are referred to as *dollar cost averaging*. Regardless of price movement, the strategy always results in protection of capital. A variation of dollar cost averaging is the investment of a fixed dollar amount over time, regardless of per-share value. This is a popular method for buying mutual fund shares. However, in the stock market, direct purchase of stock makes more sense when buying in round lot increments.

ANALYZING STOCKS

Stock selection is the starting point for covered call writing. Remember that options themselves are valued based on market value of the stock in comparison to striking price and expiration date of the option. As such, options do not contain any fundamental or technical features of their own. Valuation is a direct result of fundamental and technical conditions in the underlying stock.

Smart Investor Tip Don't look for fundamental or technical indicators in options when you should be studying the attributes of the underlying stock.

Many novice investors buy stocks on recommendations from others, without understanding the source of the recommendation. They make a second mistake in failing to question whether the particular stock is a good match for them, given their own individual risk tolerance level, long-term investing goals, and available capital. It is easier for investors to make mistakes when buying on the word of someone else and without doing their own research; but that is a lazy approach and, unfortunately for inexperienced investors, it may lead to losses that they cannot afford. Options traders are especially vulnerable to the temptation to buy stocks for the wrong reason—namely, to take advantage of high-priced option opportunities. The failure to investigate the reasons for exceptionally high premiums leads,

dollar cost averaging
a strategy for investing over time, either buying a fixed number of shares or investing a fixed dollar amount, in regular intervals. (The result is an averaging of overall price. If market value increases, average cost is always lower than current market value; if market value decreases, average cost is always higher than current market value.)

again, to selection of stocks that might be too risky for their own situation, given their goals, risk tolerance, and available capital.

Fundamental analysis—the study of financial information, management, competitive position within a sector, dividend history, volatility, volume, and more—is a common and popular method for analyzing stocks. The fundamentals provide you with comparative analysis of value, safety, stability, and the potential for growth and increase in the stock's long-term value. Collectively, the fundamentals are referred to as the "strength" of a corporation. Financial and economic information, corporate management, sector and competitive position, and other indicators involving profit and loss all are part of fundamental analysis. The fundamentalist studies a corporation's balance sheet and income statement to judge a stock's long-term prospects as an investment. Other economic indicators may influence a person's decision to invest or not, such as pending lawsuits, product-related problems, labor troubles, and competition—in other words, anything that could affect profitability.

The technician, in comparison, is not as interested in historical or current information as in indicators that predict future price movement of the stock. The technician uses financial data only to the extent that it affects a current trend, believing that trends provide the key to anticipating the future. The primary concern for technicians is price movement and patterns of price change. Many market analysts believe that price change is random, especially short-term price movement; but some technicians, notably the *chartist*, prefer to believe that patterns of price movement can be used to predict the direction of change in the stock's price.

The relative value of either fundamental or technical analysis is debated continuously. The fundamental approach is based on the assumption that short-term price movement is entirely random and that long-term value is best identified through a thorough study of a corporation's financial status and strength. The technical approach relies on patterns in price of the stock and other price-related indicators that are associated more with the market's perception of value and less with financial information. Obviously, a current report on the corporation's

 chartist
an analyst who studies charts of a stock's price movement in the belief that recent patterns can be used to predict upcoming price changes and directions.

net income will affect price, at least temporarily, and technicians acknowledge this. However, their primary interest is in studying pricing trends.

Many successful investors recognize that both schools have value, so they apply parts of fundamental and technical analysis in their own monitoring program. The purpose of monitoring the market is in order to make the four important decisions that every investor needs to be able to make: buy, hold, sell, or stay away. The wise investor knows that analysis in all of its forms is a tool for decision making, and that no analysis provides insights that dictate decisions on their own. Common sense and discriminating personal judgment based on experience are the extra edge that successful investors bring to their investments. Even so, there remains a large contingent of people in the market who cling to the belief that some particular analytical tool does, indeed, point the way to beating the market every time. The reality is that everyone is wrong at times. Smart investors know that successful investing results when they are able to use analysis so that their estimates are right more often than they are wrong.

Smart Investor Tip   There are no formulas that will make you right all of the time. Investing success comes from applying good judgment, increasing your chances of being right about market decisions.

Call writers should never overlook the need to continuously track their stocks. They tend at times to ignore changing attributes of the stock over time because their interest is in watching the options. So call writers may be inclined to ignore signals relating to the stock when, if they were not involved with writing options, they might be more inclined to watch their portfolios. Call writers are preoccupied with other matters: movement in the stock's price (but only insofar as it affects their option positions); chances of exercise and how to avoid or defer it; opportunities to roll forward; and other matters relating to immediate strategies. As important as all of these matters are for call writers, they do not address the important questions that every stockholder needs to ask continuously: Should I keep the stock or sell it? Should I buy more shares? What changes have occurred that could also change my opinion of this stock?

The time will come when, as a call writer, you will want to close an open call position and sell the stock. For example, if you own 100 shares of stock on which you have written several calls over many months or years, when should you sell the stock? For a variety of reasons, you might conclude that the stock is not going to hold its value into the future as you once believed. Even investors buying stock for the long term need to rethink their positions through constant monitoring. It would be a mistake to continue holding stock because it represents a good candidate for covered call sales, when in fact that stock no longer makes the grade based on analytical tests that you use.

Fundamental Tests

The successful call writer tracks ever-changing call status *and* the stocks on which those calls are written. A number of fundamental indicators are useful in deciding when to buy or sell; and these tests should always override the considerations that attract you to call writing.

The current market value of the stock reflects the buying public's current perception of its current and future value. This perception is affected by virtually all information available in the market at any time, including financial as well as nonfinancial data, fact and rumor, and industry or sector news not directly related to the company itself.

One indicator that enjoys widespread popularity is the *price/earnings ratio* (P/E ratio). This is a measurement of current value that uses both fundamental and technical information. The technical side (price of a share of stock) is divided by the fundamental side (*earnings per share* of common stock) to arrive at a numerical value.

Example: A company's latest annual income statement showed $220 million in profit; the company had 35 million shares outstanding. Earnings per share ($220 ÷ 35) works out to a net profit of $6.29 per share. The company's stock recently sold at $35 per share. The P/E ratio is:

$35 ÷ $6.29 = 5.6

Example: A company earned $95 million and has 40 million shares outstanding, so its earnings per share is $2.38. The stock sells at $28 per share. The P/E is calculated as:

price/earnings ratio a popular indicator used by stock market investors to rate and compare stocks. The current market value of the stock is divided by the most recent earnings per share to arrive at the P/E ratio.

earnings per share a commonly used method for reporting profits. Net profits for a year or other period are divided by the number of shares of common stock outstanding as of the ending date of the financial report. (The result is expressed as a dollar value.)

$28 \div \$2.38 = 11.8$

The P/E ratio can be described as a relative indicator of what the market believes about the particular stock. It reflects the current point of view about the company's prospects for future earnings. As a general observation, lower P/E ratio means lower risk for investors. Any ratio is only useful when it is studied in comparative form. This means not only that a company's P/E ratio may be tracked and observed over time, but also that comparisons between different companies can be instructive, especially if they are otherwise similar (in the same sector, same product profile, etc.). In these examples, the first company's 5.6 P/E would be considered a less risky investment than the second, whose P/E is 11.8. However, P/E ratio is not always a fair indicator of a stock's risk level, nor of its potential for future profits, for several reasons. These include:

1. *Financial statements may themselves be distorted.* A company's financial statement may be far more complex than it first appears, in terms of what it includes and what it leaves out. For example, the income statement might include adjustments, called extraordinary items. These are transactions affecting profit and loss that are not part of recurring operations, and which are not expected to be repeated again the following year. They may result from large gains or losses in currency exchange, payments resulting from lawsuits, changes in inventory valuation methods, and accounting adjustments for previous years.

2. *The financial statement might be unreliable for comparative purposes.* The financial reports of companies whose stock is listed must be audited by an independent auditing firm every year. While many investors take assurance from this and trust the accuracy of financial reports, it is less widely acknowledged that companies have considerable leeway in the way that they report income, costs and expenses, and profits. In fact, differences of opinion between auditors and company accountants may even be negotiated to a degree so that an accepted final version can be arrived at. Anyone who has studied the profit reports of some of the largest corporations may be impressed at the consistency of profits as reported from year to year. The perception among many corporate managers is that investors want reliability and consistency, so some transactions may be deferred to the following period. This is not necessarily deceptive as defined within the auditing rules. The leeway enables corporate management to make some adjustments in their current reports. The auditor's job is to ensure that no outright fraud is taking place. As a general rule, corporate financial reporting is a reliable science with rules that have to be followed. As long as the Securities and Exchange Commission is satisfied that reports are accurate, and auditors accept the reports within their guidelines, investors are being protected. Still, the adjustments do raise the question of how reliable the P/E ratio is as a result.

3. *The number of shares outstanding might have changed.* Because shares outstanding is part of the P/E ratio equation, its comparative value can be altered when the number of shares changes from one year to another. A corporation may issue additional shares, for example, so that any comparison from one year to the next is distorted. Some companies buy their own shares on the market when they consider current price to be low. Shares purchased in that way are called treasury stock, and they are retired, which means that the number of outstanding shares is lowered as well.

4. *The ratio becomes inaccurate as earnings reports go out of date.* If the latest earnings report of the company was issued last week, then the P/E ratio is based on relatively updated information. However, if that report was published three months ago, then the P/E is also outdated. The status of the company's earnings might be vastly different today than it was as of the last published report. The greater the time lag between the latest report and today, the less reliable the P/E ratio. However, most market watchers accept and compare P/E ratios on all issues without considering the problem of outdated earnings reports.

5. *The comparison is between dissimilar forms of information.* The P/E ratio compares a stock's price—a technical value based on perceptions about current and future value—with earnings, which are historical and fundamental in nature. In one regard, this is the advantage of the P/E ratio; it bridges technical and fundamental in a logical manner to report on perceptions. However, it can also be problematical in the sense that these forms of information are entirely separate from one another. It raises the question about whether a purely technical matter such as market price can even be compared to a purely historically and fundamental matter such as earnings.

6. *Perceptions about P/E ratio are inconsistent.* This indicator is widely used and accepted as a means for evaluating and comparing stocks. However, not everyone agrees about how to interpret P/E to select stocks. A higher P/E generally means that, in the market's overall perception, the company has better-than-average prospects for high future stock price appreciation. So to some people, a high P/E translates to an investment more likely to do well in the future. Conversely, a lower-than-average P/E would indicate that the stock is less likely to appreciate in the future. Historically, however, lower P/E stocks have outperformed the market, and higher P/E stocks have been poor performers. This may reflect the market's tendency to overrate the potential of popular issues, and to underrate the earnings potential of less interesting ones.

How, then, should you use the P/E ratio? This remains a valuable indicator for measuring market perception about value of a stock, especially if you are tracking the P/E ratio for a single stock and watching how it changes over time. Comparing P/E between two different stocks may be more of a problem in terms of reliability. Companies in different industries, for example, may have widely different norms for judging profits. In one industry, a 3% or 4% return on sales might be considered average, and in another an 8% return is expected. So comparing P/E ratios between companies with dissimilar profit expectations is inaccurate.

The P/E ratio is a useful method for tracking changes in perception about a stock, and to a degree for comparing a stock to a broader standard. For example, you might decide to narrow down a selection of likely stock candidates by setting a rules based on P/E ratio. You might exclude stocks whose P/E exceeds a mid-range P/E, for example. This tends to eliminate stocks on which market perception may be too high. The test may serve as one of several methods you use to reduce the range of stock purchase candidates.

An additional fundamental test that every investor will want to consider is the *dividend yield*. This shows the current yield from dividends, expressed as percentage of the share price. The result is expressed as a percentage. Of course, as the stock's market price changes, so does the dividend yield. Compare:

dividend yield
measurement computed by dividing dividends paid per share of common stock by the current market value of the stock.

$3.50 ÷ $65 per share = 5.4%

$3.50 ÷ $55 per share = 6.4%

$3.50 ÷ $45 per share = 6.8%

As the price per share falls, the dividend yield rises. When you are considering buying stock, the dividend yield is a useful method for calculating your return from dividends—*based on the price per share that you pay*. However, once you own stock, your return from dividends is fixed as it represents a return on the price you paid (as long as the dividend per share paid by the corporation does not change). For purposes of ongoing analysis, the comparison between dividend per share and price per share has no ongoing value.

When you consider which stock to buy from among several, dividend yield should be seen as potentially a large portion of your total return. More generous dividend yield could reflect a buying opportunity at the moment. That yield, added to capital gains as well as returns from selling covered calls, could add up to a very healthy overall return. Like comparisons between P/E ratios, the dividend yield is a useful indicator you can use for narrowing the field when you are picking stocks for investment.

A corporation's profitably is another important test. After all, long-term price appreciation occurs as the result of the corporation's ability to generate profits year after year. Short-term stock price changes are less significant when thinking about long-term growth potential of the stock, and for that, you want to compare *profit margin* from one company to another, This is the most popular system for judging a company's performance. It is computed by dividing the dollar amount of net profit by the dollar amount of gross sales. The result is expressed as a percentage.

profit margin
the most commonly used measurement of corporate operations, computed by dividing net profits by gross sales.

The profit margin, as useful as it is for comparative purposes between companies, and for year-to-year analysis, often is not fully understood by investors. As a consequence, many market analysts and investors develop unrealistic expectations about profit margin. A couple of points worth remembering:

1. *An "acceptable" level of profit varies between industries.* One industry may experience lower or higher average profit margin than another. For example, attributes of the insurance industry are vastly different than attributes of companies in computer technology. They cannot be realistically expected to generate the same profit margin, given the operational differences and structure of their company. One sells a service, while the other sells a profit. One depends on investment returns, while the other competes in a retail marketplace. These and many more differences make it impractical to arrive at a singular standard for measuring profitability; the unique aspects of each sector should be used to differentiate between corporations. Comparisons should be restricted to those between corporations in the same sector.

2. *It is not realistic to expect that one year's profit margin should always exceed that gained in the previous year.* Once a corporation reaches what is considered a respectable profit margin, it is unrealistic to expect it to continuously grow it terms of higher percentage returns. The financial elements and nature of costs and expenses naturally restrict the degree of profitability that is possible. So if a corporation's earnings only match the previous year or even come up short, that is not a negative indicator. Even so, analysts and investors often react by selling stock when earnings reports fail to meet their expectations, even the unrealistic ones.

profit on invested capital
a fundamental test showing the yield to equity investors in the company, computed by dividing net profits by the dollar value of outstanding capital.

A less frequently used method for evaluating your investments measures return to you as an investor. While this makes perfect sense, it often is overlooked. It is ironic that the market is preoccupied with stock prices, but its analysis is restricted in many instances to measurements of sales and profits. In practical terms, it is equally significant to judge how well a corporation performs in terms of what it returns to its investors (i.e., stockholders). Divide net profits by outstanding capital to arrive at the percentage of *profit on invested capital*.

This indicator demonstrates how well a corporation is

able to maintain consistent returns to its investors. It is related to a study of sources of capitalization. Corporations capitalize their operations through equity (stock) and debt (bonds and notes), and both forms of capitalization require compensation. Stockholders are paid dividends, and bondholders are paid interest. An important point for stockholders to remember is that as debt capitalization increases, an increasing portion of operating profit is paid out in interest. That means that, in turn, there remains less operating profit available for dividends. If debt capitalization increases steadily over time, stockholders lose out as their dividend income is eroded. The study of sources of capital is more complex than a simple ratio, but profit on invested capital does provide you with the means for tracking a company's management of its capitalization over several years.

Closely related to this should be a continuing analysis of your own return on invested capital. Whenever you buy stock, you may be compensated through capital gains and dividends, as well as covered call premium. Collectively, these represent your overall profit on invested capital. It is the means by which you judge your own investment performance, not only for one stock against another, but for your portfolio at large as well.

All of these fundamental tests are best reviewed in comparison with past statistics, and always computed in the same manner. Only then will you have a valid and useful analysis. Financial information is worthwhile only when tracked over time, and when it reveals the direction of a trend.

No single indicator should ever be used as the sole means for deciding what actions to take in the market. Fundamental analysis should be comprehensive. You can employ combinations of information, including a thorough study of all of the tests that reveal trends to you. They may confirm a previous opinion; or they may lead you to change your mind. Either way, the purpose in using the fundamentals is to gather information and then to act upon it.

Technical Tests

A well-rounded method for judging the value of a stock does not have to be arrived at with only one method. The combination of both fundamental and technical tests helps you to review the question of viability of a stock from several different points of view. While the fundamentals help you to gain insights into a company's overall financial and capital strength, technical indicators help you to judge market perception about future potential. In this regard, the fundamentals look back at a company's history to estimate the future; and technical indicators are used to make estimates based on current market information.

Most investors are aware of the importance in tracking a stock's price over time. In fact, price is the most popular indicator used by technicians. Even those describing themselves as acting based on the fundamentals often are, in fact, more interested in the market value of stock from day to day. It is an easy value to find; it is widely reported in the financial press. And while the short-term price movement of a stock is not valuable as a long-term indicator, it is interesting in technical terms. It is also of utmost importance to every options trader.

Often overlooked in this analysis is the study of volume in a stock. You may apply volume tests to the market as a whole and several popular technical tests review trading volume on a daily basis. It can also be applied to individual stocks. When volume increases, it indicates increased market interest in the stock. Of course, if that interest is led by buyer interest, then it means the price probably will rise. If the interest is generated by sellers, then the price will be driven downward. The direction of movement of the stock indicates which of these applies. Obviously, all trades will have both buyer and seller. The point is that high volume can have two opposite conclusions, and that will be manifested in the direction that the stock's price is moving on a particular day. You often see a mix of buying and selling—high volume with little change in price. This is important information as well. It indicates that while shares of stock are changing hands, the current price range is considered reasonable by the market as a whole.

You can watch the movement in volume as well as in price in the financial press or on the Internet. Charting is widely available and free on numerous sites. Look for those offering easy directions and combination price and volume charts. The analysis of price and volume together reveals trading patterns in stocks that will improve your insight into the way that a stock acts in the market. There are no universal formulas. Each stock will develop its own trading pattern and the price will vary with changing volume, often in ways unique to the stock itself. This may be affected by the mix of ownership. If a stock is heavily invested through mutual funds, for example, then trading would tend to occur in large blocks. Thus, changes in volume may appear more drastic than volume in stocks owned more by individual investors, where a large volume of relatively small lots of stock would be expected. The point is, you need to assess each stock based on the mix of ownership, historical price and volume patterns, and overall volatility in the stock's market price.

Smart Investor Tip   For free charts of stock price and volume, check these web sites:

Investor Guide   http://investorguide.com
Stockmaster   www.stockmaster.com
Wall Street Directory   www.wsdinc.com

A chartist, one who tracks patterns and trends in a stock's price, believes that by identifying patterns it is possible to predict how a stock's price will act in coming days, weeks, or months. While most people believe that short-term price movement, in fact, is random and unreliable as an indicator, chartists do present some valuable observations concerning trading ranges of a stock.

For example, the chartist is especially interested in watching a stock's *support level*, which is a range of price identified as the lowest likely price level, given current conditions. On the other side of the chart is the *resistance level*, the highest price or price range a stock is trading under current conditions. The concept of support and resistance not only are keys to the chartist's approach to studying stock price movement; they also are revealing because they indicate a stock's relative volatility. The wider the range between support and resistance, the more volatile a stock; and of course, the thinner that trading range, the more stable the stock. In this respect, the visualization of a stock's trading pattern can help every investor to identify a stock in terms of volatility over time.

 support level
the price for a stock identifying the lowest likely trading price under present conditions, below which the price of the stock is not likely to fall.

 resistance level
the price for a stock identifying the highest likely trading price under present conditions, above which the price of the stock is not likely to rise.

As long as the price remains within the trading range between support and resistance, the chartist is satisfied that the stock's price is stable. However, eventually the stock's price will test either support or resistance by threatening to break through on the downside or on the upside. When the price does move beyond the trading range, it is described as going through a *breakout* pattern. The essence of charting is to try to identify in advance of the breakout when it is going to occur. The chartist believes that by studying the trading patterns, it is possible to predict price movement.

breakout
the movement of a stock's price below support level or above resistance level.

Predictions concerning future price movement are based on detailed analysis of the patterns in the trading range. Chartists point to past patterns as confirming evidence that in fact the movement in a stock's price is predictable. However, looking ahead to future price changes, chartists probably do not perform much better than anyone else in trying to predict what is likely to occur next. It will be difficult to convince a serious market watcher that charting has any predictive value. Its value is found, however, in the definition of the trading range. The idea of support and resistance is a valuable tool for judging volatility.

Options traders can make good use of the support and resistance concepts. By observing the pattern of recent trading ranges, you may better judge a stock's price stability. The problem with a purely mathematical analysis of volatility is that it presents a year's summary in a single number. That volatility could be the result of a single change in price, or part of a pattern of widely varying prices. You cannot differentiate the two with the traditional volatility formula.

The chart reveals more for options traders. By studying the chart's pattern over time, you can judge whether the trading range is broad or thin; whether it is changing and, if so, to what degree; and how often previously established trading ranges have been changed by breakouts. The length of time a trading range remains unchanged is also revealing, as it helps options traders to determine a stock's tendency to react to market changes in general, or to go along on its own timing and trading pattern. Remembering that all of these observations may change at any time, charting is nonetheless valuable for comparing stocks to one another and for arriving at conclusions about volatility that cannot be revealed through the price range formula that looks at an entire year.

Accompanying an in-depth review of volatility, a sound analysis of a stock may include a study of the high and low price ranges over time. This demonstrates several things. For example, the more volatile stocks—those with broader high and low ranges—may, in fact, be volatile at the beginning of the period but not at the end, or vice versa. A simple one-year summary is not reliable in terms of today's tendency. In addition, the study of high and low price ranges reveals where that stock's price stands today in relation to the longer-term trading range. Is it at the high end, low end, or somewhere in the middle?

The stock reports in the financial press present only the 52-week high and low price ranges. Given the many possible varieties of trading patterns that can result in the same high and low summary, this information is highly unreliable. A more detailed study is required.

Example: Three different stocks have what appear to be highly volatile status today. They all have 52-week trading ranges with a spread of 40 points. However, upon more detailed examination, you discover three different scenarios, making the simple 52-week summary unreliable for your comparative analysis:

Stock "A" began the year at $22 per share and has risen consistently throughout the past 52 weeks. Today, the stock is valued at $62 per share.

Stock "B" has been trading between $56 and $58 for most of the year. Eight months ago, it was rumored to be a takeover candidate and the stock soared to $96 per share, at which point trading was halted. The rumor proved to be untrue, and when trading was reopened the stock resumed trading at $64, quickly falling back to its previous three-point range.

Stock "C" began the year at $107 per share. This stock is in a highly competitive market sector and is one of the less strongly capitalized corporations in the field. It began losing share value early in the 52-week range, slipped over the first three months to the 90s, and has been falling more since then. It currently is trading at $67, its lowest point in the past year.

In each of these three scenarios, the summarized 52-week high and low analysis means a completely different thing. In fact, stock "A" is trading at the high point in its 52-week range but few people would describe it as trading too high today, given its trading pattern. Stock "B" appears volatile, but in fact it is a very stable stock with an exceptionally small trading range. And stock "C" might look like a well-timed buying opportunity because it currently is at its 52-week low. However, a closer look at the stock's history points to some competitive problems that are perceived by the market as making it a high-risk alternative.

Some investors pick stocks by religiously studying the 52-week high and low ranges. The use of this information cannot be restricted to the conclusions as shown in the financial press, however. It is essential that the character of the high and low range be more fully explored so that its exact nature can be identified.

No single fundamental or technical test can be used reliably to identify good purchase candidates. The high and low ranges, for example, might represent a fair starting point for stock selection, but the analysis should explore further into the timing and attributes of the stock and its trading range. The more information available, the more accurate your analysis. You can evaluate stocks by tracking key indicators over time, looking not only for patterns, but also for the emergence of *new* pricing trends. For example, you might decide to track a stock you are thinking of buying, combining dividend rate, P/E ratio, high and low range, and current price (close each day) of a stock. The worksheet in Figure 6.3 can be used for this purpose. You might use the close each Friday to track a particular stock. After entering information on each line, you can begin to see how each piece of information changes or interacts with the others.

The problem with analysis is that it takes time. And the more time you spend on analysis, the more quickly it goes out of date. Having online charting services available without charge makes your task much easier. As an options trader, you may also be able to limit your analysis to the relatively small number of stocks on which options are traded.

stock name _____

DATE	DIVIDEND RATE	P/E RATIO	HIGH	LOW	CLOSE

FIGURE 6.3 Stock evaluation worksheet.

Deciding Which Tests to Apply

Entire books have been written about the hundreds of possible fundamental and technical tests you may use for picking stocks, tracking them, and deciding when to sell. How do you determine which of these tests is most useful to you? This is no easy question, since the answer depends on your own opinion. Before deciding how to pick one form of analysis over another, be aware of these important points:

1. *Many analysts love complex formulas.* A difficult-to-understand theory that requires a lot of mathematical ability is probably entirely useless in the real world. An academic approach to the market might be interesting in an academic setting, where professors and students take a theoretical approach to studying stocks but are likely to have no actual investing experience. Avoid the complex, recognizing that useful information also tends to be straightforward and easily comprehended.

2. *Price has nothing to do with the fundamentals.* This is one of the often overlooked realities in the market. The price of any stock (or option) reflects the market's perception about future potential value, whereas the financial condition of that company is historical. A study of fundamentals certainly indicates good long-term investment prospects, but it has nothing to do with today's price or the way that the price is likely to change tomorrow or next week.

3. *The actual net worth of a company has nothing to do with price.* Some investors fall into the mistaken belief that the price of stock represents the value of the company. That is not true; the two have nothing to do with one another. Current market value is determined through auction between buyers and sellers, and not by accountants at the company's headquarters. The actual value of the stockholders' equity in a corporation is found in the *book value* of shares of stock. This is the net worth of a company, divided by the number of outstanding shares. However, book value per share has little to do with current market value per share; it often is considerably lower and in some instances might even be higher. Most investors and analysts completely ignore book value.

4. *The past is not an infallible indicator.* You may attempt to use past patterns to predict future patterns of price, profits, or competitive posture within an industry; but in fact, the past is unreliable. In corporate offices, accountants continuously try to estimate future sales, costs, expenses, and profits through the budgeting process. This itself is more art than science. When investors attempt to predict price movement through studying the fundamentals, they face an even more elusive task, since the fundamentals do not affect short-term price movement as much as other fac-

book value

the actual value of a company, more accurately called book value per share; the value of a company's capital (assets less liabilities), divided by the number of outstanding shares of stock.

tors, such as perception of the market as a whole. As much as investors would like to be able to predict the future, it simply cannot be done. Every investor is well advised to remember the wisdom that "the stock market has no past."

5. *Predictions abound, but reliable predictions do not exist.* Anyone can get lucky and make an accurate prediction once in a while. Doing so with any consistency is far more difficult. You can study any number of factors, either fundamental or technical, but none will enable you to accurately predict future price movement of stocks. Technicians spend a lot of time trying to prove that there is a correlation between market prices and other events; some have attempted to tie market trends with social, political, or even sporting events. Some have been even more far-fetched, including studies trying to show that market prices are affected by weather patterns or the thickness of tree rings!

None of these unrelated factors are related to pricing of stocks and the elements that make them change. No one really knows what causes price changes overall. Numerous theories address part of the cause, and it is certain that all market, economic, financial, and technical indicators play a part. An entire predictive industry convinces subscribers that a particular formula will provide insight, and the desire to beat the averages results in many dollars going into the pockets of newsletter and newspaper subscriptions. The truth, though, is that no one can predict price movements of the market as a whole, or of individual stocks. However, you can gain informed insight that will help you to make an intelligent decision.

6. *Common sense is your best tool.* Investing is more likely to be a successful experience if you employ common sense, backed up with study, analysis, and comparison. If you seek fast riches through easy formulas, you are more likely to lose money than to make money in the stock market. Getting rich without hard work is no easier in the stock market than anywhere else. All too often, promoters of schemes or tricks appeal to many inexperienced people; and now that the Internet is accessible to so many investors, new schemes like day trading are being promoted as the way to get rich—but the promotions often fail to mention that opportunities are accompanied with exceptionally high risks as well.

7. *Stock prices, especially in the short term, are random.* Most predictive theories acknowledge that, while long-term analysis can narrow down the guesswork, short-term price movement is completely random. In the stock market, where opinion and speculation are so widespread, no one can control the way stock prices change from one day to the next. Long-term investment prospects can be identified through a study of the fundamentals; but trying to guess where a stock's price will be within the next few months is virtually impossible, and any system that attempts to provide a means for such predictions should be viewed with great skepticism.

The two major theories directing opinions about stock prices are the *random walk* theory and the *Dow Theory*. Both of these deserve consideration, because while they differ in their approach, they agree on one important issue: Short-term prices cannot be used as reliable indicators, because they cannot be predicted. This idea has ramifications for options traders and, since both theories agree on that point, it probably has considerable merit.

A third idea about market pricing only supports the theory about pricing as expressed in the two broad theories. This idea is called the *efficient market hypothesis*. An efficient market is one is which current prices reflect all information known to the public. Thus, prices are reasonable based upon perceptions about markets and the companies whose stock is listed publicly. If the efficient market hypothesis is correct, then all current prices are fair and reasonable. Again, this idea has ramifications for all options traders.

All three of these theories deserve some further study, at least regarding short-term price movement. Options traders deal exclusively in the short term, so the theories about market pricing should be observed carefully. Of course, no theory is absolutely right. A theory is intended only to offer observations about price behavior. Understanding how and why a theory is developed can help you to understand markets and stock prices, but no theory can ever be used as a guiding force for making decisions about when (or if) to buy or sell.

The Random Walk In one regard, the random walk contradicts the other theories. If, in fact, prices are en-

 random walk
a theory about market pricing, stating that prices of stocks cannot be predicted because price movement is entirely random.

 Dow Theory
a theory that market trends are predictable based on changes in market averages.

 efficient market hypothesis
a theory stating that current stock prices reflect all information publicly known about a company.

tirely random, then there is no explanation for price behavior. There is a 50–50 chance that prices will rise, and a
50–50 chance that prices will fall. Thus, if the theory were
absolute, then there would be no need for market analysis. Fundamental and technical indicators would provide
no useful information.

However, in another sense, the random walk makes
a point about short-term price movement that conforms
to the principles of the Dow Theory and the efficient market hypothesis. There is no way to know how short-term
prices will change. Virtually everyone agrees that short-
term price changes are highly unreliable, and that they do
not act or react with any consistent logic whatsoever. The
random walk emphasizes the absolute importance of selecting stocks with strong fundamental and technical
characteristics. For options traders, the strength of the
underlying stock is a long-term attribute; the value of
stock selection is the most important consideration for
option sellers. It is the proper selection of stock for long-
term value that determines whether your portfolio has intrinsic strength. Only after selecting stocks through
careful research should you ever consider writing calls.

Remembering the random walk, an option seller
cannot know how short-term price changes will occur. So
the need to look at all possible outcomes is always essential to succeeding in an option writing plan. Only when
you will be satisfied will all possible outcomes does it
make sense to sell options against stock. It is one of the
few strategies that can be designed so that you will profit
no matter what happens to the underlying stock. Some
outcomes are going to be more desirable than others, but
it is possible to create situations where profits are virtually
guaranteed. (The one exception being an unexpected significant drop in the stock's market value, in which case
the writer can only wait for a rebound.)

The Dow Theory The Dow Theory has been around for
more than 100 years, its origins going back to Charles
Dow, who developed the system as a means for tracking
business trends. He did not originally intend for this analysis to be used in the stock market. However, he and his
partner, Edward Jones, founded the Dow Jones Company

and began publishing a newsletter, which grew into the *Wall Street Journal*. Dow's editorial comments and ideas were expanded upon by his successors.

What was originally a rather straightforward idea has developed into an overall market theory based largely on the premise that the averages concocted by the Dow Jones Company can be used to predict market price changes. Among the tenets of the Dow Theory is the identification of three movements in the stock market: primary, secondary, and daily. The primary movement is an overall trend in the market, most often described as bull or bear. The secondary movement is a reaction to the first, characterized by opposite movements—a rally in a bear market or a correction during a bull market. The daily movements are variously described as unimportant or meaningless.

If you select stocks based on the Dow Theory, you face a difficult task. Used primarily to predict overall price movement, the Dow Theory is less reliable for selection of individual stocks, whose price changes may more accurately be traced to the company's fundamentals. The Dow Theory utilizes a number of precepts concerning the identification of changing trends, but it is of little use in picking out one stock from among thousands. However you select stocks, the significant point to remember as an options trader is that daily movement is considered as mere ripples within the tide (primary movement) or the wave (secondary movement).

The Efficient Market The theory of the efficient market, in some people's view, is the most cynical. It is particularly resisted by market professionals whose livelihood depends on convincing customers that their analysis is valuable. The efficient market theory essentially debunks all analysis that might be used to time market decisions. If it is correct, then both fundamental and technical analysis are useless.

Anyone who has observed how the market works understands that the efficient market is a pure theory, but it is not always applicable. For example, Value Line divides the stocks it studies into five groups, from the highest-rated for safety and timeliness down to the lowest. The first two tiers beat market averages with consistency, proving that there is value in going through the analysis of prices, price movement, and the range of fundamentals. A reasonable approach is to believe that the market is efficient, but only to a degree. Market observers will acknowledge that the investing public tends to overreact to news in the market. Prices rise beyond a reasonable level on good news, and decline beyond a reasonable degree on bad news. So in short-term trading, prices cannot be called efficient by any means. However, the often unrealistic pricing swings present momentary opportunities for speculators.

In intermediate timing—meaning weeks or months rather than the short term, hours or days—the efficient market theory might hold a degree of truth. In other words, news, whether true or not, has an effect on prices. However, it takes some time for the overreaction to simmer down to produce the end result that appears more "efficient." If a rumor proves untrue, the intermediate-term effect is that the stock price is not affected at all. If it is true, then the intermediate-term effect is more reasonable than the initial price reaction.

Like the other two theories, the efficient market points out the danger and opportunity for options traders. Short-term price changes cannot be predicted with any reliability whatsoever, even in the efficient market; so options traders really have no reliable *options-related* method for selecting which ones to trade. However, the characteristics of the underlying stock can be used reliably to select a profitable portfolio. It is fair to surmise that a stock with strong fundamental and technical characteristics is not only a good long-term investment, but also a viable candidate for writing covered calls. The option buyer, on the other hand, undertakes considerable risks, remembering that none of the theories place any reliability on short-term price changes.

Smart Investor Tip   All theories agree that short-term price changes provide no useful information. This presents problems for options buyers; but for option sellers, the volatility of short-term prices can have a positive effect on time value, meaning opportunities for profits.

APPLYING ANALYSIS TO CALLS

To select stocks for writing calls, the essential requirement is that you pick stocks with strong long-term growth potential. Keep the major market theories in mind when you study stocks, and emphasize the characteristics that should be used for picking stocks. These characteristics do not include exceptionally rich option premium. The volatility test is appropriate for picking stocks, given that you are able to distinguish between different causes of volatility; is it a general tendency, a momentary spike in an otherwise stable price range, or an upward or downward pricing trend? Volatility needs to be studied in more detail than is normally provided in the financial press. A study of a yearlong stock price chart yields more useful information.

Many investors believe that moderate volatility is a positive sign, as it demonstrates investor interest. A stock that has little or no volatility is, indeed, not a "hot" stock and such conditions will invariably be accompanied by very low volume as well. So some short-term volatility might demonstrate not only that investor interest is high, but also that option activity and pricing will be more interesting as well. As a technical test of a stock's price stability, volatility should be analyzed for short-term and long-term levels. Ideally, your stocks will contain long-term stability, but relatively volatile price movement in the short term. The volatility test will not be a constant, and stocks that are popular in the market will change in terms of volatility as markets change and as their price moves from one moment to another.

With the distinctions in mind between different causes and patterns of volatility, the selection of stock may be based on a comparative study of the past 12 months. First, ensure that the stocks you are considering as prospects for purchase have approximately the same causes for their volatility. Then apply volatility as a test for identifying relative degrees of safety.

Example: You are considering buying several stocks. Their volatility patterns are similar, with price ranges tending to be consistent over the past 12 months. (You have eliminated stocks whose volatility resulted from price spikes.) One stock's price range over the past 12 months was between $28 and $49 per share. To compute volatility, divide the difference between high and low, by the low. Multiply the result by 100 to arrive at a percentage representing volatility:

$$\frac{\$49 - \$28}{\$28} \times 100 = 75.0\%$$

Example: A second stock in your comparison had a 12-month price range between $67 and $72 per share. Volatility is computed as:

$$\frac{\$72 - \$67}{\$67} \times 100 = 7.5\%$$

The stock in the second example is considerable less volatile than the one in the first example. The trading ranges of each might contain similar pattern characteristics, but it is the degree of change, or the width of that gap, that defines volatility.

For call writers, the degree of volatility is an indication of risk as well as potential richness in call premiums. Obviously, you will want to seek stocks with long-term price appreciation potential but high short-term volatility. This attribute is easy to spot in hindsight, but difficult to predict—especially since short-term volatility also means difficulty in predicting any price movement over the next few months. So a lower volatility, as in the second example, indicates more predictability is stock price movement, but lower likelihood of call premium richness. The obvious choice for call writers is to select stocks with a history of short-term volatility, and the best possible long-term growth potential.

Fundamental and technical tests are complemented with the use of another feature in a stock's price used to define volatility—that is, the stock's *beta*. This is a test of relative volatility; in other words, the degree to which a stock tends to move with an entire market or index of stocks. A beta of 1 tells you that a particular stock tends to rise or fall in the same degree as the market as a whole; a beta of 0 implies that price changes of the stock are independent of price changes in the broader market; and a beta of 2 indicates that a stock's price tends to overreact to market trends, often by moving to a greater degree than the market as a whole.

beta

a measurement of relative volatility of a stock, made by comparing the degree of price movement in comparison to a larger index of stock prices.

Example: Over the past year, the composite index—the overall value of the stock market—rose by approximately 7%. Your stock also rose 7%, so its beta is 1. If your stock had risen 14%, its beta would be 2.

As a general rule, the more volatile stocks will also tend to have greater time value premiums associated with their options. That is because the stocks represent greater risks, and option premium reflects that risk. It is an advantage for sellers, and a problem for buyers, because high-beta stocks will also experience more rapid decline in their options' time value than the rate of decline for low-beta stocks. So if your portfolio contains high-beta stocks, you will receive higher premiums for selling calls, but your stock will be more volatile as well.

Because time value tends to be higher than average for high-beta stocks, premium value, like the stock's market value, is less predictable. From the call writer's point of view, exceptionally high time value that declines rapidly is a clear advantage, but it would be shortsighted to trade only in such stocks, especially if you also want stability in your stock portfolio.

delta
the degree of change in option premium, in relation to changes in the underlying stock. (If the call option's degree of change exceeds the change in the underlying stock, it is called an "up delta"; when the change is less than the underlying stock, it is called a "down delta." The reverse terminology is applied to puts.)

Example: You own 100 shares of stock that you bought at $62 per share. You recently sold a May 65 call at 5. Last week, the stock fell 6 points and the call's value fell to 1. You buy to close the position, realizing a profit of $400 on the call. However, you lost $600 in the underlying stock.

In this example, the fast turnaround in the option reflected high volatility and was offset by a paper loss in the stock. Investors often choose volatile stocks in full awareness of the risk, planning to move in and out of short option positions several times—trading on volatility, in other words. In this example, you walked away with a profit of $400 and you still own the stock. If it were to jump in value above your basis, you could sell another call and wait for yet another decline in value. You cannot control the frequency or the direction of price changes in the stock, but when its price moves in the desired direction, you can profit by selling calls with high time value.

A more elusive but interesting indicator that helps select options is called the *delta*. When the price of the underlying stock and the premium value of the option change exactly the same number of points, the delta is 1.00. As delta increases or decreases for an option, you are able to judge the responsiveness (volatility) of the option to the stock. This takes into consideration the distance between current market value of the stock and striking price of the call, fluctuations of time value, and changes in delta as expiration approaches. The delta provides you with the means to compare interaction between stock and option pricing for a particular stock.

The inclination of a typical option is to behave predictably, tending to approach a delta of 1.00 as it goes in the money. So for every point of price movement in the underlying stock, you would expect a change in option premium very close to 1 point when in the money. Time value tends to not be a factor when options are deep in the money. Time value is more likely to change predictably based on time until expiration. Many beginning options traders overlook this important fact, forgetting that time value does not rise in most situations; it tends to fall as expiration approaches.

When the option is at the money, you can best judge option tendency by observing delta. For example, if the option's delta is 0.80 when at the money, you would expect a change of eight-tenths of a point for every change in the stock's market price. In addition, however, the direction of the stock's movement may also affect response in the option's premium. This is true because movement in one direction puts the option in the money; and movement in the other direction moves the option out of the money.

Example: You are tracking an in-the-money call. Its striking price is 35, and the underlying stock's market value is $47 per share. You notice that each point of movement in the stock's market price is paralleled by a corresponding change in the option's premium value. The only variance is evaporating time value.

Example: An option is at the money. You observe that as the underlying stock's price changes, it affects premium value by about 80%. This option's delta is 0.80.

Example: A call is out of the money. The striking price is 65 but current market value of the stock is $52 per share.

Minor changes in the stock's market value have little or no effect in the call's premium value, all of which is time value. As the gap widens between striking price of the call and current market value of the stock, you observe that there is even less effect on the call's premium value. In this case, delta is almost inapplicable, since the call is so far out of the money. Time value premium declines as expiration approaches; the only factor that could increase the time value would be the sudden closing of that gap, presenting a prospect that the call could move into the money.

Being aware of delta enables you to take advantage of conditions and improve your timing, whether you are operating as a buyer or as a seller.

open interest

the number of open contracts of a particular option at any given time, which can be used to measure market interest.

Accompanying these indicators of relative volatility, you may also follow *open interest*. This is the number of open option contracts on a particular underlying stock. For example, one stock's July 40 calls had open interest last month of 22,000 contracts; today, only 500 contracts remain open. The number changes for several reasons. As the status of the call moves higher into the money, the number of open contracts tends to change as the result of closing sale transactions, rolling forward, or exercise. Sellers tend to buy out their positions as time value falls, and buyers tend to close out positions as intrinsic value rises. And as expiration approaches, fewer new contracts open. In addition to these factors, open interest changes when perceptions among buyers and sellers change for the stock as well. Unfortunately, the number of contracts does not tell you the reasons for the change, nor whether the change is being driven by buyers or by sellers.

Applying the Delta

The delta of a call should be 1.00 whenever it is deep in the money. As a general rule, expect the call to parallel the price movement of the stock on a point-for-point basis, an observation that is more true closer to expiration than at other times. In some instances, a call's delta may change unexpectedly. For example, if an in-the-money call increases by 3 points but the stock's price rose by only 2 points (a delta of 1.50), the aberration represents an *in-*

crease in time value, which rarely occurs. It may be a sign that investors perceive the option to be worth more than its previous price, relative to movement in the stock. This can be caused by any number of changes in market perception. For example, buyers might drive delta by way of increased time value when an in-the-money call is viewed as having profit potential based on rumors about the company. Figure 6.4 summarizes movement in option premium relative to the underlying stock, with corresponding delta.

Time value does not move in a completely predictable manner, since perceptions about the option are changing constantly. However, it is fair to say that increases in time value are rare. Of course, perceptions about both the stock and the option will affect time value to a degree, and increases in time value premium can occur, especially if the option has several months to go until expiration. You can track a call's delta in order to better time a covered call write.

Example: You bought 100 shares of stock at $48 per share. During yesterday's market, the stock rose from $51

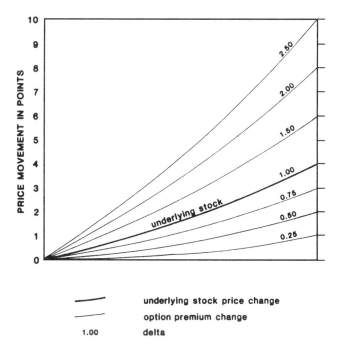

FIGURE 6.4 Changes in an option's delta.

to $53, based largely on rumors of higher quarterly profits than predicted by analysts. The 60 call rose from 4 to 8, an increase of 4 points (and a delta of 2.00).

In this example, it is apparent that the market overreaction to current news presents a buying opportunity. Increases in time value are invariably corrected in the future. Once the news hits and is absorbed, the time value is likely to correct itself as quickly as it appeared. Distortions in value often are momentary and require fast action. The covered call writer needs to be able to move quickly when opportunities are presented.

The same strategy can be applied when you already have an open covered call position and you are thinking of closing it. Suppose, for example, your call is in the money and the stock falls 2 points. At the same time, option premium falls by 3 points, for a delta of 1.50. This could be a temporary distortion, so profits can be taken immediately on the theory that the distortion will be corrected within a few days.

FOLLOWING YOUR OWN PERSPECTIVE

All market analysts depend on their best estimates in making decisions. You cannot time your decisions perfectly or consistently, so you have to depend on a combination of fundamental and technical indicators to provide yourself with an edge. That means you improve your percentages, and not that you will be right every time. As a call writer, it is crucial that you base your entire strategy on the thorough analysis and well thought-out selection of stocks. You should always pick a stock on its merits as a long-term investment and not merely to provide coverage for short option positions.

Also recognize that covered call writing is one way you create downside protection and improve overall return from your stock portfolio. In exchange for much-improved returns, you might lose the occasional sudden rise in market value of a stock. The fixed striking price ensures a limited but consistent profit. If writing covered calls is contrary to your overall long-term objectives, you should not participate in this market. For example, if you buy a stock because you believe it is grossly underpriced, then you expect its market value to rise in the future. In that case, it would not make sense to sell calls and fix the striking price.

Example: You bought 300 shares of stock last year as a long-term investment. You have no plans to sell and, as you hoped, the market price has been inching upward consistently. Your broker is encouraging you to write calls against your shares, pointing to the potential for additional profits as well as downside protection. Your broker also observes that if exercised, you will still earn a profit. However, remembering your reasons for buying the stock, you reject the advice. Call writing is contrary to your goal in buying the stock.

You usually can avoid exercise by rolling up and forward, as long as the price increase in the stock is not too severe. Exercise could be unavoidable when a stock's market price takes off. Call writers should understand such risks before entering into short positions; the loss of potential market value in the stock might not be worth a relatively small call premium. Exercise is always possible when a call is in the money, so you need to be completely satisfied with the return from call premium and the capital gain if the option is exercised.

As an options trader, never overlook the need for continued monitoring of the stock. By preparing a price performance chart like the one shown in Figure 6.5, you can track movement by week. A completed chart helps you to time decisions, notably on writing covered calls. If you have access to the Internet, you can also use free sites to produce price and volume charts. Three out of the many sites that provide this free benefit were listed earlier in this chapter.

Successful call writers have learned that it is important to track both the option and the underlying stock. If profits in one are offset by losses in the other, there is no point to a strategy. By observing changes in the option and the stock, you will be able to spot opportunities and dangers as they emerge.

Example: You bought 100 shares in each of four companies last year. Within the following months, you wrote

stock _____ dates: _____ to _____

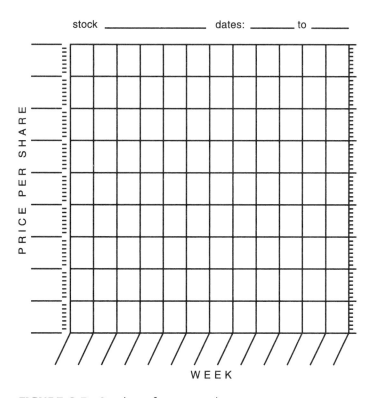

FIGURE 6.5 Stock performance chart.

covered calls in all four. Today, three of the four have market values below your basis, even though the overall market is higher. You add up the total of call premiums, dividends, and paper capital gains and losses, and realize that if you were to close out all of your positions today, you would lose money.

This example indicates that stocks were poorly chosen or poorly timed. While paper losses might have been greater had you not written calls, it also raises questions about why a particular mix of stocks was chosen. A critical review of your selection criteria might reveal that you are picking stocks based on option premium value rather than on the stock's fundamental and technical indicators. Relatively safe stocks tend to have little options appeal, because time value is minimal in stocks that do not change much. So more volatile stocks are far more likely candidates for premium action. That does not mean they are worthwhile investments; it could mean that option profits will be offset by capital losses in your portfolio.

Perhaps the greatest risk in call writing is the tendency to buy stocks that are overly volatile because they also have higher time value premium in their options. You will do better if you look for moderate volatility as a secondary strategy.

First, select stocks with good growth potential and hold them for a while without writing options. Give the stocks a chance to appreciate. This gives you much more flexibility in picking options and ensuring profits regardless of the outcome. The combination of premium, dividends, and capital gains can be built into your strategy with ease, assuming that current market value is higher than your original cost per share.

Second, time your decision to sell calls on stock you already own, to maximize your potential for gains from the options.

Third, remember the importance of patience. You might need to wait out a market that seems to be moving too slowly. Your patience will be rewarded if you select stocks properly. Opportunity does come around eventually, but too many novice call writers give in to their impatience, anxious to write calls as soon as possible. This is a mistake.

Putting Your Rules Down on Paper

Setting goals helps you to succeed in the options market. This is equally true if you buy stocks and do not write options. By defining your personal rules, you will have a better chance for success. Define several aspects of your investment plan, including:

1. Long-term goals for your entire portfolio.
2. Strategies you believe will help you reach those goals.
3. Percentages of your portfolio that are to be placed in each type of investment.
4. Definitions of risk in its many forms, and the degree of risk you are willing to assume.

5. Purchase and sale levels you are willing and able to commit.

6. Guidelines for review and possible modification of your goals.

Those investors who write down their rules tend to succeed more than those who do not have clearly defined rules of practice. If guidelines are overly vague or generalized, it is easy to modify them as you go, giving in to temptation that you cannot afford in the market. In a sense, hard-and-fast rules provide you with a programmed response to evolving situations, and improve your performance and profits. This does not mean you have to be inflexible; only that you know the limits of risk you are willing to take.

The next chapter explains how the strategy of selling puts can be used to achieve several different goals, including the protection of long positions in the market.

7

Selling Puts

A wise man turns chance into good fortune.
—Thomas Fuller, *Gnomologia*, 1732

Options traders are well aware of the special risks involved in selling calls. The underlying stock could rise indefinitely, so that in theory risk is un-limited when the call is not covered; even those writing covered calls face the risk of lost future profits because striking prices lock in the option seller to a fixed price in the event of exercise.

The situation is completely different when you sell puts. Recalling that a put is the opposite of a call, a put seller hopes that the value of the underlying stock will rise. As the stock rises, the value of the put falls, creating a profit for the put seller. The seller also faces the risk that the stock's market value will fall. In that case, the seller will experience a loss. However, this loss is finite. The greatest loss possible, in theory, occurs if the stock falls to zero. However, for practical reasons, a stock is unlikely to fall that far. A well-selected company's stock will have a limited likely range of market price; for example, while market value could fall below a company's book value per share, it does not stand to reason that market price would decline far below that level.

Even a drastic decline in a stock's market value has

limited consequences for the put seller. It could be defined as the difference between striking price and book value as the "lowest likely" price level. This is no guarantee, as the market has shown time and again that price levels are not governed by the intrinsic value of stock. In other words, fundamentals serve as valuable means for evaluating a company's long-term growth potential, but short-term price changes are unreliable; the fundamentals mean little in terms of pricing over the next few months.

Book value per share is a fundamental support level for the valuation of stock. It is today's value in terms of financial worth, without considering any prospects for future growth. A stock's value could fall below book value per share, however. For example, if the market perception is that a company will not be able to maintain its position in the market sector, or that current problems will spell disaster for sales and profits, or other significant defects in products and services spell problems in the future, then current price could reflect a dire outlook. The consequence could be that market price plummets well below book value per share, at least temporarily. For the put seller, a temporary drop in price could present a problem; at such a time, exercise is possible.

By and large, a put seller takes a reasonable position is assuming that book value per share is a fair support level, and it is unlikely that the stock's price will fall below that level. So a stock selling at $50 per share with book value of $20 per share could be assessed at having a maximum risk range of 30 points.

A put is an option to *sell* 100 shares of the underlying stock, at a fixed price by a specific date in the near future. So when you sell a put, you grant the buyer the right to "put" 100 shares of stock to you, or to sell you those shares. In exchange for receiving a premium at the time of your opening sale transaction, you assume the risk of exercise. You are willing, then, to buy 100 shares of the underlying stock even though at the time of exercise current value of the shares will be lower.

Smart Investor Tip It makes sense to sell puts as long as you believe that the striking price is a fair value for that company's stock.

As a put seller, you reduce your exposure to risk by selecting stocks within a limited price range. For example, if you sell puts with striking prices of 50 or less, your maximum loss is 50 points, or $5,000; that, of course, would occur only if a stock were to become worthless by expiration date. If you sell puts with striking price of 25 or lower, that cuts the maximum exposure in half, to $2,500 per contract. However, the more realistic way to assess maximum risk is to identify book value per share in comparison to striking price. That gap represents a more likely range of risk.

EVALUATING STOCK VALUES

If you consider the striking price to be fair and reasonable for 100 shares of the underlying stock, selling puts has two advantages:

1. You receive cash at the point that you sell a put.
2. The premium discounts the price of the stock in the event of exercise.

If you are willing to purchase shares of stock at the striking price, then selling puts is a smart strategy. In one regard, there is no actual risk because you think the price is reasonable. Of course, in the event of exercise, you would own 100 shares whose current market value would be lower than your purchase price, and that ties up capital.

Buying shares above market value may be acceptable if you plan to keep those shares as a long-term investment. Remember, however, that if the difference between striking price and current market value at the time of exercise is greater than the amount you received in premium, you have a paper loss at the point of exercise. You will need to wait out the time required for the stock's price to rebound before you recapture that loss. It might be true that, over the long term, that company represents a profitable investment. But put sellers would prefer not to experience exercise, so they use the same techniques to avoid it—rolling forward and rolling down, for example.

Once you identify the degree of risk involved with exercise, you need to compare that to the premium income in order to determine whether placing yourself in a short position is worth that risk exposure. If you embark on a heavy program of put writing, you will need to have available adequate capital to purchase the shares of stock involved, an important factor that limits the degree of put writing you are likely to undertake. If you experience a high degree of exercise, you will use up your available capital and fill your portfolio with shares of stock acquired above current market value. So you should limit put writing to those stocks you would like to own, whether or not you write puts.

Example: You sold a put with a striking price of 55 and received 6. You considered $55 per share a reasonable price for those shares. Before expiration, the stock's market value fell to $48 and your put was exercised. You paid $55 per share, 7 points above current market value.

Several observations need to be made concerning this transaction:

1. The outcome is acceptable as long as you believe that $55 per share is a fair price for the stock. You would then also believe that current market value represents a temporary depression in market value, and that is likely to rebound in the future. If your assumption is correct, the loss is a paper loss only and it will turn out to be a worthwhile investment.

2. The premium you received of $600 discounted your basis in the stock to $49 per share. So your true basis after exercise is only 1 point above current market value.

3. If the stock's market value had risen, you would have profited from selling the put. It would not have been exercised and would have expired worthless; or time value would have evaporated, enabling you to buy to close at a profit. In those outcomes, the put sale would have produced a

profit. So selling puts in a rising market can produce profits for investors unable or unwilling to tie up capital to buy 100 shares, with limited risk exposure.

Put sellers who seek only the income from premiums need to select stocks that they consider to be good prospects for price increase. Fundamental and technical tests of a company and its stock can be applied to a degree against the market in general, but it makes more sense to apply such tests to individual issues, because you cannot depend on a stock to follow market trends. Premium value is only half the test of a viable put sale; the other half is careful selection of stocks. If risks are too great, then you cannot justify the strategy.

EVALUATING RISKS

Stock selection contains specific risks for call sellers, as shown in the previous chapter. More attractive option premiums are associated with more volatile stocks. So covered call writers may be prone to selecting higher-risk stocks in order to sell higher-than-average time value.

The same risks apply to put sellers. You will find that higher time value premiums for puts are going to be found on stocks with higher-than-average volatility. The direction of price movement you desire is different with puts than with calls, but the risks in the underlying stock are the same. Put sellers face the risk that the underlying stock's market value will fall. The more drastic the fall, the greater the risk of exercise. However, a put seller's perception of risk has to be different than that of the call seller. The key to selecting puts should not be the size of the premium, but your willingness to buy the stock at the striking price in the event of exercise.

With this in mind, the evaluation of risk is different than for call selling. The put seller needs to apply those fundamental and technical tests to a stock in the same way as call sellers. The difference, however, is that while covered call writers own shares of the stock when they sell a call, the put writer can only be willing to buy the stock if exercise does occur. Because not every put will be exercised, put sellers enjoy greater leverage than call sellers. Your risk is limited to the degree of short position risk you can assume at one time and, of course, the risk exposure your brokerage firm will allow you to carry in your portfolio. You will need to be able to demonstrate that you have equity available to pay for shares in the event of exercise. A short position always carries a degree of risk, and if the market trend turns downward, several puts could be exercised within a short period of time.

PUT STRATEGIES

There are four popular strategies you may have in mind for selling puts: to produce short-term income, to make use of idle cash deposits in a brokerage account, to buy stocks, or to create a tax put.

Strategy 1: Producing Income

The most popular reason for selling puts is also the most apparent: the purely speculative idea of earning short-term profits from put premiums. The ideal outcome would be a decline in put value from declining time and intrinsic value, enabling the put seller to purchase and close the position at a profit. The passage of time is on your side when you sell, so the more time value in the total premium, the better your chances for profit. A corresponding higher risk will be associated with high time value.

Example: Last January, you sold a June 45 put for 4. At that time, the underlying stock's market value was $46 per share. Because market value was higher than the striking price, the entire premium was time value. (Remember that for puts, in-the-money is opposite that for calls.) If the stock's market value remained at or above $45 per share, the put would eventually expire worthless. If by exercise date the stock is valued between $41 and $45 per share, you would earn a limited profit or break even in the event of exercise (before trading costs). The $41 per share level is 4 points below striking price, and you received $400 for selling the put.

A short position can be canceled at any time. As a seller, you can close the position by buying the put at the current premium price. However, remember that an open put can also be exercised at any time by the buyer. So whenever you sell a put, you are exposed to exercise whenever that put is in the money (when the stock's market value is lower than striking price). For the premium you receive, you willingly expose yourself to this risk.

Smart put sellers are always aware of the profit and loss zones in their positions, and they decide in advance at what point to close their positions and when to keep them open. This self-imposed goal is related to premium level, of course, the status of current market value in relation to striking price, and the degree of time value premium still in the premium value. If a profit becomes unlikely or, in the seller's opinion, impossible, it might be necessary to close the position and limit the loss.

Smart Investor Tip Options traders recognize that they cannot be right all of the time. It often is wisest to accept a small loss rather than continue to be exposed to potentially greater losses.

An example of profit and loss zones for selling a put is shown in Figure 7.1. This is based on a striking price of 50 with put premium of 6. The premium creates a 6-point limited profit zone between $44 and $50 per share. Below that, the put seller will have a loss. This visual range analysis helps you to define when and where you will close a position, based on proximity between a stock's current market value and loss zone.

Example: You sold a 50 put for 6. Your profit zone is any price above the striking price of 50. If the stock's market value falls below $50 per share, the put will be in the money. As long as the price range remains between $44 and $50 per share, the loss upon exercise is limited because the premium you received discounts your potential basis in the stock in the event of exercise. If the stock's

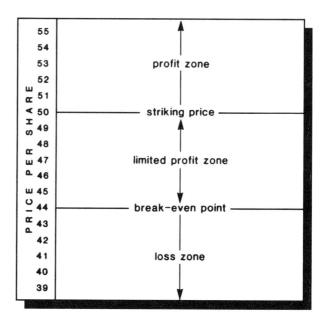

FIGURE 7.1 Put selling profit and loss zones.

market value falls below $44 per share, you will experience a loss upon exercise.

It is possible for a stock's market value to fall below striking price by several points and still enable you to close the put at a profit. This relies, of course, on time value decline. The analysis of profit and loss zones in the previous example is based on the worst-case assumption of where a stock's price will lie at the point of expiration. If the premium contains a good amount of time value, a put seller can profit merely by trading in the put.

Conceivably, you could select stocks that will remain at or above the striking price and earn premium profits repeatedly, without ever experiencing exercise. However, foresight about which stocks will achieve such consistent price support is difficult. It takes only a single, temporary dip in price to be exposed to exercise, a risk that cannot be overlooked. Exercise is not necessarily a drastic step; but it does tie up your capital because it requires that you buy stock above current market value. While you wait for the stock's price to rebound, you might miss other market opportunities.

Remember the basic guideline for selling puts: You need to be willing to buy 100 shares of the underlying stock at the striking price, which you consider a fair price for that stock. If current market value is lower than the striking price, you should believe that the price is going to rebound, justifying the purchase you will be required to make upon exercise.

If you consider the price a fair one, that does not mean you would welcome exercise. It only means that you would not mind owning those shares. You might still want to avoid exercise whenever possible by rolling positions, remembering that exercise of many puts means you end up with an overpriced portfolio of stocks.

Example: You sold several puts in the past few months. This month the entire market fell several hundred points. Five of your puts were exercised at the same time, requiring you to purchase 500 shares of stock. All of your available capital is now tied up in these shares. Consequently, your portfolio's basis is higher than current market value for *all* of the shares you own. The market is recovering, but very slowly. Even considering your premium income, you are in a large paper loss position. You have no choice but to sit out the market and hope for a rebound in the future.

The net cost level for stock acquired through exercise of puts is the striking price, minus premiums you received when you sold the puts. Allowing for transaction fees paid (both when you sold the put and when you bought the shares), your basis will be higher still. You should not overlook the potential paper loss position you could experience in the event of a market correction. The tendency in such times is for a broad-based drop in most stock prices, meaning you could have many exercised puts at the same time.

You reduce the risk somewhat by not selling puts with the same expiration month, and by spreading your put sales among different market sectors. Diversification takes many forms, for put sellers need to be aware of the strategic spreading of exposure to risk. Even if you believe that the striking price represents a reasonable price for shares, your point of view could change in the event of a large market correction.

Your brokerage firm will require cash or securities to satisfy margin requirements if you want to sell puts. Whenever you open a short position, the brokerage firm will want to ensure that it will not be stuck picking up losses because its clients do not have the resources. If you have numerous short positions open at the same time, the brokerage firm will want to be assured that in the event of exercise, you are able to honor your commitments and buy the shares assigned to you. If you are unable to honor your commitment, the brokerage firm is stuck with overpriced shares.

The brokerage firm is also aware that you cannot cover short puts as you can cover short calls. The call writer who owns 100 shares of stock faces no risk in the event of unexpected market rallies, because the shares can be delivered upon exercise. The put seller, however, cannot cover a potential exercise. So the put seller has to be able to demonstrate the financial ability to pay for shares upon exercise.

Example: You have $12,000 available to invest in the market today. Taking the traditional route, you could buy shares of stock up to $12,000 in market value. However, you may also decide to sell puts as an alternative. Your brokerage firm will decide how much your $12,000 deposit will allow you to write in puts—in other words, the brokerage firm will define how much risk you can expose yourself to for your $12,000 equity.

A brokerage firm might allow you to exceed your maximum point value (in this example, $12,000 deposit is also called 120 points, so option premium can add up to that point value under the brokerage firm allowance). Your brokerage firm might allow you to exceed the 120-point level in written puts, in two circumstances. First, the put premium you earn upon sale may be deposited in your account and held as a reserve, increasing your maximum point level. Second, you might be allowed to exceed total point exposure on the condition that you would be required to finance exercise in excess of your reserves through a margin account. In that outcome, you not only end up with a portfolio of overpriced stocks, but a portion of your purchase price would be accumulating interest.

Short put positions cannot be covered through stock,

as is the case with calls. However, it is possible to cover puts with the use of other option positions (see Chapter 8). There is no put strategy comparable to the coverage of short calls through stock ownership. The strategy sometimes referred to as a "covered put" involves selling a put and selling short 100 shares of the underlying stock. But this protects the stock only to the number of points the seller receives for the put and does not truly cover the short stock position. If the stock's value rises above the premium point level, then the short position begins to lose money.

With these differences in mind between selling calls and selling puts, the put seller needs to evaluate strategies differently. Call sellers will not always see exercise as a negative; in many circumstances, it is viewed as the most desired outcome. Profits can be built into the strategy. But when a put is exercised, stock is always going to be bought at a level above current market value, without exception. This outcome is advantageous only when the put premium exceeds the number of points between striking price and the stock's current market value; and this is a limited advantage only.

As a put seller, you can avoid exercise by using rolling techniques. Rolling forward buys time and might help avoid exercise, remembering that while exercise can occur at any time, it is most likely near expiration. Avoid increasing the number of puts in a rolling technique on a single issue, because that only increases your risk. Since rolling is most likely to occur in the money, it does not make sense to increase risks through rolling forward *and* picking up more short puts.

Example: You sold a put two months ago for 4. The stock's market price recently declined below striking price and you would like to avoid exercise. The put expires later this month, but you believe the stock's price will rebound. Premium level currently is 6. You close the position and replace it with two puts expiring in four months, each with a premium of 4. You receive $800 for opening the new puts, less the $600 you paid to purchase and close the original put.

A problem in this strategy is that it also increases your risk. You buy extra time and get an additional $200 in premium, but you end up with two puts instead of one. If both are exercised, you will be required to buy 200 shares above market value. An alternative is to roll forward the single put and replace it with another. In this example, you would purchase the first put at 6 and sell a later one at 4. That creates a cash outlay of $200. You originally received $400 when you sold the put; now you reduce that profit to $200 for the purchase of extra time. Another alternative to avoid exercise would be to buy the put and take a $200 loss. The decision depends on how much you want to avoid exercise, how willing you are to buy 100 shares at the striking price, your basis in the stock discounted by premium received, and how much value you place on the current premium level.

Strategy 2: Using Idle Cash

When investors sell uncovered options, their brokerage firm requires deposits of cash or securities for a portion of potential losses. With puts, the maximum risk is identified easily. It is equal to the striking price of the put minus premium received.

Investors may hold their capital on the sidelines, believing that stocks they want to buy are overpriced and will be attractive buying opportunities in the future. The dilemma is that the longer cash is held in reserve, the more they miss opportunities to put that money to work. Idle cash does not earn money, and there is no way to know how long it will take for conditions to present themselves, making the desired move practical.

One way to deal with this problem is by selling puts on the targeted stock. In this way, capital is still kept in reserve, yet you earn money from put premiums *and* you discount the basis in the stock in the event of exercise. You will profit from selling the put if the stock's price rises; and you will end up buying shares at the striking price (less premium discount) if the stock's market value falls. In either event, the premium you receive will be yours to keep.

Example: You are interested in buying stock as a long-term investment. However, you believe that the current market price is too high, and that a correction is likely to occur in the near future. One possible solution: Sell one put for every 100 shares you want to buy, instead of buying the stock. Place your capital on deposit with the brokerage firm as security against your short position in the puts. If the current market value of the stock rises, your short puts will fall in value and can be closed at a profit or allowed to expire worthless. In this way, you benefit from rising market value without placing all of your capital at risk.

If market value of the stock declines, you will purchase the shares at the striking price. Your basis will be discounted by the value of premiums you received for selling the puts. As a long-term investor, you will be confident that the share price will grow over time, and the current paper loss will be partially offset by the premium.

Strategy 3: Buying Stock

The third reason for selling puts is to intentionally seek exercise. Selling a put discounts the basis in stock in the event of exercise, and using the strategy of looking for exercise, you will not be concerned with price drops in the stock.

Example: You have been tracking a stock for several months, and you have decided that you are willing to buy 100 shares at or below $40 per share. The current price is $45. You could wait for the stock to drop to your level, which might or might not happen. However, an alternative is to sell a November 45 put, which has a current premium value of 6. This is all time value. If the market value of stock rises, the put will become worthless and the $600 you received is yours to keep. You could then repeat the transaction on the same argument as before, at a higher price increment. If the stock's market value falls, the put will be exercised. Your basis would be $39—striking price of 45 less 6 points received in put premium—which is one dollar per share below your target purchase price.

In this example, the put was sold at the money and the premium—all time value—was high enough to create a net basis below your target price. Even if the stock's market value were to fall below $40 per share, your long-term plans would not be affected. You considered $40 per share a reasonable purchase level for the shares. Long-term investors are not concerned with short-term price changes.

Simply waiting for the right price to come along means you expose yourself to the risk of losing the opportunity to get the stock at your price. Selling puts discounts current market value and makes it worthwhile to wait for exercise.

Example: You are interested in buying stock at $40 per share. Current market value is $45. You sell a put with a striking price of 45 and receive 6. Willing to take exercise, you have reduced your potential basis to $39 per share by selling the put. However, instead of falling, the stock's market value rises 14 points.

In this scenario, the put will expire worthless and you keep the $600 as profit. But if you had bought shares instead of selling the put, you would have earned $1,400 in profit. However, once your put expires, you are free to sell another one, offsetting the lost opportunity and perhaps exceeding that potential profit. Remember, the lost $1,400 is easy to recognize after the fact; however, at the time of making the decision to sell a put, you have no way of knowing whether the price will rise or fall. If share price were too high, you could risk *losing* $1,400 just as easily as you miss the opportunity for profiting by the same degree. This is why selling puts sometimes presents an attractive alternative to buying shares outright.

You risk losing future profits in two ways as a put seller, so you need to be willing to assume these risks in exchange for the premium income:

1. If the price of the underlying stock rises beyond the point value you received in premium, you lose the opportunity to realize profits in owning the stock. You settle for premium income only. However, when this occurs, your put expires worthless and you are free to sell another and receive additional premium.

2. If the price of the underlying stock falls significantly, you are required to buy 100 shares at the striking price, which will be above current market value. It might take considerable time for the stock's market value to rebound to the striking price level. Meanwhile, your capital is tied up in stock you bought above current market value.

While the risks of put selling are far more limited than those associated with uncovered call selling, you can also miss opportunities for profits in the event of stock price movement in either direction.

Strategy 4: Creating a Tax Put

A fourth reason to sell puts is to create an advantage for tax purposes, which is known as a *tax put*. However, before employing this strategy, you should consult with your tax adviser to determine that you time the transaction properly and legally, and to ensure that the tax rules have not changed. You also need to be able to identify the risks and potential liabilities involved with the tax put.

> **tax put**
> a strategy combining the sale of stock at a loss—taken for tax purposes—and the sale of a put at the same time. (The premium received on the put offsets the stock loss; if the put is exercised, the stock is purchased at the striking price.)

An investor who has a paper loss position on stock has the right to sell and create a capital loss at any time, even if the timing is intended to reduce income tax liability. Such losses are limited to annual maximums. You can deduct capital losses only up to those maximums, and the excess is carried over to future years. By selling puts at the same time that you take a tax loss, you offset part of the loss. The tax put is maximized when the put's expiration occurs in the following tax year. (For example, expiration will occur in January or later, but you sell the put in December or earlier.) If your net stock loss is greater than the maximum allowed, the profit on the put is absorbed by that over-the-limit loss. By selling a put as you also sell stock at a loss, one of three possible outcomes will occur:

1. The stock's market value rises and the option expires worthless. The stock loss is deducted in the year stock is sold, but profit on the short put is taxed in the following year, when it expires. This has the effect of enabling you to take stock losses in the current year, but deferring put premium gains until the following year.

2. The stock's market value rises and you close the position in the put, profiting by the premium difference.

3. The stock's market value falls below the striking price, and you are assigned the stock. In this case, your basis in the stock is discounted by the amount received for selling the put.

A potential problem arises in the event that the put is exercised within 30 days from the date you sold the shares of stock. Under the wash sale rule, you cannot claim a loss in stock if you repurchase the same stock within 30 days.

The tax put's advantage is twofold: First, you take a current-year loss on stock, reducing your overall tax liability, while deferring tax on the put sale until the following tax year. Second, you profit from selling the put, as shown in Figure 7.2, in the following two ways:

1. The premium income offsets the loss in stock.

2. In the event of exercise, your basis in the stock is discounted by the put premium.

Example: You bought stock at $38 per share, and it is valued currently at $34. You sell shares in December and take a $400 loss. At the same time, you sell a March 35 put at 6. The $400 loss in stock is offset by a $600 pre-

DATE	ACTION	RECEIVED	PAID
Aug. 15	buy 100 shares at $50		$5000
Dec. 15	sell 100 shares at $47	$4700	
Dec. 15	sell 1 Feb 50 put at 6	$ 600	
	total	$5300	$5000
	net cash	$ 300	

PRICE MOVEMENT	RESULT
stock rises above striking price	$300 profit
	put is bought at a profit
stock falls below striking price	put is exercised at $50, net cost $47 (with $300 profit from tax put)

FIGURE 7.2 Example of tax put.

mium from selling the put. If exercised, adjusted basis in the stock is discounted by the put premium.

Put sellers enjoy an important advantage over call sellers: Their risk is not unlimited because the stock's market value can fall only so far. An example of a put write is described next and illustrated with profit and loss zones in Figure 7.3.

Example: You sold one May 40 put at 3. The outcome of taking this short position will be profitable as long as the stock's market value remains at or above the striking price of $40 per share. If at expiration the market value is below $40, the put will be exercised and you will buy 100 shares at $40 per share. Losses are limited between striking price and $37 due to the put premium received. If the stock's market value falls below $37, you will take a loss at the point of exercise.

You may look at losses upon exercise of a put as paper losses in one regard: While the premium you receive for the put is yours to keep, you acquire stock above market value and you can wait until the price rebounds. So selling puts does require you to spend money on overpriced shares, but the condition may be a temporary one.

The most dire outcome for put sellers is that the stock may become worthless. As remote a possibility as

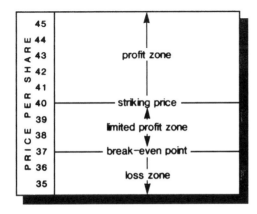

FIGURE 7.3 Example of put write with profit and loss zones.

this might be, it remains within the realm of possible outcomes. The possibility only emphasizes the importance of selecting stock carefully before writing puts. In the event a stock became worthless, your put would be exercised and you would buy 100 shares at the striking price. Current market value would be zero. The more likely true risk level, of course, is book value. Remember, however, that it is always possible for a stock's market value to fall below book value. The fundamental value of a company's equity has little to do with market pricing, especially in the short term. Tangible net worth often is overlooked in the more important factor affecting price—the *perception* of future potential value, which might be positive or negative and certainly will affect current share price. Even when a stock is associated with the fundamental strength of a well-capitalized company, the market might discount that value entirely. Market pricing is far from rational, and every put seller needs to keep that reality in mind.

As with all options strategies, the best stocks to select for put selling are those that tend to experience price movement within a limited trading range. The ideal stock has experienced moderate volatility in the recent past in order to create attractive time value, but has not had ever-broadening support and resistance ranges or exhibited unpredictable and sudden price changes. Highly volatile stocks are high-risk alternatives for selling puts, and a loss could require many months, perhaps even years to recover.

Put sellers should always be willing to buy 100 shares at the striking price, recognizing that exercise is always possible when the put is in the money. This is essential because your exercised price will always be above current market value. As long as you believe that striking price is reasonable, short-term price movement does not affect the stock's long-term growth potential. If you have studied thoroughly the company's strength and prospects as a long-term investment, selling puts can be a smart way to increase current income while discounting potential basis in the stock.

In the next chapter, you will see how mixing various buying and selling strategies can be used to decrease (or increase) risks and returns.

Chapter 8

Combined Techniques

Decision making isn't a matter of arriving at a right or wrong answer, it's a matter of selecting the most effective course of action from among less effective courses of action.
— Philip Marvin, *Developing Decisions for Action*, 1971

Options traders can employ only four basic strategies: buying calls, selling calls, buying puts, and selling puts. These basic approaches can be applied in numerous methods and strategies, as shown in previous chapters. For example, you can modify risks in long positions with offsetting short positions in options.

Your reasons for buying or selling options define the level and degree of risk that you are willing to assume. In that regard, the utilization of options defines another investment, specifically your ownership of stock. Consider, for example, the difference between one investor who wants only to profit from buying and selling options and another who covers calls with shares of stock in order to maximize returns. The risks are on opposite sides of the spectrum, and the uses of options by each person define and distinguish their perceptions of risk and opportunity, their desired outcomes, and even the basic idea about how to operate within the market.

This chapter expands on the variations of the four basic strategies, and demonstrates how they can be structured and combined in many ways. Long and short positions can be engaged in at the same time, so that risks offset one another. Some combined strategies are designed to create profits in the event that the underlying stock moves in either direction; others are designed to create profits if the stock remains within a specific range of price. There are three major classifications of advanced strategies: spread, straddle, and hedge.

A *spread* is the simultaneous opening of both a long position and a short position in options on the same underlying stock. The spread increases potential profits while also reducing risks in the event that the underlying stock behaves in a particular manner, as illustrated shortly.

In order to meet the definition of a spread, the options should have different expiration dates, different striking prices, or both. When the striking prices are different but the expiration dates are the same, it is called a *vertical spread*. This is also referred to as a *money spread*.

Example: You buy a 45 call and, at the same time, sell a 40 call. Both expire in February. Because expiration dates are identical, this is a vertical spread.

Example: You buy a 30 put and, at the same time, sell a 35 put. Both expire in December. This is also a vertical spread.

The vertical spread is created using either calls or puts. The spread can have different expiration dates or a *combination* of different striking prices and expiration dates. Spreads can be put together in numerous formations.

The combined strategy called a *straddle* is defined as the simultaneous purchase and sale of an identical number of calls and puts with the same striking price and expiration date. While the spread requires a difference in one or more of the terms, the straddle is distinguished by the fact that the terms of each side are identical. The exception, of course, is that a straddle consists of combining calls on one side with puts on the other.

The advanced strategy called the *hedge* has been discussed many times throughout this book. For example, you hedge a short sale in stock by purchasing a call. In the event the stock rises, the short seller's losses will be offset by a point-for-point rise in the call. A put also protects a

spread
the simultaneous purchase and sale of options on the same underlying stock, with different striking prices or expiration dates, or both.

vertical spread
a spread involving different striking prices but identical expiration dates.

money spread
alternate name for the vertical spread.

combination
any purchase or sale of options on one underlying stock, with terms that are not identical.

long stock position against a decline in price. So one use of a hedge is to utilize options as insurance. In some respects, both spreads and straddles contain hedging features, since two dissimilar positions are opened at the same time; price movement reducing the value on one side of the transaction tends to be offset by price increase on the other side.

straddle
the simultaneous purchase and sale of the same number of calls and puts with identical striking prices and expiration dates.

If you are new to the options market, you will want to keep your strategies fairly simple at first. If you venture beyond the basic strategies, you will most likely begin with a vertical spread. Other, more advanced strategies are used by more experienced options traders and are included here to explain the full range of possibilities in options trading. However, they often produce minimal profits for each option contract, given the need to pay trading fees upon opening and closing. Such marginal outcomes do not justify risks in many cases, so advanced options traders apply these strategies with large multiples of option contracts.

Remember, too, that what appears simple and logical on paper does not always work out the way you expect in the real world. Changes in option premium levels are not always logical or predictable as you might hope, and short-term variations can occur for a number of reasons. This is what makes option investing so interesting; such experiences also test your true risk tolerance level. You could discover that your risk tolerance is much different than you thought, once you begin dabbling in advanced option strategies. The experience of being at risk can be daunting, and it is important that you understand the full range of possible risks and costs before embarking on any advanced strategies.

VERTICAL SPREAD STRATEGIES

Options traders use spreads to take advantage of the predictable course of changes in option premium values. These changes are predictable because everyone knows what happens to time value as expiration approaches. And when options are in the money, it is reasonable to expect intrinsic value premium to react dollar-for-dollar with movement in the price of the underlying stock. The relationship between intrinsic value and time value is what makes the spread an interesting and challenging strategic tool for the options investor.

Smart Investor Tip   As with most option strategies, time value spells the difference between profit and loss in most spreads.

You have an advantage when offsetting long and short positions in the spread. The spread is most likely to involve one side in the money and the other side out of the money. The in-the-money side will tend to change in value at a different rate than the out-of-the-money side, because it contains intrinsic value—and because when in the money, time value tends to act differently as well. By observing the differences on either side of the striking price, you can anticipate advantages that you gain through the spread strategy, whether the market moves up or down.

Bull Spreads

bull spread
a strategy involving the purchase and sale of calls or puts that will produce maximum profits when the value of the underlying stock rises.

A *bull spread* provides the greatest profit potential if and when the underlying stock's market value rises. With the bull spread, you buy an option with a lower striking price and sell another with a higher striking price. You can employ either puts or calls in the bull spread.

Example: You open a bull spread using calls. You sell one December 55 call and buy one December 50 call, as shown in Figure 8.1. At the time of this transaction, the underlying stock's market value is $49 per share. After you open the spread, the stock's market value rises to $54 per share. When that occurs, the 50 call increases in value point for point once it is in the money. The short 55 call does not change in value as it remains out of the money and, in fact, will drop in value as its time value falls. Because of the advantage the spread creates at the time the stock has reached the $54 per share level, both sides of the spread will be profitable. The long 50 call rises in value and the short 55 call remains out of the money, so it loses time value.

This example describes the ideal situation, in which both sides of the spread are profitable, because the stock's price

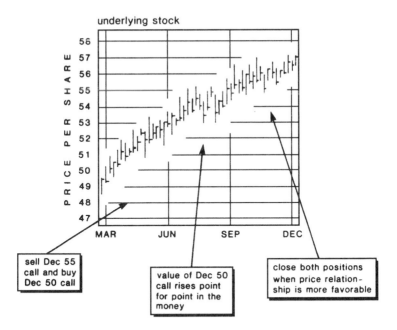

FIGURE 8.1 Example of bull spread.

behaves perfectly to suit the spread. Of course, you have no control over price movement, so this outcome will not always occur. Even when only one side is profitable, however, the strategy works as long as you achieve an overall profit.

Smart Investor Tip The spread is most profitable when the stock's price changes in the desired timing and pattern. Both sides of the spread can work out well. Of course, this would be much easier if stock price movement could be controlled or predicted—but it cannot.

A bull vertical spread is profitable when the underlying stock's price moves in the anticipated direction. For example, a lower-priced call will be profitable if the stock rises in value, whereas the higher-priced short call will not be exercised as long as it remains out of the money, as illustrated in the example just given.

A bull vertical spread, with defined profit and loss zones, is shown in Figure 8.2.

Example: You sell one September 45 call for 2, and buy one September 40 call for 5. The net cost before brokerage

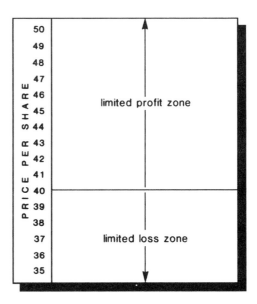

FIGURE 8.2 Bull vertical spread profit and loss zones.

fees is $300. When the stock rises between $40 and $45 per share, the September 40 call rises dollar for dollar with the stock, while the short September 45 call remains out of the money. Its premium value will decline as time value disappears. As long as the stock remains within this 5-point range, both sides can be closed at a profit (as long as closing the positions would exceed your initial cost of $300). If the stock's price rises above $45 per share, the 5-point spread in striking prices will be offset by the long and short positions. Both calls will be in the money. So this strategy limits both profits and losses.

bear spread
a strategy involving the purchase and sale of calls or puts that will produce maximum profits when the value of the underlying stock falls.

Bear Spreads

Compared to the bull spread, the *bear spread* will produce profits if the stock's market value falls. In this variety of the spread, the higher-value option is always bought, and the lower-value option is always sold.

Example: You open a bear spread using calls. You sell one March 35 call and buy one March 40 call. The stock's market value is $37 per share. The premium value of the lower call, which is in the money, will decline point for point as the stock's market value falls; if the stock's value does fall, the position can be closed at a profit.

Example: You open a bear spread using puts. As shown in the example in Figure 8.3, you sell one December 50 put and buy one December 55 put. The underlying stock's market value is $55 per share. As the price of the stock moves down, the long 55 put will increase in value point for point with the change in stock price. By the time the stock's price moves down to $51, both puts will be profitable—the long put from increased intrinsic value, and the short put from lower time value.

This scenario assumes ideal conditions in which the stock's price moves the desired number of points in the maximized time frame, which enables the bear spread writer to profit. This does not always happen, of course, but this illustrates the ideal outcome you would desire upon using a bear spread.

Smart Investor Tip Bear strategies often are overlooked by investors, who tend more often than not to be

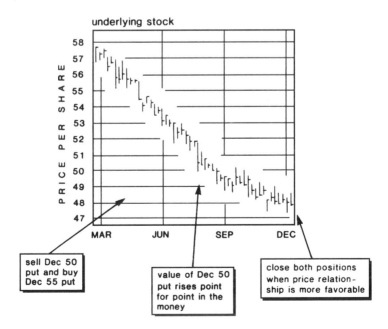

FIGURE 8.3 Example of bear spread.

optimists. Look at *all* of the possibilities. You can make money when the stock goes down in value, too.

A detailed bear spread with defined profit and loss zones is illustrated in Figure 8.4.

Example: You sell one September 40 call for 5 and buy one September 45 call for 2; your net proceeds are $300. As the stock's market value falls below the level of $45 per share, the short 40 call will lose point value matching the stock's decline; the lower long call will not react in the same way, as it remains out of the money. As the $40 per share price level is approached, the spread can be closed with profits on both sides.

Consider how this example would work with puts instead of calls. In that scenario, the higher long put would *increase* point for point with a decline in the stock's market value.

When the bear spread employs calls, profits are frozen once both sides are in the money, at least to the degree that intrinsic value changes; one side's increase will be offset by the other side's decrease. The only remaining opportunity to increase profits at that point would lie in time value premium remaining in the short position.

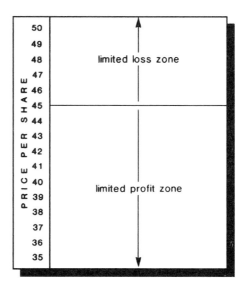

FIGURE 8.4 Bear vertical spread profit and loss zones.

In all of these examples, the most significant risk is that the stock will move in the direction opposite that desired. Be prepared to close a spread in that event before the short position increases to value (meaning you will lose). You risk exercise on the short side at any time that option is in the money, and you might need to close to avoid exercise and to reduce potential losses as well. Your maximum risk other than that of exercise is limited to the point difference between the two striking prices (minus net premium received when the position was opened; or plus net premium paid). In the preceding examples, a 5-point spread was used, so that maximum point-spread risk was $500 per spread. The point-spread risk increases as the gap between striking price changes, as shown in Table 8.1. It becomes apparent that as the striking price interval and the number of spreads grows, the risk grows as well.

Example: You open a spread. The difference between striking prices on either side is 5 points. Your maximum risk is $500 plus brokerage fees, plus net premium paid when you opened the position (or minus net premium received).

	TABLE 8.1 Spread Risk Table	
Number of Option Spreads	*Striking Price Interval*	
	5 Points	*10 Points*
1	$ 500	$ 1,000
2	1,000	2,000
3	1,500	3,000
4	2,000	4,000
5	2,500	5,000
6	3,000	6,000
7	3,500	7,000
8	4,000	8,000
9	4,500	9,000
10	5,000	10,000

Example: You open a spread buying and selling four options on either side. The difference between striking prices is 5 points. Your maximum risk is $2,000 (modified as in the previous example), because four positions are involved, each with a 5-point difference between striking prices.

Box Spreads

box spread
the combination of a bull spread and a bear spread, opened at the same time on the same underlying stock.

When you open a bull spread *and* a bear spread at the same time, using options on the same underlying stock, it is called a *box spread*. This limits risks as well as potential profits, and is designed to produce a profit in one side or the other, regardless of which direction the stock moves.

Example: As illustrated in Figure 8.5, you create a box spread by buying and selling the following option contracts:

Bull spread: Sell one September 40 put and buy one September 35 put.

Bear spread: Buy one September 45 call and sell one September 40 call.

If the underlying stock's price moves significantly in either direction, portions of the box spread can be closed at a profit. One important reminder: It makes sense to close corresponding long and short positions in the event of a profit opportunity, to avoid the risk of leaving yourself exposed to an uncovered short situation. In the ideal situation, the stock's price will move first in one direction (enabling half the box spread to be closed at a profit) and then in the other (enabling the close of the other half at a profit).

Smart Investor Tip   Remember, when one side of the box spread expires, you might be left exposed on the other side. Keep an eye on the changing situation to avoid unacceptable risks.

The detailed profit and loss zones of a box spread are summarized in Figure 8.6. The net proceeds from this box spread result from the following outcomes:

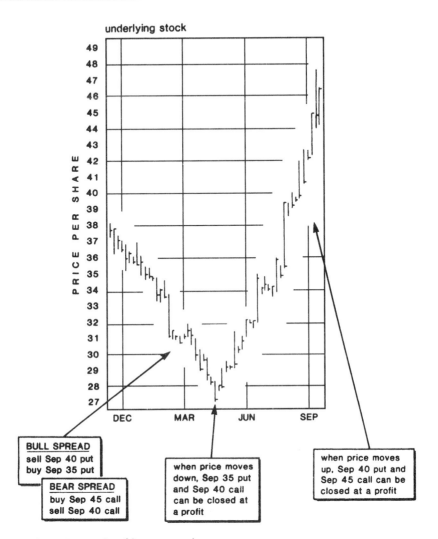

underlying stock

BULL SPREAD
sell Sep 40 put
buy Sep 35 put

BEAR SPREAD
buy Sep 45 call
sell Sep 40 call

when price moves
down, Sep 35 put
and Sep 40 call
can be closed at
a profit

when price moves
up, Sep 40 put and
Sep 45 call can be
closed at a profit

FIGURE 8.5 Example of box spread.

Bull spread: Sell one September 45 put for 6 (+$600) and buy one September 40 put for 2 (–$200).

Bear spread: Sell one December 35 put for 1 (+$100) and buy one December 40 put for 4 (–$400).

If the stock's market price rises between $40 and $45 per share, the bull spread can be closed at a profit. Above that level, the difference in bull spread values will move to the same degree in the money, offsetting one another. If the

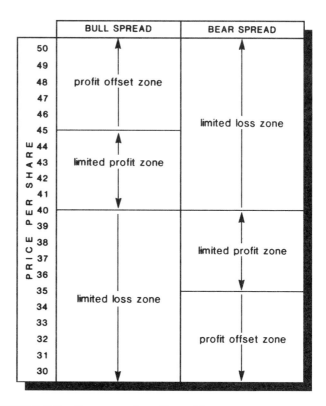

FIGURE 8.6   Box spread profit and loss zones.

stock falls to between $35 and $40 per share, the bear spread can be closed at a profit. The long December 40 put will be in the money and will change point for point with change in the stock's price. Below the level of $35 per share, the long and short position will change in intrinsic value levels, offsetting one another.

Smart Investor Tip   Whenever you close part of a box spread, close both long and short positions to avoid unintended short positions that are not covered or hedged.

Debit and Credit Spreads

The simultaneous opening of long and short positions involves receipt *and* payment of money. When you go short, you receive a premium, and when you go long you are required to pay. While it is always desirable to receive more money than you pay out, it is not always possible. Some strategies will involve making a net payment. When you receive cash when you open a position, that provides you flexibility, because you need less price movement to produce a net profit. When you make a payment to open the position, more profit is required in changes in option premium to offset the amount paid.

Smart Investor Tip When a spread involves a net receipt, that broadens your profit potential; a net payment is accompanied by the requirement for greater profits in changed option premium to make up the difference.

A spread in which more cash is received than paid is called a *credit spread*. When the net outcome requires you to make a payment, it is called a *debit spread*.

HORIZONTAL AND DIAGONAL SPREAD STRATEGIES

In the previous section, vertical spreads were illustrated (involving options with identical expiration dates but different striking prices). Another variation of spread involves simultaneous option transactions with different expiration months. This is a *calendar spread*, also called a *time spread*.

The calendar spread can be broken down into two specific variations, *horizontal spread* and *diagonal spread*:

> *Horizontal spread:* In this variation, options have identical striking prices but different expiration dates.
>
> *Diagonal spread:* In this variation, options have different striking prices *and* different expiration dates.

Example: You enter into transactions that create a horizontal calendar spread. You sell one March 40 call for 2; and you buy one June 40 call for 5. Your net cost is $300. Two different expiration months are involved. The earlier, short call expires in March, while the long call does not expire until June. Your loss is limited in two ways: by amount and time. This point is illustrated in Figure 8.7. If

credit spread
any spread in which receipts from short positions are higher than premiums paid for long positions, net of transaction fees.

debit spread
any spread in which receipts from short positions are lower than premiums paid for long positions, net of transaction fees.

calendar spread
a spread involving the simultaneous purchase or sale of options on the same underlying stock, with different expirations.

time spread
alternate name for the calendar spread.

horizontal spread
a calendar spread in which offsetting long and short positions have identical striking prices but different expiration dates.

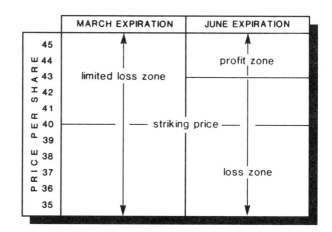

FIGURE 8.7 Profit and loss zones for an example of horizontal calendar spread.

diagonal spread
a calendar spread in which offsetting long and short positions have both different striking prices and different expiration dates.

in March the first call expires worthless, you have a profit in that position and the second phase goes into effect. The short position no longer exists. If the stock rises at least 3 points above striking price before expiration, the overall position is at breakeven; above that, it will be profitable.

Example: You create a diagonal calendar spread. You sell one March 40 call for 2; and you buy one June 45 call for 3. Your net cost is $100. This transaction involves different striking prices *and* expiration months. If the earlier-expiring short position is exercised, the long call can be used to satisfy the call. In other words, as owner of the long position, you can exercise the call when your short position call is exercised. If the earlier call is not exercised, the overall risk is restricted to the net cost of $100. After expiration of the short call, breakeven is equal to the long call's striking price plus the cost of the overall transaction. In this case, the net cost was $100, so $46 is the break-even price (not allowing for trading costs). This is illustrated in Figure 8.8.

Giving different spread strategies the names vertical, horizontal, and diagonal helps distinguish them from one another, and provides a way to visualize the relationships between expiration and striking prices. These distinctions are summarized in Figure 8.9.

A horizontal spread is an attractive strategy when

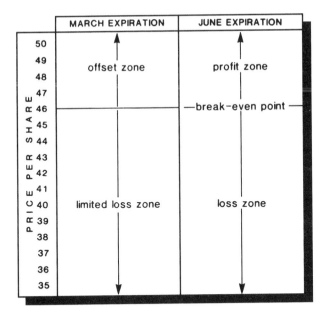

FIGURE 8.8 Profit and loss zones for an example of diagonal calendar spread.

the premium value between two related options is temporarily distorted, or when the later option's features protect the risks of the earlier-expiring short position.

Example: You open a horizontal spread using calls. You sell a March 40 call for 4, and you buy a June 40 call for 6. Your net cost is $200. If the market value of the underlying stock rises, the long position protects against the risks of the short position. The risk is no longer unlimited. The maximum risk in this situation is the $200 paid to open the spread. If the stock remains at or below striking price,

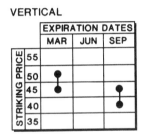
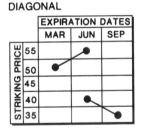

FIGURE 8.9 Comparison of spread strategies.

the short call will lose value and expire worthless; or it can be bought and closed at a profit. For example, if its value fell to 1, you could buy and realize a profit of $300. Compared to the net cost of opening the spread, this puts you $100 ahead overall, but you still own the long call. If the premium value were to rise above the $600 paid for this call, it could be sold at a profit.

A horizontal spread is useful for reducing existing risks when one position is already open. For example, if you previously sold a call and the stock begins to change in value so that you are at risk of exercise, you can reduce that risk by buying an option with a later expiration, which offsets the short position. This may be a less expensive alternative than buying the short position at a loss, because the long position has the potential to increase in value.

Smart Investor Tip   Devices like the horizontal spread sometimes come about in stages, and can be used to avoid exercise in a previously established short position.

Example: You sold a covered June 45 call last month. The stock's market value is above striking price. You do not want to close the position because that will create a loss, but you also would like to avoid exercise. By buying a September 45 call, you create a horizontal spread. If the June 45 call is exercised, you will be able to exercise the September 45 call, offsetting the assignment. However, if the call is not exercised, you own a later-expiring call that has its own potential for profit within a time span of an additional three months.

A diagonal spread combines vertical and horizontal features. Long and short positions are opened with different striking prices and expiration dates.

Example: You create a diagonal spread. You sell a March 50 call for 4; and you buy a June 55 call for 1. You receive $300 net for these transactions. If the stock's market value falls, you profit from the decline in premium value on the short position. If the stock's market value rises, the long position call rises as well, offsetting increases in the short call. Maximum risk in this situation is 5 points; however, because you received net premium of $300, real exposure is limited to 2 points (5 points between striking prices, less 3 points net premium). If the earlier short call expires worthless, you continue to own the long call. With its longer term, you continue to enjoy potential profit for three more months.

ALTERING SPREAD PATTERNS

The vertical, horizontal, and diagonal patterns of the spread can be employed to reduce risks, especially if you keep an eye on relative price patterns, and you see a temporary price distortion. Going beyond reduction of risk, some techniques can be employed in advanced strategies to make the spread even more interesting.

Varying the Number of Options

The *ratio calendar spread* involves the employment of a different number of options on each side of the spread, and the use of different expiration dates as well. The strategy is interesting because it creates two separate profit and loss zone ranges, broadening the opportunity for interim profits.

Example: You enter into a ratio calendar spread by selling four May 50 calls at 5, and buying two August 50 calls at 6. You receive $800 net ($2,000 received less $1,200 paid) before transaction fees are deducted. Between the time you open these positions and expiration, you hope that the underlying stock's market value will remain below striking price; that would produce a profit on the short side. Your breakeven is $54 per share.

If the stock is at $54 at the point of expiration, you break even due to the ratio of four short calls and two long calls. Upon exercise, the two short calls will cost $800—the same amount that you received upon opening the ratio calendar spread. If the price of stock is higher than $54 per share, the loss occurs at the ratio of 4 to 2 (since you sold four calls and bought only two). If the May expiration date were to pass without exercise, the

ratio calendar spread
a strategy involving a different number of options on the long side of a transaction from the number on the short side, when the expiration dates for each side are also different. (This strategy creates two separate profit and loss zone ranges, one of which disappears upon the earlier expiration.)

four short positions would be profitable, and you would still own the two August 50 calls.

The profit and loss zones in this example are summarized in Figure 8.10. Note that no consideration is given to transaction costs, time value of the longer-expiration premiums, or the outcome in the event of early exercise.

Another complete ratio calendar spread strategy with defined profit and loss zones is summarized in Figure 8.11 and explained in the following example.

Example: You sell five June 40 calls at 5, and buy three September 40 calls at 7. Net proceeds are $400. The short position risk is limited to the first expiration period, with potential losses partially covered by the longer-expiration long calls. As long as the stock's market value does not rise above the striking price of 40, the short calls will ex-

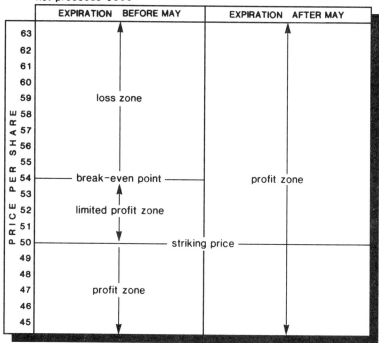

FIGURE 8.10 Example of ratio calendar spread.

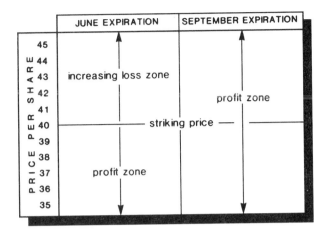

FIGURE 8.11 Ratio calendar spread profit and loss zones.

ratio calendar
combination
spread

pire worthless. However, there are two open, uncovered calls up until the point of the earlier expiration.

Once the June expiration passes, the $400 net represents pure profit, regardless of stock price movement after that date. However, if the stock's market value were to rise above the long calls' striking price, they would increase in value 3 points for each point of increase in the stock. Of course, the calls can also be sold at any time prior to expiration, to create additional profit.

Table 8.2 shows a summary of the values for this strategy at various stock price levels as of expiration. No time value is considered in this summary. If the stock remains at or below the $40 per share level, the ratio calendar spread will be profitable. However, that profit will be limited as long as all positions remain open.

Expanding the Ratio

The ratio calendar spread can be expanded into an even more complex strategy through employment of the *ratio calendar combination spread*. This adds yet another dimension to the ratio calendar spread by adding a box spread to it.

Example: As illustrated in Figure 8.12, you open the following option positions:

ratio calendar combination spread a strategy involving both a ratio between purchases and sales and a box spread. (Long and short positions are opened on options with the same underlying stock, in varying numbers of contracts and with expiration dates extending over two or more periods. This strategy is designed to produce profits in the event of price increases or decreases in the market value of the underlying stock.)

TABLE 8.2 Profits/Losses for Ratio Calendar Spread Example			
Price	June 40	Sep. 40	Total
$50	-$5000	+$3000	-$2000
49	- 4500	+ 2700	- 1800
48	- 4000	+ 2400	- 1600
47	- 3500	+ 2100	- 1400
46	- 3000	+ 1800	- 1200
45	- 2500	+ 1500	- 1000
44	- 2000	+ 1200	- 800
43	- 1500	+ 900	- 600
42	- 1000	+ 600	- 400
41	- 500	+ 300	- 200
40	+ 2500	- 2100	+ 400
39	+ 2500	- 2100	+ 400
38	+ 2500	- 2100	+ 400
Lower	+ 2500	- 2100	+ 400

Buy one June 30 call at 3 (pay $300).

Sell two March 30 calls at 1¾ (receive $350).

Buy one September 25 put at ¾ (pay $75).

Sell two June 25 puts at ⅝ (receive $125).

(After decimalization, the values in this list are denoted differently. The value 1¾ becomes 1.75; ¾ becomes 0.75; and ⅝ becomes 0.625.)

The net result of these transactions is a receipt of $100, before calculation of trading charges. This complex combination involves 2 to 1 ratios between short and long positions on both sides (two short option positions for each long option position). In the event of unfavorable price movements in either direction, you risk exercise on at least a segment of this overall strategy. The ideal price change pattern would enable you to close parts of the total combination at a profit, while leaving other parts. Ideally, short positions should be closed in advance of long positions, because the long positions provide at least partial coverage against exercise.

buy 1 Jun 30 call for 3 (−300)
sell 2 Mar 30 calls for 1¾ (+350)
buy 1 Sep 25 put for ¾ (− 75)
sell 2 Jun 25 puts for ⅝ (+125)
net proceeds $100

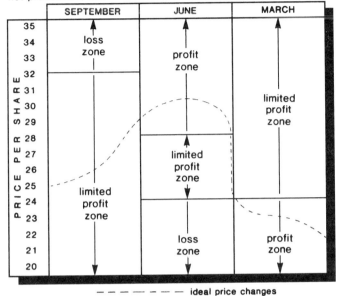

FIGURE 8.12 Example of ratio calendar combination spread.

Smart Investor Tip You normally will need to close short positions in advance of long positions to avoid unacceptable risk—a point worth remembering when you open the positions when initiating the spread.

Because trading fees add up quickly, a combination using only a small number of options is a costly strategy. Considering the risk exposure, potential profits would not justify the action in many cases; the previous example is a case in point. However, for the purpose of illustration, this shows how the strategy works. In practice, such actions would be likely to involve much larger numbers of option contracts, and thus more money—and more risk exposure.

Exercise risk is reduced by owning shares in the underlying stock, providing full or partial coverage against short call positions. For example, when writing two calls and buying one, the risk of a price increase is eliminated if you also own 100 shares. Those shares cover one call, and the other is covered by the long call.

Example: A complete ratio calendar combination spread, with defined profit and loss zones, is shown in Figure 8.13. In this example, you open the following positions:

Buy one July 40 call for 6 (–$600).

Sell two April 40 calls for 3 (+$600).

Buy one October 35 put for 1 (–$100).

Sell two July 35 puts for 2 (+$400).

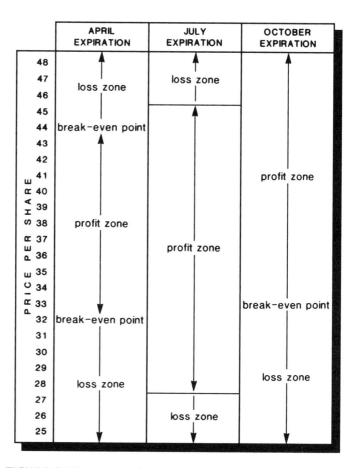

FIGURE 8.13 Ratio calendar combination spread profit and loss zones.

The net result of these transactions is a receipt of $300, before calculation of trading charges. This example consists of two separate ratio calendar spreads, boxed together. Profits would occur if the stock's market value were to move in either direction, whereas losses are limited. Three separate expiration dates are involved. One danger in this elaborate strategy is that, as earlier options expire, later open positions become exposed to uncovered losses, so risks are increased. This situation can be reversed—so that chances for profits are greater—by building a combination using later-expiring long positions instead of short positions. Table 8.3 provides a breakdown of profit and loss produced at various price levels based on the example.

A Strategy with a Middle Range

Another technique calls for the opening of offsetting options in middle striking price ranges, with opposing positions above *and* below. This is known as the *butterfly spread*. It can involve long and short positions, in calls or puts. There are several possible variations of the butterfly spread. For example:

 butterfly spread
a strategy involving open options in one striking price range, offset by transactions at higher and lower ranges at the same time.

- ✔ Sell two middle-range calls and buy two calls, one with a striking price above that level and one with a striking price below that level.
- ✔ Sell two middle-range puts and buy two puts, one with a striking price above that level and one with a striking price below that level.
- ✔ Buy two middle-range calls and sell two calls, one with a striking price above that level and one with a striking price below that level.
- ✔ Buy two middle-range puts and sell two puts, one with a striking price above that level and one with a striking price below that level.

Example: You sell two September 50 calls at 5, receiving $1,000. You also buy one September 55 call at 1 and one September 45 call at 7, paying a total of $800. Net proceeds are $200. This is a credit spread, since you received more than you paid. You will profit if the underlying

| | April 40 | July 40 | July 35 | Oct. 35 | |
Price	Call	Call	Put	Put	Total
$47	+$100	−$800	$ 0	+$400	−$300
46	0	− 600	0	+ 400	− 200
45	− 100	− 400	0	+ 400	− 100
44	− 200	− 200	0	+ 400	0
43	− 300	0	0	+ 400	+ 100
42	− 400	+ 200	0	+ 400	+ 200
41	− 500	+ 400	0	+ 400	+ 300
40	− 600	+ 600	0	+ 400	+ 400
39	− 600	+ 600	0	+ 400	+ 400
38	− 600	+ 600	0	+ 400	+ 400
37	− 600	+ 600	0	+ 400	+ 400
36	− 600	+ 600	0	+ 400	+ 400
35	− 600	+ 600	0	+ 400	+ 400
34	− 600	+ 600	0	+ 200	+ 200
33	− 600	+ 600	+ 100	0	+ 100
32	− 600	+ 600	+ 200	− 200	0
31	− 600	+ 600	+ 300	− 400	− 100
30	− 600	+ 600	+ 400	− 600	− 200
29	− 600	+ 600	+ 500	− 800	− 300
28	− 600	+ 600	+ 500	−1000	− 500
27	− 600	+ 600	+ 500	−1200	− 700
26	− 600	+ 600	+ 500	−1400	− 900

TABLE 8.3   Profits/Losses for Ratio Calendar Combination Spread Example

stock's price falls. And no matter how high the stock's price rises, the combined long positions' value will always exceed the values in the two short positions.

Smart Investor Tip   Exotic combinations are more often good for studying strategy than for actual use in the market. Trading costs are likely to offset potential limited profits in such strategies.

Butterfly spreads often are created when a single open position is expanded by the addition of other calls or puts, most often to protect a short position when a stock moves in a direction other than anticipated. It is difficult to find situations in which you can create a risk-free combination such as the one in the previous example.

Example: You sold two calls last month with a striking price of 40. The underlying stock's market value has declined to a point that the 35 calls are cheap, so you buy one to partially cover your short position. At the same time, you also buy a 45 call, which is deep out of the money. This series of trades creates a butterfly spread.

The trading fees charged by your brokerage firm make butterfly spreads impractical when using a small number of options. A credit spread is even less likely. The potential gain should be evaluated against the potential loss, commission costs, and ongoing exposure to risk.

Butterfly spreads can involve either calls or puts. A bull butterfly spread will be most profitable if the underlying stock's market value rises, and the opposite is true for a bear butterfly spread.

A detailed butterfly spread, with defined profit and loss zones, is shown in Figure 8.14. In this example, the following transactions are involved:

Sell two June 40 calls at 6 (+$1,200).

Buy one June 30 call at 12 (–$1,200).

Buy one June 50 call at 3 (–$300).

The net cost is $300. This butterfly spread will either yield a limited profit or result in a limited loss. In the butterfly spread, the potential yield often does not justify the strategy, since trading costs will offset the limited potential profit. That is why the butterfly spread is often created in increments rather than all at once.

Table 8.4 summarizes profit and loss status at various prices of the underlying stock, based on the previous example. It is based on values at expiration and includes no time value. If the stock's market value rises to $50 or more, the short position losses will be offset by an equal number of long position profits. And if the stock's market value declines, the maximum loss is $300, the net cost of opening these positions.

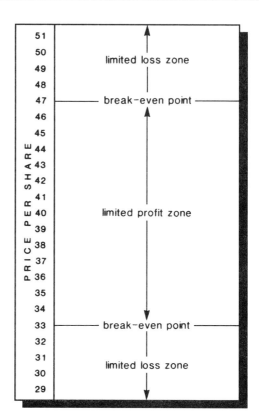

FIGURE 8.14 Butterfly spread profit and loss zones.

long hedge
the purchase of options as a form of insurance to protect a portfolio position in the event of a price increase, a strategy employed by investors selling stock short and insuring against a rise in the market value of the stock.

short hedge
the purchase of options as a form of insurance to protect a portfolio position in the event of a price decrease, a strategy employed by investors in long positions and insuring against a decline in the market value of the stock.

HEDGE STRATEGIES

Whenever options are bought or sold as part of a strategy to protect another open position, the combination of positions represents a hedge.

Two Types of Hedges

A *long hedge* protects against price increases.

Example of a long hedge: You are short on 100 shares of stock. This puts you at risk in the event the market value of that stock were to rise. You buy one call on that stock, which hedges your short stock position.

A *short hedge* protects against price decreases.

	TABLE 8.4 Profits/Losses for Butterfly Spread Example			
Price	June 30	June 40	June 50	Total
$51	+$900	−$1000	−$200	−$300
50	+ 800	− 800	− 300	− 300
49	+ 700	− 600	− 300	− 200
48	+ 600	− 400	− 300	− 100
47	+ 500	− 200	− 300	0
46	+ 400	0	− 300	+ 100
45	+ 300	+ 200	− 300	+ 200
44	+ 200	+ 400	− 300	+ 300
43	+ 100	+ 600	− 300	+ 400
42	0	+ 800	− 300	+ 500
41	− 100	+1000	− 300	+ 600
40	− 200	+1200	− 300	+ 700
39	− 300	+1200	− 300	+ 600
38	− 400	+1200	− 300	+ 500
37	− 500	+1200	− 300	+ 400
36	− 600	+1200	− 300	+ 300
35	− 700	+1200	− 300	+ 200
34	− 800	+1200	− 300	+ 100
33	− 900	+1200	− 300	0
32	−1000	+1200	− 300	− 100
31	−1100	+1200	− 300	− 200
30	−1200	+1200	− 300	− 300
29	−1200	+1200	− 300	− 300
Lower	−1200	+1200	− 300	− 300

Example of a short hedge: You own 100 shares of stock and, due to recent negative news, you are concerned that the market value could drop. You do not want to sell the shares, however. To hedge against the risk of lost market value, you have a choice of either buying one put or selling one call. Both positions hedge the 100 shares. The put provides unlimited protection because it would increase in value for each point lost in the stock's value. The call provides limited downside protection, only to the extent of the points received in premium.

An expanded example of a long hedge, with defined profit and loss zones, is shown in Figure 8.15.

Example: You sold short 100 shares of stock at $43, and hedged that position with a May 40 call bought at 2. The cost of hedging your short position reduces potential profits by $200, but protects you against potentially greater losses without requiring that you close the position. The risk is eliminated until the call expires. At that point, there are three choices:

1. Close the short position to eliminate risk.
2. Replace the call with another, later-expiring one.
3. Do nothing since perception of the risk might have changed.

In this example, if the underlying stock's market value increases, then profit potential is limited to the offsetting price gap between the stock's market value and the call's premium value. If the stock's market value falls, the short stock position will be profitable, with profits reduced by 2 points for the call premium you paid.

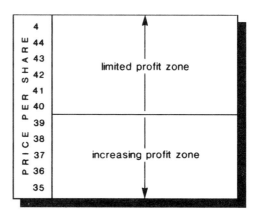

FIGURE 8.15 Long hedge profit and loss zones.

Table 8.5 summarizes this hedged position's overall value at various stock price levels.

Hedging beyond Coverage

One of the disadvantages to the hedge when matched precisely is that potential profits may be limited. A solution is to modify the hedge to increase profit potential, while still minimizing the risk of loss.

A *reverse hedge* involves providing more protection than needed just to cover another position. For example, if you are short on 100 shares of stock, you need to purchase only one call to hedge the position. In a reverse hedge strategy, you buy more than one call, providing protection for the short position *and* potential for additional profits that would outpace adverse movement in the stock's price. With two calls, the call profits would outpace stock losses 2 to 1, for example; with three calls, the ratio would be 3 to 1.

An expanded example of a reverse hedge, with defined profit and loss zones, is shown in Figure 8.16. In this example, you sold short 100 shares of stock at $43 per share, and the value now has declined to $39. To protect the profit in

reverse hedge an extension of a long or short hedge in which more options are opened than the number needed to cover the stock position; this increases profit potential in the event of unfavorable movement in the market value of the underlying stock.

TABLE 8.5 Profits/Losses from the Long Hedge Example			
Price	Stock	Call	Total
$45	−$200	+$300	+$100
44	− 100	+ 200	+ 100
43	0	+ 100	+ 100
42	+ 100	0	+ 100
41	+ 200	− 100	+ 100
40	+ 300	− 200	+ 100
39	+ 400	− 200	+ 200
38	+ 500	− 200	+ 300
37	+ 600	− 200	+ 400
36	+ 700	− 200	+ 500
35	+ 800	− 200	+ 600

the short position and to insure against losses in the event the price rises, you bought two May 40 calls at 2.

This reverse hedge solves the problem of risk in the short stock position, while also providing the potential for additional gain in the calls. In order for this profit to materialize, the stock's value would have to increase enough points to offset your cost in buying the calls. This hedge creates two advantages: First, it protects the short position in the event of unwanted price increase in the stock. Second, the 2-to-1 ratio from calls to stock means that if the price were to increase in the stock, the calls would become profitable.

Smart Investor Tip   The reverse hedge protects an exposed position while adding the potential for additional profits (or losses). This makes the hedge more than a form of insurance.

Table 8.6 summarizes this position's value as of expiration at various stock prices.

The reverse hedge works in the opposite direction as well. For example, you may own 100 shares of stock that has risen in value. To protect against a decline in value, you may buy two puts, a reverse hedge that would produce 2 to 1 profits in calls over decline in the stock's value. You may also sell two calls for the same reason. One would be covered while the other would be uncovered. Or, looking at this another way, the hedged position would be one-half covered overall. If the stock's market

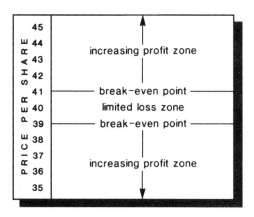

FIGURE 8.16 Reverse hedge profit and loss zones.

	TABLE 8.6 Profits/Losses from Reverse Hedge Example		
Price	Stock	Call	Total
$45	−$200	+$600	+$400
44	− 100	+ 400	+ 300
43	0	+ 200	+ 200
42	+ 100	0	+ 100
41	+ 200	− 200	0
40	+ 300	− 400	− 100
39	+ 400	− 400	0
38	+ 500	− 400	+ 100
37	+ 600	− 400	+ 200
36	+ 700	− 400	+ 300
35	+ 800	− 400	+ 400

value were to fall, the calls would lose value, providing downside protection to the extent of the total premium received. However, if the stock were to rise, profits in the stock would be reduced by losses in the calls.

Hedging Option Positions

Hedging can protect a long or short position in an underlying stock, or it can reduce or eliminate risks in other option positions. Hedging is achieved with various forms of spreads and combinations. By varying the number of options on one side or the other, you create a *variable hedge*, which is a hedge involving both long and short positions. However, one side will contain a greater number of options than the other.

Example: You buy three May 40 calls and sell one May 55 call. This variable hedge creates the potential for profits while completely eliminating the risk of selling an uncovered call. If the underlying stock's market value were to increase above the level of $55 per share, your three long positions would increase in value by 3 points for every point in the short position. If the stock's market

variable hedge
a hedge involving a long position and a short position in related options, when one side contains a greater number of options than the other. (The desired result is reduction of risks or potentially greater profits.)

value were to decrease, the short position would lose value and could be closed at a profit.

This particular situation would be difficult to create all at once with a credit, because the lower-striking-price calls would tend to cost more than the higher-priced short position call. However, the variable hedge may be created at different times, when a singular position needs to be protected due to future price changes in the underlying stock.

Long and short variable hedge strategies, with defined profit and loss zones, are shown in Figure 8.17. In the long variable hedge example, you buy three June 65 calls for 1, paying $300; and you sell one June 60 call for 5. Net proceeds are $200. This long variable hedge strategy achieves maximum profits if the underlying stock's market value rises. Above the striking price of 65, long call values would increase 3 points for every point increase in the underlying stock. If the stock's market value decreases, all of the calls lose value and the net $200 proceeds will be all profit.

Table 8.7 summarizes this position's value as of expiration at various stock price levels. The problem in this strategy is that the short positions expire later than the long positions; in most circumstances, this is the most

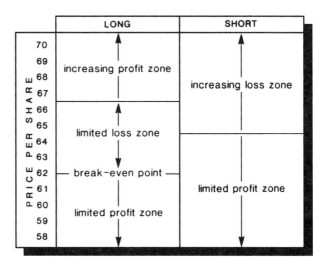

FIGURE 8.17 Variable hedge profit and loss zones.

TABLE 8.7 Profits/Losses from the Long Variable Hedge Example			
Price	Stock	Call	Total
$70	+$1200	−$500	+$700
69	+ 900	− 400	+ 500
68	+ 600	− 300	+ 300
67	+ 300	− 200	+ 100
66	0	− 100	− 100
65	− 300	0	− 300
64	− 300	+ 100	− 200
63	− 300	+ 200	− 100
62	− 300	+ 300	0
61	− 300	+ 400	+ 100
60	− 300	+ 500	+ 200
59	− 300	+ 500	+ 200
58	− 300	+ 500	+ 200

likely way to create a credit in a variable hedge. So you need to experience price movement that creates an acceptable profit before expiration of the long position options, or be prepared to close out the short positions once the long ones expire to avoid exposure to the risk of exercise.

The previously discussed Figure 8.17 also shows an increasing loss zone and limited profit zone in the example of a *short* hedge. In that example, you sold five June 60 calls for 5, receiving $2,500; and you bought three June 65 calls for 1, paying $300; net proceeds were $2,200. This short variable hedge strategy is a more aggressive variation than the long example, with more proceeds up front and a corresponding higher risk level overall. When the offsetting call positions are eliminated, two of the calls remain uncovered. A decline in the value of the underlying stock would create a profit. However, an increase in the stock's market value creates an increasing level of losses. Beyond striking price, the loss is 2 points for every point of movement in the stock's price. Outcomes for this short hedge at various price levels of the stock are summarized in Table 8.8.

TABLE 8.8 Profits/Losses from the Short Variable Hedge Example			
Price	Stock	Call	Total
$70	−$2500	+$500	−$2000
69	− 2000	+ 400	− 1600
68	− 1500	+ 300	− 1200
67	− 1000	+ 200	− 800
66	− 500	0	− 500
65	0	− 300	− 300
64	+ 500	− 300	+ 200
63	+ 1000	− 300	+ 700
62	+ 1500	− 300	+ 1200
61	+ 2000	− 300	+ 1700
60	+ 2500	− 300	+ 2200
59	+ 2500	− 300	+ 2200
58	+ 2500	− 300	+ 2200

Partial Coverage Strategies

ratio write
a strategy for partially covering one position with another for partial rather than full coverage. (A portion of risk is eliminated, so that ratio writes can be used to reduce overall risk levels.)

Another variation of hedging involves cutting partial losses through partial coverage. This strategy is known as a *ratio write*. When you sell one call for every 100 shares owned, you have provided a one-to-one coverage. A ratio write exists when the relationship between long and short positions is not identical. The ratio can be greater on either the long side or the short side. See Table 8.9.

Example: You own 75 shares of stock and you sell one call. Because some of your shares are not covered, this position actually consists of two separate positions: 75 shares of stock are long, and one call is short. In practice, however, in the event of exercise, your 75 shares would satisfy three-quarters of the assignment. You would need to buy 25 shares at the striking price. Your short position is 75 percent covered. The ratio write is 1 to $^3/_4$.

Example: You own 300 shares of stock and you recently sold four calls. You have two positions here: 300 shares

TABLE 8.9 Ratio Writes			
Calls Sold	*Shares Owned*	*Percent Coverage*	*Ratio*
1	75	75%	1 to $^3/_4$
2	150	75	2 to 1$^1/_2$
3	200	67	3 to 2
4	300	75	4 to 3
5	300	60	5 to 3
5	400	80	5 to 4

that are associated with covered calls, and one uncovered short call. In practice, however, you have a 4 to 3 ratio write.

Smart Investor Tip   The ratio write is appropriate when you are willing to accept some of the risk. Consider ratio writes when you think the chances of loss are minimal.

An expanded example of the ratio write, with defined profit and loss zones, is shown in Figure 8.18.

In this example, you buy 50 shares of stock at $38 per share and you sell one September 40 call for 3. This creates a partially covered call. Half of the risk in the short call position is offset by the 50 shares. The other half of the risk is uncovered. If the value of the underlying stock rises, the risk is cut in half in the event of exercise. However, if the stock's market value falls, a loss in the stock will be offset by premium received from selling the call. A summary of this strategy is shown at various prices of the stock at expiration in Table 8.10.

STRADDLE STRATEGIES

While spreads involve buying and selling options with different terms, straddles are the simultaneous purchase and sale of options with the same striking price and expiration date.

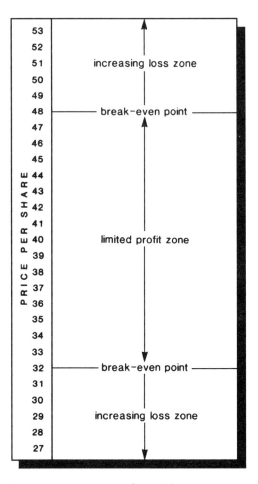

FIGURE 8.18   Ratio write profit and loss zones.

Middle Loss Zones

A *long straddle* involves the purchase of calls and puts at the same striking price and expiration date. Because you pay to create the long positions, the result is a middle-zone loss range above and below the striking price, and profit zones above and below that zone.

Example: You open a long straddle. You buy one February 40 call for 2; and you buy one February 40 put for 1. Your total cost is $300. If the underlying stock's value remains within 3 points above or below the striking price, the straddle will lose money. If the stock's market value

---

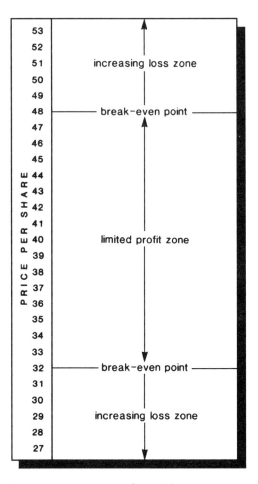 labels:
- increasing loss zone
- break-even point
- limited profit zone
- break-even point
- increasing loss zone

PRICE PER SHARE (vertical axis): 53, 52, 51, 50, 49, 48, 47, 46, 45, 44, 43, 42, 41, 40, 39, 38, 37, 36, 35, 34, 33, 32, 31, 30, 29, 28, 27

---

long straddle
the purchase of an identical number of calls and puts with identical striking prices and expiration dates, designed to produce profits in the event of price movement of the underlying stock in either direction adequate to surpass the cost of opening the position.

	50 Shares	Sept. 40	
Price	of Stock	Call	Total
$50	+$600	–$700	–$100
49	+ 550	– 600	– 50
48	+ 500	– 500	0
47	+ 450	– 400	+ 50
46	+ 400	– 300	+ 100
45	+ 350	– 200	+ 150
44	+ 300	– 100	+ 200
43	+ 250	0	+ 250
42	+ 200	+ 100	+ 300
41	+ 150	+ 200	+ 350
40	+ 100	+ 300	+ 400
39	+ 50	+ 300	+ 350
38	0	+ 300	+ 300
37	– 50	+ 300	+ 250
36	– 100	+ 300	+ 200
35	– 150	+ 300	+ 150
34	– 200	+ 300	+ 100
33	– 250	+ 300	+ 50
32	– 300	+ 300	0
31	– 350	+ 300	– 50
30	– 400	+ 300	– 100

TABLE 8.10 Profits/Losses from the Ratio Write Example

moves higher or lower by more than 3 points from striking price, then the long straddle will be profitable.

Another example of a long straddle is summarized with defined profit and loss zones in Figure 8.19. In this example, you buy one July 40 call for 3 and one July 40 put for 1; total cost is $400. The long straddle strategy will be profitable if the underlying stock's market price exceeds the 4-point range on either side of the striking price.

The 4 points required on either side of the striking price highlight the most important fact about long straddles:

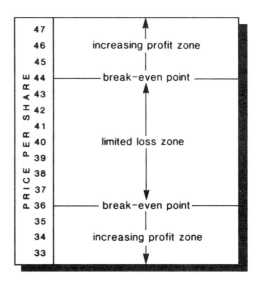

FIGURE 8.19 Long straddle profit and loss zones.

The more you pay in overall premium, the greater the required stock point movement away from striking price. It does not matter which direction the price moves, as long as its total point value exceeds the amount paid to open the position. Table 8.11 summarizes the outcome of this example at various stock price levels.

You have some flexibility in the long straddle. Since both sides are long, you are free to sell off one portion at a profit while holding onto the other. In the ideal situation, the stock will move in one direction and produce a profit on one side; and then it will move in the opposite direction, enabling you to profit on the other side. A long straddle may be most profitable in highly volatile stocks, but of course premium value of the options will tend to be greater as well in that situation. To show how the price swing can help to double profit potential, let's say that the stock's price moves up 2 points above striking price. The call can then be sold at a profit. If the stock's market value later falls 3 points below striking price, the put can also be sold at a profit. The strategy loses if the stock remains within the narrow loss range and time value premium offsets any minor price movements. In other words, time works against you as a buyer; and when you buy both calls and puts, you have a time value premium problem on both sides of the transaction.

	TABLE 8.11 Profits/Losses from the Long Straddle Example		
Price	50 Shares of Stock	Sept. 40 Call	Total
$47	+$400	–$100	+$300
46	+ 300	– 100	+ 200
45	+ 200	– 100	+ 100
44	+ 100	– 100	0
43	0	– 100	– 100
42	– 100	– 100	– 200
41	– 200	– 100	– 300
40	– 300	– 100	– 400
39	– 300	0	– 300
38	– 300	+ 100	– 200
37	– 300	+ 200	– 100
36	– 300	+ 300	0
35	– 300	+ 400	+ 100
34	– 300	+ 500	+ 200
33	– 300	+ 600	+ 300

Middle Profit Zones

In the previous example, two related long positions were opened, creating a middle loss zone on either side of the striking price. The opposite situation—a middle profit zone—is created through opening a *short straddle*. This involves selling an identical number of calls and puts on the same underlying stock, with the same striking price and expiration date. If the stock's market price moves beyond the middle profit zone in either direction, this position would result in a loss. Short straddles offer the potential for profits when stocks do not move in an overly broad trading range, and when time value premium is higher than average. Of course, less volatile stocks also tend to contain lower time value, whereas more volatile stocks have higher time value and higher risks with short straddles. Because time value decreases as expiration approaches, the advantage in this position

short straddle

the sale of an identical number of calls and puts with identical striking prices and expiration dates, designed to produce profits in the event of price movement of the underlying stock only within a limited range.

is the same for sellers of calls and puts—time works for the short seller.

Example: You open a short straddle. You sell one March 50 call for 2 and one March 50 put for 1; total proceeds are $300. As long as the underlying stock's market value remains within 3 points of the striking price—on either side—any intrinsic value in one option is offset by the other side. But if current market value of the stock exceeds the 3-point range, the short straddle will produce a loss.

The problem with the short straddle is that one side or the other is always at or in the money, so the risk of exercise is constant. And the preceding example does not allow for the transaction costs. In a practical application, the profit zone would be smaller for single options. The best outcome for this strategy, assuming that exercise does not take place, is that both sides will lose enough time value so that they can both be closed at a profit. Considering that the profit margin will be slim and risks are considerable, you need to evaluate whether this two-sided short position would be worth the risk. As with other examples of advanced strategies, the short straddle might be the result of opening one position and later adding the other.

Smart Investor Tip   For each and every strategy with limited profit potential, always ask the critical question: Is it worth the risk?

An example of a short straddle with defined profit and loss zones is shown in Figure 8.20. In this example, you sell one July 40 call at 3, and one July 40 put at 1; total proceeds are $400. This creates a 4-point profit zone on either side of the striking price.

The short straddle in this example creates a middle profit zone extending 4 points in both directions from striking price. Unless the stock's market value is at the money when expiration is imminent, the likelihood of exercise of one side or the other is high. Table 8.12 summarizes the outcome of this short straddle at various stock price levels.

Actual profits and losses have to be adjusted to allow for trading costs on both sides of any position. So a thin

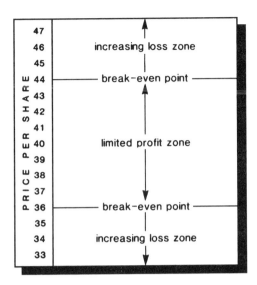

FIGURE 8.20 Short straddle profit and loss zones.

margin of profit can be entirely wiped out by those fees, making more elaborate option strategies less than practical, notably when using only single options on either side. To compare outcomes of long and short straddles, refer to Figure 8.21, which shows profit and loss zones in a side-by-side format for each strategy.

THEORY AND PRACTICE OF COMBINED TECHNIQUES

Advanced option strategies expose you to the risk of loss, which could be significant—especially when short positions are involved. If you do decide to employ any of these strategies, remember the following critical points:

1. *Brokerage fees are part of the equation.* Transaction fees reduce profit margins significantly, especially when you are dealing in single-option increments. The more contracts involved, the lower the transaction fees per contract—and the greater your risks. A marginal potential profit could be wiped out by fees, so approach advanced strategies from a practical point of view.

	July 40	July 40	
Price	Call	Put	Total
$47	−$400	+$100	−$300
46	− 300	+ 100	− 200
45	− 200	+ 100	− 100
44	− 100	+ 100	0
43	0	+ 100	+ 100
42	+ 100	+ 100	+ 200
41	+ 200	+ 100	+ 300
40	+ 300	+ 100	+ 400
39	+ 300	0	+ 300
38	+ 300	− 100	+ 200
37	+ 300	− 200	+ 100
36	+ 300	− 300	0
35	+ 300	− 400	− 100
34	+ 300	− 500	− 200
33	+ 300	− 600	− 300

TABLE 8.12 Profits/Losses from the Short Straddle Example

Remember that profits could be minimal, but risks could be high.

2. *Early exercise can change everything.* Buyers have the right of exercise at any time, so whenever your short positions are in the money, you could face early exercise. It is easy to forget this point and to assume that exercise is only a risk at the point of expiration. What seems a straightforward, easy strategy can be thrown into complete disarray by early exercise. In evaluating combined strategies, be sure to consider the possibility of exercise and study what its effects would be on the position.

3. *Potential profit and risk are always related directly to one another.* Many options traders tend to pay attention only to potential profits, while overlooking potential risks. Remember that the greater the possibility of profit, the higher the potential for losses. The relationship between risk and return is inescapable.

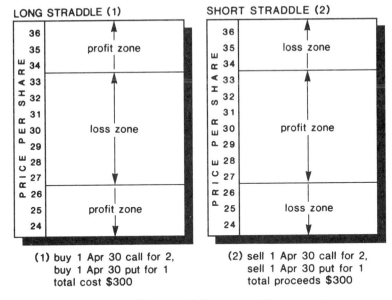

FIGURE 8.21 Comparison of long and short straddle strategies.

4. *Your degree of risk will be limited by your brokerage firm.* You may devise a complex series of trades that, in your opinion, limit your risks while providing potential for significant gains. However, remember that as long as your strategy includes short positions, your brokerage firm will restrict your exposure to risk—because if you cannot meet assignment obligations, the firm will be stuck with them. The brokerage firm might not be willing to view the coverage you provide in offsetting positions, but is more likely to look at your short positions on their own merit, recognizing that you can always close long positions and be left with significant risk exposure.

5. *You need to thoroughly understand a strategy before opening positions.* Never employ any strategy before you understand how it will work out, given all possible outcomes. You need to evaluate risks carefully, not only for the most likely results but for the worst-case possibilities as well. You will need to know what to do if and when price movement happens that you were not expecting, whether the result is positive or negative in its effect on your strategy. You will not have time to think it through in every case, because changes happen quickly in the options market. You need to know how to react to every possible situation.

6. *It doesn't always work out the way it was planned on paper.* When working out an option strategy on paper, it is easy to convince yourself that a particular strategy cannot fail, or that failure is only a remote possibility. However, once you enter into a transaction, prices may not move as you expect. Remember that option premium changes are not completely predictable, and neither are stock prices. Risk is only fully understood once it is experienced directly, and only experience can demonstrate the difference between theory and practice. Sudden changes in market value of an underlying stock, or in the market as a whole, could throw a paper model into disarray.

Options add a new dimension to your portfolio. You can protect existing positions, insure profits, and take advantage of momentary opportunities. However, every potential profit is associated with an offsetting risk. The market is efficient at least in that regard: Pricing of options reflects the risk level, so while a price is an opportunity, it also reflects exposure to the inherent risk in opening a position. Only through evaluation and analysis can you identify strategies that make sense for you, that protect your stock positions, and that you believe have a reasonable chance of producing profits at risk levels you are willing to undertake.

The next chapter explains why each investor needs to develop a personalized, individual strategy. No one approach is a proper fit for everyone.

Choosing Your Own Strategy

Happiness, wealth, and success are by-products of goal setting; they cannot be the goals themselves.
—Denis Waitley and Remi L. Witt, *The Joy of Working*, 1985

You will ultimately decide to employ options in your portfolio upon concluding that they are appropriate in your particular circumstances. If your personal risk tolerance and goals dictate that you should *not* employ options at any level, then you should avoid the strategy altogether. Keep in mind, however, that there is a broad range of reasons to use options—some high-risk and others very conservative.

Your success as an investor depends on how well you are able and willing to set policies based on your long-term goals, and then to identify appropriate strategies and investment choices to achieve those goals. All investors, and particularly those using options, need to be able to establish standards and then follow the rules they set for themselves, ignoring the temptation to deviate from a preestablished course.

With options, perhaps more than with most other forms of investing, the establishment of firm policies is critical. There are so many variations on the use of options that you need to examine with great care what you need and what you can afford. Most important in the mix of analyzing your portfolio requirements and long-term goals is the identification of what will be considered an acceptable risk. Your personal risk standards identify and define which forms of option investing—if any—fit with your profile and long-term goals. Perhaps they fit today, but will not fit tomorrow. Or perhaps the reverse is true. Your personal investment requirements do not remain stationary. Your financial environment is dynamic, and it changes as your circumstances change. Along with changing long-term goals, your risk standards change with time, age, and experience.

Options might provide you with a convenient form of diversification, protection, or income—or all of these in various combinations. First, though, you need to decide what type of investor you are today and what type of investor you expect to be in the future. For so many people, the process of definition and goal-setting involves setting down ways to accumulate wealth. Along the way, the accumulation needs to be protected, altered, and properly invested so that it increases rather than remaining at the same level or shrinking. Wise investors are aware not only of the need to accumulate wealth, but also to offset the double effect of taxation and inflation, which together can erode an overly conservative and low-yielding portfolio. The loss of buying power can be as damaging in the long term as failing to plan altogether.

Option investing contains many traps, making it one of the more challenging specialties you can find. It has a complex and specialized language; it changes rapidly; and it requires a high degree of comfort with mathematics. Thus, it is easy for people to become lost in terminology, to fail to act quickly enough to take advantage of the momentary situation, or to become confused by the calculations required to assess risk and potential profit. It is also easy to become distracted by the theoretical profit of options, ignoring the associated risks—the result being taking on risks that in fact are unacceptable. Novice options traders often fail to realize how important it is to monitor the market regularly and to look for action points in their open positions.

ESTABLISHING YOUR OWN PLAN

To properly determine what risks are acceptable to you, the first step is to arrive at a series of definitions. What kinds of risks can you take? If you are a speculator, you will seek short-term income and you will have little interest in long-term growth potential. You will be willing to take exceptionally high risks while seeking higher than average profits. Selling uncovered calls or buying near-expiration options will appeal to you. You may also gravitate toward the more exotic spreads and straddles for maximum profit with limited loss exposure. If you also speculate in your stock portfolio, you will be interested in using options along with highly volatile stocks, or for coverage of short positions. The big danger for speculators is that they tend to be attracted to exotic strategies not always because they are appropriate, but because they are exotic.

Smart Investor Tip Speculators should be certain that they use a complex strategy because it makes sense, and not just because it is complex.

If you are a conservative investor and you seek long-term growth more than immediate income, your primary interest will be in the proper selection of stocks. However, even in this situation, options can supplement your portfolio. You can sell puts as one means for acquiring stocks that you consider well-priced at a particular striking price. Covered calls can be used to supplement dividend income and capital gains. And puts can be bought for temporary insurance against downside movement in the stock's price, especially during market corrections.

Many investors diversify their portfolios so that options do not jeopardize longer-term plans. You may set aside a small portion of your investment capital to use in option speculation—for example, to take advantage of short-term market price movement. Or the fund can be used to provide insurance against downside corrections when a stock's price has gone up in what you consider an overreaction to current news. Since such changes in price often are corrected in the short term, buying puts at such times could be a wise move. The opposite is true as well. If the price of a stock falls, buying calls in anticipation of an upward correction could produce short-term profits in the speculative side of your portfolio.

The definition of yourself as a speculator or conservative investor is only the beginning of the process. You also need to define the long-term purpose in investing. Young couples plan for the purchase of a home or saving for their child's college education. Some people want to accumulate a fund to start their own business, or to supplement retirement income. All of these long-term goals define the kinds of risks you can take. Of course, all situations require a more comprehensive planning point of view than investments. Most people need various forms of insurance (life, health, homeowners, disability); and virtually everyone needs an emergency reserve, a fund of easily accessible money that can be used for emergencies. How much to set up in a reserve depends on your situation. For example, if you have a line of credit secured by your home or available through credit cards, you may not need to put a large sum of cash in a low-yielding savings account.

In the past, much has been made of financial planning. An entire industry offers to help people define their goals, usually for a fee. The financial plan might involve a written document that carefully defines your risk tolerance, long-term goals, and identification of investments that are appropriate for you. A problem with most financial planners is that they are compensated by commissions. So their investment recommendations often are self-serving. For example, a financial planner will invariably recommend a load mutual fund over a no-load fund, because the latter does not pay a commission. However, there are no significant differences in market performance between load and no-load funds, so it makes no sense to pay a commission to a financial planner.

All too often, individuals representing themselves as planners or advisers are functioning as salespeople. Thus, you need to protect yourself by ensuring that you are getting objective advice. If you hire a planner, make sure that he or she is properly licensed by the state and qualified by education and experience to make recommendations. A Certified Financial Planner (CFP) has the proper training and experience to understand investing—which does not necessarily mean the individual understands *all* of the investment choices available to you.

Smart Investor Tip   Before hiring anyone as your financial planner, check the person out thoroughly. Check the CFP web site for more information, at www.cfp-board.org. Also check to see if the individual belongs to the Financial Planning Association (FPA), whose web site is www.fpanet.org.

Of course, you also need to ask whether you really need to hire someone. Most people who believe they need the advice of a planner think that it is their lack of knowledge that makes that necessary. However, so much free information is available online today that it is easier than ever to educate yourself.

If you are considering using options as part of your portfolio, it is unlikely that you will find a planner or adviser who is knowledgeable in this area. It is even less likely that such a person will be willing to help you set up a program for options trading. The commissions simply will not be high enough to make it practical for the planner. Some planners are "fee-based," meaning that they are supposed to work for a flat fee and not for commission. In practical application, however, a fee-based planner often is not justified, either. If you plan to use options as part of your investment program, you are going to need to educate yourself and make your own decisions.

By the same argument, you are not going to benefit by using a full-commission brokerage firm. One of the dozens of discount brokerage firms is adequate for the execution of your trades. If you believe that you can trade in options but also need a broker's advice, it might not be a practical route to take just yet.

Select a discount broker based not only on price, but also on level of service. If you will trade by telephone, how hard is it to get through? If you use an online brokerage firm, how easy is it to get connected? Ask for referrals from friends and locate the brokerage firm offering reasonable price and excellent service. Remember, the cheapest trading cost is not necessarily going to be the best service source.

In practical terms, you will operate most effectively as an options trader without any outside help or interference. You do not need a financial planner or a stockbroker for advice. As an options trader, you will need to develop your confidence and knowledge to the point that you are able to make decisions on your own. One of the myths about the stock market is that professional help is necessary to make wise decisions. More often than not, the help you get from paying a professional is not better than decisions you make on your own. Successful investors recognize that no matter how much professional help they pay for, they are responsible for their own profits or losses. Many people have discovered at great expense that no one will care for their money as much as they do. As an options investor—or as an experienced investor employing any strategy—you do not need to pay for advice from a market professional.

Smart Investor Tip   Options traders, because of the type of market, do not serve themselves well by paying someone else for advice.

IDENTIFYING THE RANGE OF RISK

Options serve the entire spectrum of risk profiles, and can be used in combinations of ways to supplement income, insure other positions, or modify exposure to loss. To determine how to use options in your portfolio, first go through these three steps:

1. *Study the full range of possible option strategies.* Before opening any positions in options, prepare hypothetical variations and track the market to see how you would have done. Track options through the Internet if you have access, which provides ongoing quotations free of charge, usually with only a 20-minute delay. Watch how values change from day to day and pay special attention to the course of time value. Note how time value decreases over time and how that rate of change is affected when stock market prices are at different levels in relation to striking prices. In other words, become familiar with valuation and changes in valuation by watching a particular series of options over time.

2. *Identify your personal risk tolerance levels.* Before picking an option strategy, first determine what levels of risk you can afford to take. Set standards and then follow them. Limit your market activities to only those strategies that fit your risk profile, and avoid the temptation to open the more exotic positions—at least when you are starting out. Also remember that your investing goals *and* risk tolerance will change over time, based on changes in your financial position, experience, and age. Be prepared to abandon outdated ideas and perceptions of risk, and continually refresh your outlook based on current information. Avoid the mistake of assuming that you can set down your entire lifetime's investing goals today, because these will change over time.

3. *Identify and understand all of the risks associated with options trading.* Consider every possible risk, including the risk that a stock's market price will not move as you expect, or that a short position could be exercised early. Anticipate even the most remote possibility, because in the options market, that possibility could materialize without warning. Remember that it is easy to be distracted by the most obvious or most likely outcome, and to overlook the complexity of the market. Develop a deeper sense of the market by tracking it and, ultimately, by experiencing it directly. In most forms of investing, perceptions about risk tend to be fixed. In option investing, it all depends on the position you assume. For example, as a buyer, time is the enemy; and as a seller, time defines your profit potential.

The obvious risk in each and every option position is that the underlying stock will do one of two things. It may move in a direction you didn't expect or want; or it will fail to move enough for a position to be profitable. Always identify and make a graph of the profit and loss zones before opening positions. The visualization of these zones helps you to identify when strategies make sense, and when the potential profit does not justify the risk.

Beyond this, be aware of the other forms of risk that are going to be involved when you trade in options.

Margin Risks

Most investors think of margin investing as buying stock on credit. That is the most familiar and common form. In the options market, margin requirements are different, and margin is used in a different way. Your brokerage firm will require that short positions be protected, at least partially, through collateral. The preferred form of collateral is owning 100 shares of stock for each call sold; in other situations, your maximum exposure will be limited by the brokerage firm.

Whenever you open uncovered short positions in options, cash or securities will have to be placed on deposit or otherwise committed to protect the brokerage firm's position. The level required will be established by minimum legal requirements, subject to increases by individual brokerage firms' policies. Any balance owed above the deposit represents risk, both for the brokerage firm and for you. If the stock moves in a direction you do not desire, the margin requirement goes up as well. In that respect, margin risk could be defined as leverage risk.

The margin requirement limits your freedom to be involved in short option positions. The amount of capital available to you defines the maximum scope of participation you can enjoy in the options market, as a short seller. Before entering any uncovered short positions, you will need to determine the policies of the brokerage firm, and ensure that you will be able to meet them. If you cannot, you could be required to close positions at a loss before you want. For positions like spreads and straddles, the brokerage firm may view each position separately, and not in combination. So a short position may be seen as representing full exposure, and the margin requirement could be significant.

Personal Goal Risks

Successful investors always establish goals. Putting it another way, they always know what they want and where they stand; they also know what they need to do in every possible change in their investment positions. For example, if you establish a goal that you will invest no more than 15% of your total portfolio in option speculation, it is important to stay with that goal. This requires constant review. Sudden market changes can mean sudden and un-expected losses, especially when you buy options and when you sell short. Getting away from the maximum goal you set is all too easy.

Your goal should also include identification of the point at which you will close positions, either to take prof-its or to limit losses. Avoid breaking your own rules by de-laying, hoping for favorable changes in the near-term future. This is tempting, but often leads to unacceptable losses or missing a profit opportunity. Establish two price points in every option position: *minimum gain* and *maximum loss*. When either point is reached, close the position.

Smart Investor Tip   Options traders, like gamblers, can succeed if they know when to fold. If they don't fold when they should, they will lose.

Unavailability of a Market Risks

One of the least talked about risks in any investment is the potential that you will not be able to buy or sell when you want. The discussion of options strategies is based on the basic idea that you will be able to place orders when-ever you want to, without problems or delays.

The reality is quite different in some situations. When market volume is especially heavy, it is difficult and sometimes impossible to place orders when you want to. In an exceptionally large market correction, volume will be exceptionally heavy as investors try to cut losses. So if you trade by telephone, your broker's lines will be over-loaded and those who do get through will experience longer than usual delays—because so much business is taking place at the same time. If you trade online, the same problem will occur. You will not be able to get through to the online brokerage web site if it is already overloaded with traders placing orders. In these extreme situations, your need to place orders will be greater than normal, as it is with all other investors. So at such times the market is unavailable to you.

Current rules require that the markets shut down when large downside losses take place, protecting you to a degree. However, this still represents the unavailability of the market. The most desirable price level for a particular strategy might come and go in moments, and if the market is unavailable to you—because of high traffic or a programmed shutdown—that opportunity will be gone and might never return. This problem is rare, but the risk is very real.

Disruption in Trading Risks

Another risk you face as an options trader is that trading could be halted in the underlying stock. For example, if rumors about a company are affecting the stock's market price, the exchange may halt trading for a day or more. A company might be rumored as a takeover candidate. If the rumors affecting price are true, when the trading halt is lifted the stock may open at a much higher or lower price than before. When trading is halted on a stock, all trading on related options is halted as well. As an options investor, this exposes you to potentially significant risks, perhaps even preventing you from being able to limit your exposure to loss.

Brokerage Risks

As with all institutions, brokerage firms can become insolvent and go out of business. As a general rule, a type of industry self-insurance protects most positions if and when a particular firm were to go out of business. This rare occurrence would not necessarily affect your open options positions, because the Options Clearing Corporation (OCC) would normally cover all of the open positions. However, in a particularly severe situation involving thousands of open positions, the risk—as remote as it is—does exist.

A more severe potential risk is the individual action of your broker. If you use a discount brokerage, you are not exposed to this risk, because the role of the broker is to place orders as you direct. However, if you are using a broker for advice on options trading, you are exposed to the risk that a broker will use his or her discretion, even if you have not granted that right. Never grant unlimited discretion to someone else, no matter how much trust you have. As an options trader, it is highly questionable that using a broker's advice makes sense; however, you need to ensure that the broker follows your instructions and does not exceed the authority you grant. In this fast-moving market, it is difficult for a broker with many clients to pay attention to your options trades to the degree required. In fact, with online free quotations widely available, you really do not need a full-commission broker at all. In the Internet environment with a lot of free information services and low-cost trading, the commission-based brokerage is becoming increasingly obsolete.

Yet another risk, even with online brokerage accounts, is that mistakes will be made in placing orders. Fortunately, online trading is easily traced and documented. However, it is still possible that a "buy" order goes in as a "sale," or vice versa. Such mistakes can be disastrous for you as an options trader. If you trade by telephone or in person, the risk is increased just due to human error. If you trade online, check your order carefully before sending it.

Trading Cost Risks

A calculated profit zone has to be reduced, or a loss zone increased, to allow for the cost of placing trades. Brokerage trading fees apply to both sides of every transaction. If you trade in single-option contracts, the cost is high on a per-option basis. Trading in higher increments is economical because the cost of trading is lower on a per-option basis.

This book has used examples for single contracts in most cases to make outcomes clear; in practice, such trading is not practical because the trading fees require more profit just to break even in many circumstances. A thin margin of profit will evaporate quickly when trading costs are added into the mix.

Every investor needs to shop for the most economical brokerage arrangement, given the need for high-quality service. With online competition, trading fees are reasonable and, in most instances, lower than in the past. However, be sure to compare option fees as well as other features of online trading. Seek a high service level combined with competitive option trading fees to minimize the cost of trading.

In cases where you exercise an option or you sell and the option is exercised by the buyer or the exchange, you not only pay the option trading fee, but you also have to pay for the cost of transacting the shares of stock, a point to remember in calculating overall return.

Lost Opportunity Risks

One of the more troubling aspects of options trading involves lost opportunity. This arises in several ways, the most obvious being that experienced by covered call sellers. You risk the loss of stock profits in the event of price increase and exercise. Your profit is locked in at the striking price. Covered call writers accept the certainly of a consistent, better-than-average return and, in exchange, they lose the occasional larger capital gain on their stock.

Opportunity risks arise in other ways, too. For example, if you are involved in exotic combinations including long and short positions, your margin requirements may prevent you from being able to take advantage of other investment opportunities. Most investors find themselves existing in an environment of moderate scarcity, so that not every opportunity may be seized. With this in mind, it is important that before committing yourself to an open position in options, you recognize how that could limit you in other choices.

EVALUATING YOUR RISK TOLERANCE

Every investor has a specific level of risk tolerance—the ability and willingness to accept risk. This trait is not fixed, however, but changes over time. Your personal risk tolerance is affected by several factors:

1. *Investment capital.* How much money do you have available to invest? How much do you have committed to long-term growth, and how much can you spare for more adventurous alternatives? Obviously, those with a large amount of what is called disposable income can afford to dispose of it, more than those who cannot afford to lose at all.

2. *Personal factors.* Your risk tolerance is significantly affected by your age, income, debt level, economic status, job, and job security. It changes drastically with major life events such as marriage, birth of a child, divorce, or death.

3. *Your investing experience.* How experienced are you as an investor? Confident investors are going to be more likely to willingly undertake option investing without the advice of a broker, and less experienced investors will hesitate to go on their own. The length of time you have been investing is also a factor. No matter how much you study investing in theory, you do not really gain market experience until you place real money at risk.

4. *Type of account.* Your risk tolerance depends on how and why you invest, and the type of account involved. For example, if you use options as part of a self-directed retirement plan, you will be limited in most cases to covered call writing. Because the portfolio is long-term, you will tend to pick stocks with good growth potential. If you invest in your personal account, you will have greater flexibility and could take a broader range of strategic risks.

5. *Your personal goals.* Every investor's goals ultimately determine how much risk is acceptable. You may wish to conserve capital, hedge against inflation, maximize short-term income, attain a consistent rate of return, accumulate capital for retirement, or a combination of these and other goals. Remember that definition of personal goals should dictate how you invest. It is easy to invest in ways that are contrary to your goals, so definition has to be applied in the market as well.

Smart Investor Tip Risk tolerance is reflected in the way you invest. You will have a better chance of succeeding if you ensure that the risks you take are risks you can afford.

As you develop your risk tolerance profile, use that profile to determine how to invest. Many investors find themselves making decisions based on rumor or unsubstantiated opinion or suggestions from others. They fail to check out information for themselves; more to the point, they do not apply the basic test to determine if a particular action fits with their own risk profiles. Your tolerance for risk should be the guiding force for all investment decisions you make. Select fundamental and technical indicators that not only provide information about trends in the company and its stock, but also identify specific risk factors that should affect your decision to take one of the four basic market actions: buy, hold, sell, or stay away.

The best investment decisions invariably are made as the result of thorough evaluation of the essential features of an investment or strategy, the most important being risk. By putting down on paper the various types of options trades in which you can engage and studying possible outcomes—including the visualized graph of profit and loss zones—you will gain a clear view of how options fit—or don't fit—into your overall plan. Of equal importance, you will discover which strategies clearly are inappropriate for you, and those can be abandoned. The evaluation process helps you to avoid mistakes and focus attention on what will be beneficial, given your risk tolerance level. The risk evaluation worksheet for option investing in Table 9.1 will help you to classify options by degrees of risk.

Applying Limits

Awareness of your personal limits is important as a guide for option investing. Whenever you have open positions in options, you need to know what your immediate goals are—when or if you will close those positions, for example, on either profit or loss side. Establishing a target rate of return or maximum bailout loss position clearly defines your policies as an options trader.

To set these limits, identify option trades you will make defined by rate of return and other features of the option: time until expiration, time value level, distance between current market value of the stock and striking price of the option, premium level, volatility of the stock, overall market conditions, and the potential for rolling forward to avoid exercise. In the case of covered calls, also identify potential rates of return if the stock is unchanged

TABLE 9.1 Risk Evaluation Worksheet
Lowest Possible Risk

____	Covered call writing
____	Put purchase for insurance (long position)
____	Call purchase for insurance (short position)

Medium Risk

____	Ratio writing
____	Combined strategies
	____ Long ____ Short

High Risk

____	Uncovered call writing
____	Combined strategies
	____ Long ____ Short
____	Call purchases for income
____	Put purchases for income

versus return if exercised. You improve your chances of success by narrowing down your choices with these points in mind:

1. *Maximum time value.* As a buyer, avoid purchasing options with a high level of time value. Remember that time works against you, and the more time value, the lower your prospects for profit. As a seller, the opposite advice applies. Look for options containing maximum time value premium. Time works *for* you as seller, so the higher the time value premium, the greater your profit potential and the higher your protection against increasing premium in the option.

2. *Time until expiration.* Buyers of very short-term options will be fortunate to earn a profit. These options tend to be very cheap as long as they are at the money or out of the money; however, you will depend on movement in the stock's market value in a short period of time. Novice options traders easily overlook the fact that time value premium declines as expiration approaches, but it rarely increases. Sellers benefit from short-term trading in options for the same reasons, but they expose themselves to risk of exercise for relatively low premium income. As a general observation, it takes time for the buyer's option to build intrinsic value; and it also takes time for the seller's option to lose time value. How much time is ideal will depend on the option, current status and volatility of the underlying stock, and the relationship between the stock's current market value and the option's striking price.

3. *The number of option contracts.* How many options should you trade at one time? You do not have to limit yourself to a single contract when it makes more sense and requires less in trading costs to use several contracts. Of course, while this increases your profit potential, it also exposes you to higher risks. You will also be limited in terms of uncovered short positions by the degree to which your brokerage firm is willing to let you face exposure to exercise, and by the regulations governing coverage of short positions.

4. *Target rate of return.* Enter every option trade with a specific target return in mind, in terms of either rate of return or dollars. Remember that if more than one outcome is possible, you need to define your target with each outcome in mind. For example, you might determine that an open long position will be closed when you double your money or lose half.

By identifying all of the features that you consider acceptable in order to employ a specific option strategy, you define your risk tolerance level. You can then select options and strategies that fit within your self-defined limits. If your limits are unrealistic, you will soon discover that no options meet your criteria.

Example: You have set a policy for yourself that incorporates several features. You desire to buy options. First, the time value should not exceed 25% of total premium. Second, the options must have at least four months to go until expiration. Third, they must be in the money. However, when you try to apply this set of rules, you cannot locate any options meeting your list of requirements. Adjustments are necessary.

When considering an option strategy of any nature, first calculate potential profits in the event of expiration or exercise, and then set criteria for other features: maximum time value, time until expiration, the number of contracts involved in the transaction, target rate of return, and the price range at which you will close. Obviously, these criteria will be drastically different for buyers than for sellers, and for covered versus uncovered option writing.

Use the option limits worksheet in Table 9.2 to set your personal limits. Then always use these limits as rules, and follow your rules to guide your option trading activity. If you discover that your standards are unrealistic, adjust them so that profit opportunities are not lost. By deciding in advance the characteristics of your option investments, and by knowing when you will close an open position, you will avoid the most common problem

---

TABLE 9.2   Option Limits

Covered Call Sale Criteria

Rate of Return If Unchanged

Dividends	$____		
Call premium	____	Total	$____
		Cost of stock	$____
		Gain	____%

Rate of Return If Exercised

Dividends	$____		
Call premium	____		
Stock gain	____	Total	$____
		Cost of stock	$____
		Gain	____%

Option Purchase Criteria

Maximum time value: ____%

Time until expiration: ____ months

Number of options: ____ contracts

Target rate of return: ____%

Sell level: increase to $____ or decrease to $____

faced by option investors: making decisions in a void. Many have invested well in the beginning, only to fail later by not knowing when to take profits, or by falling into the second common trap: impatience.

LOOKING TO THE FUTURE

Besides setting immediate standards and goals for option strategies in your portfolio, set long-term investing policies for yourself. Then fit option strategies that conform to those policies.

It is a mistake to open an option position on the advice of a broker or friend without first considering how it fits into your long-term investing policy and how the move corresponds with your risk profile. Options, like all investments, should always be used in the context of your individual plans. This is one of the long-term problems with taking advice from individuals whose compensation depends on generating trades: They tend to think in terms of volume rather than starting from the point of view of what works for the client.

Example: You have written down your personal investing goals, and have identified what you hope to achieve in the intermediate and long-term future. You are willing to assume risks in a low to moderate range, so all of your capital is invested in shares of blue-chip companies. In order to increase portfolio value, you consider one of the following two possible strategies:

Strategy 1: Hold shares of stock as long-term investments. Aim for appreciation and continuing dividend income.

Strategy 2: Increase the value of your portfolio by purchasing shares as in the first strategy and waiting for a moderate increase in value; then begin writing covered calls. As long as your minimum rate of return if exercised or unchanged always exceeds 35%, you will write a call, and then avoid exercise through rolling techniques. If a call is exercised and stock is called away, you plan to reinvest the proceeds in additional purchases of other blue-chip company shares.

In this comparison, the rate of return from the second strategy will always be higher than the first, due to the yield from writing covered calls. A 35% rate of return is not unreasonable, because it includes the capital gain from selling shares in the event of exercise, and because calls can be closed and replaced several times per year. So an annualized double-digit rate is not only possible, it is likely under this strategy. In addition to providing impressive returns, writing covered calls also provides downside protection by discounting your basis in shares of stock.

An interesting point to remember about the covered call strategy, especially as described in strategy 2: The common argument *against* writing covered calls is that you may lose future profits in the event the stock's price rises dramatically, because your striking price locks you in. It is true that, were the stock's market value to climb dramatically, you would experience exercise and "lose" those profits. However, remember that well-selected stocks will also tend to be less volatile than average, so that the chances of such increases—while they can happen—are lower than average. In addition, covered call writers take their double-digit returns consistently in exchange for the occasional lost paper profit. The goal of long-term growth is not inconsistent with writing covered calls, as long as you have a plan and stick to it, and as long as exercised shares are replaced with other shares of equal growth potential.

The long-term goal of building a portfolio can be achieved while also using options in appropriate ways. Covered call writing is a conservative strategy that yields exceptionally high returns when done correctly, especially for the patient investor who is willing to build some profit into the basis before embarking on a covered call writing program. The impatient investor is constantly tempted to take unacceptable risks, and ultimately will lose, not because a strategy is wrong but because such an investor sabotages his or her own plans. A smart approach is first to create and build a portfolio of strong growth-oriented stocks, wait for some price appreciation, and then embark on a program of income enhancement through covered call writing. For example, you might decide that you need a stock's market value to grow by 5 points or 10% above your basis before you will begin writing covered calls. With that policy, exercise ensures profits with properly selected calls.

Each form of investing contains its own set of opportunities and risks. Options can be used to reach your goals overall, to reduce risks, and to insure other positions through hedging strategies. Investors who lose money consistently in options tend to share many characteristics: They do not set goals, so they do not have a preestablished plan for closing positions profitably. They do not select strategies in their own best interests, often describing themselves as conservative while using options in a highly speculative manner. They have not taken the time to define their risk tolerance level, so they do not know when the risks they are taking are too high. A popular maxim in the investing community is, "If you don't know where you're going, any road will get you there." This is as true for option investors as for anyone else.

Successful investors are focused. They take the time to define their goals carefully, and they narrow down their risk tolerance with great care. In other words, they define themselves in terms of what works for them, and what doesn't work. This enables them to use strategies that make sense, *and* to resist temptation when they receive advice from others. They also tend to be patient, and are willing to wait for the right opportunities rather than taking chances even when conditions are not right for them.

To succeed in the market, place yourself in the second group of investors. Work from clear definition of goals and risk tolerance levels; avoid the temptation to chase fast profits; start by selecting stocks wisely; and wait for the right opportunities to use options to enhance your portfolio. Also study option terminology and trading rules so that you are completely comfortable with the market before risking your money. Success does not come to the unprepared—a cliché to be sure, but still a true observation. Success with options can be both predictable and controllable. If you gain knowledge, learn the rules of the playing field, research stocks thoroughly, and stay disciplined in your decisions, then you will succeed.

To some extent, you may also need to experiment, to try out a strategy to find out whether you are comfortable in a particular risk profile and to see how you react when markets move in the opposite direction than you expected. You cannot really know your risk tolerance until you have your money at risk—no matter how much time you spend on the theory of the market. There is no substitute for experience.

Devising a personal, individualized strategy is a rewarding experience. Seeing clearly what you need to do and then executing the strategy successfully gives you a well-deserved sense of achievement and competence, not to mention control. You will profit from devising and applying options strategies based on calculation and observation. You will also benefit from the satisfaction that comes from mastering a complex investment field, and from finding yourself completely and totally in control.

Glossary

The most bloodthirsty language in the newspapers today is not found in the international pages. It's found in the business pages.
— Al Ries and Jack Trout, *Marketing Warfare*, 1986

annualized basis   a method for comparing rates of return for holdings of varying periods, in which all returns are expressed as though investments had been held over a full year. (It involves dividing the holding period by the number of months the positions were open, and multiplying the result by 12.)

assignment   the act of exercise against a seller, done on a random basis or in accordance with orderly procedures developed by the Options Clearing Corporation and brokerage firms.

at the money   the status of an option when the underlying stock's value is identical to the option's striking price.

auction market   the public exchanges in which stocks, bonds, options, and other products are traded publicly and in which values are established by ever-changing supply and demand on the part of buyers and sellers.

automatic exercise   action taken by the Options Clearing Corporation at the time of expiration, when an in-the-money option has not been otherwise exercised or canceled.

average down   a strategy involving the purchase of stock when its market value is decreasing. (The average cost of shares bought in this manner is consistently higher than current market value, so a portion of the paper loss on declining stock value is absorbed, enabling covered call writers to sell calls and profit even when the stock's market value has declined.)

average up   a strategy involving the purchase of stock when its market value is increasing. (The average cost of shares bought in this manner is consistently lower than current market value, enabling covered call writers to sell calls in the money when the basis is below the striking price.)

bear spread   a strategy involving the purchase and sale of calls or puts that will produce maximum profits when the value of the underlying stock falls.

beta   a measurement of relative volatility of a stock, made by comparing the degree of price movement in comparison to a larger index of stock prices.

book value   the actual value of a company, more accurately called book value per share; the value of a company's capital (assets less liabilities), divided by the number of outstanding shares of stock.

box spread   the combination of a bull spread and a bear spread, opened at the same time on the same underlying stock.

buy 100 shares per month:

MONTH	PRICE	AVERAGE
Jan	$40	$40
Feb	38	39
Mar	36	38
Apr	34	37
May	27	35
Jun	29	34

buy 100 shares per month:

MONTH	PRICE	AVERAGE
Jan	$40	$40
Feb	44	42
Mar	45	43
Apr	47	44
May	54	46
Jun	52	47

FIGURE G.1 Average down.

FIGURE G.2 Average up.

break-even price (also called the **break-even point**) the price of the underlying stock at which the option investor breaks even. (For call buyers, this price is the number of points above striking price equal to the call premium cost; for put buyers, this price is the number of points below striking price equal to the put premium cost.)

breakout the movement of a stock's price below support level or above resistance level.

bull spread a strategy involving the purchase and sale of calls or puts that will produce maximum profits when the value of the underlying stock rises.

butterfly spread a strategy involving open options in one striking price range, offset by transactions at higher and lower ranges at the same time.

buyer an investor who purchases a call or a put option; the buyer realizes a profit if the value of stock moves above the specified price (call) or below the specified price (put).

calendar spread a spread involving the simultaneous purchase or sale of options on the same underlying stock, with different expirations.

call an option acquired by a buyer or granted by a seller to buy 100 shares of stock at a fixed price.

called away the result of having stock assigned. (Upon exercise, 100 shares of the seller's stock are called away at the striking price.)

chartist an analyst who studies charts of a stock's price movement in the belief that recent patterns can be used to predict upcoming price changes and directions.

class all options traded on a single underlying security, including different striking prices and expiration dates.

closing purchase transaction a transaction to close a short position, executed by buying an option previously sold, canceling it out.

closing sale transaction a transaction to close a long position, executed by selling an option previously bought, closing it out.

combination any purchase or sale of options on one underlying stock, with terms that are not identical.

contract a single option, the agreement providing a buyer with the rights the option grants. (Those rights include identification of the stock, the cost of the option, the date the option will expire, and the fixed price per share of the stock to be bought or sold under the right of the option.)

conversion the process of moving assigned stock from the seller of a call option or to the seller of a put option.

cover to protect oneself by owning 100 shares of the underlying stock for each call sold. (The risk in the short position in the call is covered by ownership of 100 shares.)

covered call a call sold to create an open short position, when the seller also owns 100 shares of stock for each call sold.

credit spread any spread in which receipts from short positions are higher than premiums paid for long positions, net of transaction fees.

current market value the market value of stock at any given time.

cycle the pattern of expiration dates of options for a particular underlying stock. The three cycles occur in four-month intervals and are described by month abbreviations. They are (1) January, April, July, and October, or JAJO; (2) February, May, August, and November, or FMAN; and (3) March, June, September, and December, or MJSD.

debit spread any spread in which receipts from short positions are lower than premiums paid for long positions, net of transaction fees.

debt investment an investment in the form of a loan made to earn interest, such as the purchase of a bond.

deep in condition when the underlying stock's current market value is 5 points or more above the striking price of the call or below the striking price of the put.

deep out condition when the underlying stock's current market value is 5 points or more below the striking price of the call or above the striking price of the put.

delivery the movement of stock ownership from one owner to another. (In the case of exercised options, shares are registered to the new owner upon receipt of payment.)

delta the degree of change in option premium, in relation to changes in the underlying stock. (If the call option's degree of change exceeds the change in the underlying stock, it is called an "up delta"; when the change is less than the underlying stock, it is called a "down delta." The reverse terminology is applied to puts.)

diagonal spread a calendar spread in which offsetting long and short positions have both different striking prices and different expiration dates.

	CALLS	PUTS
48	deep in	deep out
47		
46		
45		
44	in the	out of the
43	money	money
42		
41		
40	striking price	
39		
38	out of the	in the
37	money	money
36		
35		
34		
33	deep out	deep in
32		

(SHARE PRICE / EXERCISE PRICE)

FIGURE G.3 Deep in/deep out.

stock price change	OPTION PREMIUM CHANGE			
	1 point	2 points	3 points	4 points
1	1.00	2.00	3.00	4.00
2	0.50	1.00	1.50	2.00
3	0.33	0.67	1.00	1.33
4	0.25	0.50	0.75	1.00
5	0.20	0.40	0.60	0.80

FIGURE G.4 Delta.

discount to reduce the true price of the stock by the amount of premium received. (A benefit in selling covered calls, the discount provides downside protection and protects long positions.)

dividend yield measurement computed by dividing dividends paid per share of common stock by the current market value of the stock.

dollar cost averaging a strategy for investing over time, either buying a fixed number of shares or investing a fixed dollar amount, in regular intervals. (The result is an averaging of overall price. If market value increases, average cost is always lower than current market value; if market value decreases, average cost is always higher than current market value.)

downside protection a strategy involving the purchase of one put for every 100 shares of the underlying stock that you own. (This insures you against losses to some degree. For every in-the-money point the stock falls, the put will increase in value by 1 point. Before exercise, you may sell the put and take a profit offsetting stock losses, or exercise the put and sell the shares at the striking price.)

Dow Theory a theory that market trends are predictable based on changes in market averages.

early exercise the act of exercising an option prior to expiration date.

earnings per share a commonly used method for reporting profits. Net profits for a year or other period are divided by the number of shares of common stock outstanding as of the ending date of the financial report. (The result is expressed as a dollar value.)

efficient market hypothesis a theory stating that current stock prices reflect all information publicly known about a company.

equity investment an investment in the form of part ownership, such as the purchase of shares of stock in a corporation.

exercise the act of buying stock under the terms of the call option or selling stock under the terms of the put option, at the specified price per share in the option contract.

expiration date the date on which an option becomes worthless, which is specified in the option contract.

expiration time the latest possible time to place an order for cancellation or exercise of an option, which may vary depending on the brokerage firm executing the order and on the option itself.

fundamental analysis a study of financial information and attributes of a company's management and competitive position, as a means for selecting stocks.

hedge a strategy involving the use of one position to protect another. (For example, stock is purchased in the belief it will rise in value, and a put is purchased on the same stock to protect against the risk that market value will decline.)

horizontal spread a calendar spread in which offsetting long and short positions have identical striking prices but different expiration dates.

incremental return a technique for avoiding exercise while increasing profits with written calls. (When the value of the underlying stock rises, a single call is closed at a loss and replaced with two or more call writes with later expiration dates, producing cash and a profit in the exchange.)

in the money the status of a call option when the underlying stock's market value is higher than the option's striking price, or of a put option when the underlying stock's market value is lower than the option's striking price.

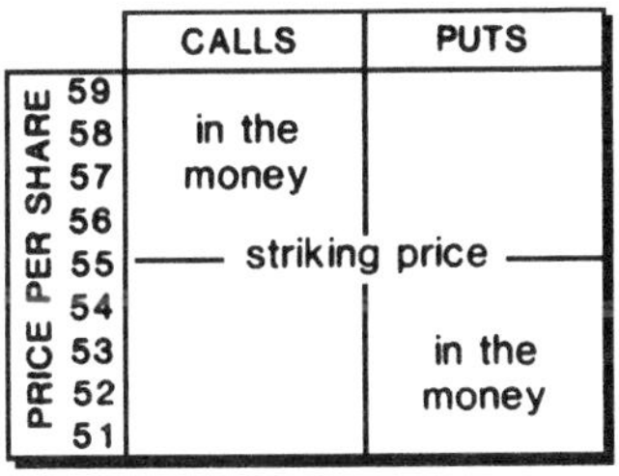

	CALLS	PUTS
59		
58	in the	
57	money	
56		
55	—— striking price ——	
54		
53		in the
52		money
51		

(left axis: PRICE PER SHARE)

FIGURE G.5 In the money.

STOCK VALUE	STRIKING PRICE	INTRINSIC VALUE
$38	$35	$3
43	45	0
41	40	1
65	65	0
21	20	1

FIGURE G.6 Intrinsic value.

intrinsic value that portion of an option's current value equal to the number of points that it is in the money. ("Points" equals the number of dollars of value per share, so 35 points equals $35 per share.)

know your customer a rule for brokers requiring the broker to be aware of the risk and capital profile of each client, designed to ensure that recommendations are suitable for each individual.

last trading day the Friday preceding the third Saturday of the expiration month of an option.

leverage the use of investment capital in a way that a relatively small amount of money enables the investor to control a relatively large value. (This is achieved through borrowing—for example, using borrowed money to purchase stocks or bonds—or through the purchase of options, which exist for only a short period of time but enable the option buyer to control 100 shares of stock. As a general rule, the use of leverage increases potential for profit as well as for loss.)

listed option an option traded on a public exchange and listed in the published reports in the financial press.

lock in to freeze the price of the underlying stock when the investor has sold a corresponding short call. (As long as the call position is open, the writer is locked into a striking price, regardless of current market value of the stock. In the event of exercise, the stock is delivered at that locked-in price.)

long hedge the purchase of options as a form of insurance to protect a portfolio position in the event of a price increase, a strategy employed by investors selling stock short and insuring against a rise in the market value of the stock.

long position the status assumed by investors when they enter a buy order in advance of entering a sell order. (The long position is closed by later entering a sell order, or through expiration.)

long straddle the purchase of an identical number of calls and puts with identical striking prices and expiration dates, designed to produce profits in the event of price movement of the underlying stock in either direction adequate to surpass the cost of opening the position.

loss zone the price range of the underlying stock in which the option investor loses. (A limited loss exists for option buyers, since the premium cost is the maximum loss that can be realized.)

margin an account with a brokerage firm containing a minimum level of cash and securities to provide collateral for short positions or for purchases for which payment has not yet been made.

market order   an order from an investor to a broker to buy or sell at the best available price.

market value   the value of an investment at any given time or date; the amount a buyer is willing to pay to acquire an investment and what a seller is also willing to receive to transfer the same investment.

married put   the status of a put used to hedge a long position. (Each put owned protects 100 shares of the underlying stock held in the portfolio. If the stock declines in value, the put's value will increase and offset the loss.)

money spread   alternate name for the vertical spread.

naked option   an option sold in an opening sale transaction when the seller (writer) does not own 100 shares of the underlying stock.

naked position   status for investors when they assume short positions in calls without also owning 100 shares of the underlying stock for each call written.

odd lot   a lot of shares that is fewer than the more typical round lot trading unit of 100 shares.

opening purchase transaction   an initial transaction to buy, also known as the action of "going long."

opening sale transaction   an initial transaction to sell, also known as the action of "going short."

open interest   the number of open contracts of a particular option at any given time, which can be used to measure market interest.

open position   the status of a transaction when a purchase (a long position) or a sale (a short position) has been made, and before cancellation, exercise, or expiration.

option   the right to buy or to sell 100 shares of stock at a specified, fixed price and by a specified date in the future.

orderly settlement   the smooth process of buying and selling, in full confidence that the terms and conditions of options contracts will be honored in a timely manner.

out of the money   the status of a call option when the underlying stock's market value is lower than the option's striking price, or of a put option when the underlying stock's market value is higher than the option's striking price.

paper profits (also called **unrealized profits**)   values existing only on paper but not taken at the time; paper profits (or paper losses) become realized only if a closing transaction is executed.

parity   the condition of an option at expiration, when the total premium consists of intrinsic value and no time value.

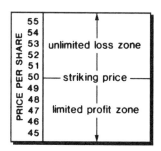

FIGURE G.7   Naked option.

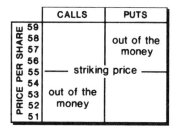

FIGURE G.8   Out of the money.

premium the current price of an option, which a buyer pays and a seller receives at the time of the transaction. (The amount of premium is expressed as the dollar value of the option, but without dollar signs; for example, stating that an option is at 3 means its current market value is $300.)

price/earnings ratio a popular indicator used by stock market investors to rate and compare stocks. The current market value of the stock is divided by the most recent earnings per share to arrive at the P/E ratio.

profit margin the most commonly used measurement of corporate operations, computed by dividing net profits by gross sales.

profit on invested capital a fundamental test showing the yield to equity investors in the company, computed by dividing net profits by the dollar value of outstanding capital.

profit zone the price range of the underlying stock in which the option investor realizes a profit. (For the call buyer, the profit zone extends upward from the break-even price. For the put buyer, the profit zone extends downward from the break-even price.)

prospectus a document designed to disclose all of the risk characteristics associated with a particular investment.

put an option acquired by a buyer or granted by a seller to sell 100 shares of stock at a fixed price.

put to seller action of exercising a put and requiring the seller to purchase 100 shares of stock at the fixed striking price.

random walk a theory about market pricing, stating that prices of stocks cannot be predicted because price movement is entirely random.

rate of return the yield from investing, calculated by dividing net cash profit upon sale by the amount spent at purchase.

ratio calendar combination spread a strategy involving both a ratio between purchases and sales and a box spread. (Long and short positions are opened on options with the same underlying stock, in varying numbers of contracts and with expiration dates extending over two or more periods. This strategy is designed to produce profits in the event of price increases or decreases in the market value of the underlying stock.)

ratio calendar spread a strategy involving a different number of options on the long side of a transaction from the number on the short side, when the expiration dates for each side are also different. (This strategy creates two separate profit and loss zone ranges, one of which disappears upon the earlier expiration.)

ratio write a strategy for partially covering one position with another for partial rather than full coverage. (A portion of risk is eliminated, so that ratio writes can be used to reduce overall risk levels.)

ready market a liquid market, one in which buyers can easily sell their holdings, or in which sellers can easily find buyers, at current market prices.

realized profits profits taken at the time a position is closed.

resistance level the price for a stock identifying the highest likely trading price under present conditions, above which the price of the stock is not likely to rise.

return if exercised the estimated rate of return option sellers will earn in the event the buyer exercises the option. (The calculation includes profit or loss in the underlying stock, dividends earned, and premium received for selling the option.)

return if unchanged the estimated rate of return option sellers will earn in the event the buyer does not exercise the option. (The calculation includes dividends earned on the underlying stock, and the premium received for selling the option.)

```
exercise price 40
purchase price 38
May 40 call sold for 3
dividends earned $80
```

```
call premium      $300
dividend income     80
capital gain       200
return            $580
                  15.3%
```

basis in stock $3800

```
sold May 40 call    $300
dividends earned      80
total               $380
return             10.0%
```

FIGURE G.9 Return if exercised.   **FIGURE G.10** Return if unchanged.

reverse hedge   an extension of a long or short hedge in which more options are opened than the number needed to cover the stock position; this increases profit potential in the event of unfavorable movement in the market value of the underlying stock.

roll down   the replacement of one written call with another that has a lower striking price.

roll forward   the replacement of one written call with another with the same striking price, but a later expiration date.

roll up   the replacement of one written call with another that has a higher striking price.

round lot   a lot of 100 shares of stock or of higher numbers divisible by 100, the usual trading unit on the public exchanges.

seller   an investor who grants a right in an option to someone else; the seller realizes a profit if the value of stock moves below the specified price (call) or above the specified price (put).

series   a group of options sharing identical terms.

settlement date   the date on which a buyer is required to pay for purchases, or on which a seller is entitled to receive payment. (For stocks, settlement date is three business days after the transaction. For options, settlement date is one business day from the date of the transaction.)

share   a unit of ownership in the capital of a corporation.

short hedge   the purchase of options as a form of insurance to protect a portfolio position in the event of a price decrease, a strategy employed by investors in long positions and insuring against a decline in the market value of the stock.

short position   the status assumed by investors when they enter a sale order in advance of entering a buy order. (The short position is closed by later entering a buy order, or through expiration.)

short selling   a strategy in the stock market in which shares of stock are first sold, creating a short position for the investor, and later bought in a closing purchase transaction.

short straddle   the sale of an identical number of calls and puts with identical striking prices and expiration dates, designed to produce profits in the event of price movement of the underlying stock only within a limited range.

speculation the use of money to assume risks for short-term profit, in the knowledge that substantial or total losses are one possible outcome. (Buying calls for leverage is one form of speculation. The buyer may earn a very large profit in a matter of days, or could lose the entire amount invested.)

spread the simultaneous purchase and sale of options on the same underlying stock, with different striking prices or expiration dates, or both.

standardized terms same as **terms**.

stop-limit order an order from an investor to a broker to buy or sell at a specified price (or within a specified range).

stop order an order from an investor to a broker to buy at or above a specified price, or to sell at or below a specified price level. (Once that level has been met or passed, the order becomes a market order.)

straddle the simultaneous purchase and sale of the same number of calls and puts with identical striking prices and expiration dates.

striking price the fixed price to be paid for 100 shares of stock specified in the option contract, which will be paid or received by the owner of the option contract upon exercise, regardless of the current market value of the stock.

suitability a standard by which a particular investment or market strategy is judged. (The investor's knowledge and experience with options represent important suitability standards. Strategies are appropriate only if the investor understands the market and can afford to take the risks involved.)

supply and demand the market forces that determine the current value for stocks. A growing number of buyers represent demand for shares, and a growing number of sellers represent supply. The price of stocks rises as demand increases, and falls as supply increases.

support level the price for a stock identifying the lowest likely trading price under present conditions, below which the price of the stock is not likely to fall.

tax put a strategy combining the sale of stock at a loss—taken for tax purposes—and the sale of a put at the same time. (The premium received on the put offsets the stock loss; if the put is exercised, the stock is purchased at the striking price.)

technical analysis a study of trends and patterns of price movement in stocks, including price per share, the shape of price movements on charts, high and low ranges, and trends in pricing over time.

terms the attributes that describe an option, including the striking price, expiration month, type of option (call or put), and the underlying security.

time spread alternate name for the calendar spread.

time value that portion of an option's current value above intrinsic value.

total return the combined return including income from selling a call, capital gain from profit on selling the stock, and dividends earned and received. (Total return may be calculated in two ways: return if the option is exercised, and return if the option expires worthless.)

uncovered option the same as a naked option—the sale of an option not covered, or protected, by the ownership of 100 shares of the underlying stock.

TOTAL PREMIUM	INTRINSIC VALUE	TIME VALUE
$4	$3	$1
2	0	2
4	1	3
1	0	1
3	1	2

FIGURE G.11 Time value.

stock exercised at
$40 (basis $34),
held for 13 months:

option premium	$ 800
dividends	110
capital gain	600
total	$1510
13 months	44.4%
annualized	41.0%

FIGURE G.12 Total return.

underlying stock   the stock on which the option grants the right to buy or sell, which is specified in every option contract.

variable hedge   a hedge involving a long position and a short position in related options, when one side contains a greater number of options than the other. (The desired result is reduction of risks or potentially greater profits.)

vertical spread   a spread involving different striking prices but identical expiration dates.

volatility   a measure of the degree of change in a stock's market value, measured over a 12-month period and stated as a percentage. (To measure volatility, subtract the lowest 12-month price from the highest 12-month price, and divide the answer by the 12-month lowest price.)

volume   the level of trading activity in a stock, an option, or the market as a whole.

wasting asset   any asset that declines in value over time. (An option is an example of a wasting asset because it exists only until expiration, after which it becomes worthless.)

writer   the individual who sells (writes) a call (or a put).

$$\frac{\text{high} - \text{low}}{\text{low}}$$

ANNUAL HIGH	ANNUAL LOW	PERCENT
$ 65	$ 43	51%
37	34	9
45	41	10
35	25	4
84	62	35
71	68	4
118	101	17
154	112	38

FIGURE G.13 Volatility.

Index

b

bear spread, 252–256
box spread, 256–258
brokerage risks, 300–301
bull spread, 250–252
butterfly spread, 269–272

c

calendar spread, 259–260
call
  analysis, 217–224
  buying, 21–22, 25–33,
    97–98
  contract, 21
  covered, 154–159
  defined, 18
  exercise, 167–178
  judging, 101–105
  limited life, 98–101
  naked, 146, 150
  return, 159–163
  selling, 21–22, 33–40, 121,
    144–146
  stock selection for writing,
    185–191
  strategies for buyers, 106–114
  timing, 163–167
  uncovered, 146–154

combination, 248
combined techniques, 287–290
cost averaging, 191–196
credit and debit spread, 258–259

d

diagonal spread, 259–261,
    262–263
disruption in trading risk, 300

e

exercise, 70–76, 167–178
expiration cycle, 64–67

h

hedge
  defined, 248–249
  long position, 137–140,
    272
  reverse, 275–277
  short, 272–273, 275
  strategies, 272–281
  variable, 277–279
horizontal spread, 259–262

i

intrinsic value, 56–62

l

long hedge, 272, 274–275
long straddle, 282–285
lost opportunity risks, 302

m

margin risk, 298
money spread, 248

o

option
    abbreviations, 82–85
    defined, 17
    evaluation, 78–80
    listings, 76–78
    opening and closing,
        67–68
    trading standards, 85–90
outcomes of trades, 68–70

p

personal goal risks, 298–299
premium, 27–28
profit zones, 114–118, 140–143,
    287–288
put
    buying, 41–44, 119–120,
        122–127, 133–140
    contract, 40
    defined, 19
    judging, 127–133
    limited life, 120–127
    risk evaluation, 233–234

selling, 44–47, 229–231
short selling, 120–121
standards, 47–49
stock valuation,
    231–233
strategies, 234–246
tax, 243–245

r

ratio calendar combination spread,
    265–269
ratio calendar spread,
    263–265
ratio write, 280–281
reverse hedge, 275–277
risk, 296–302
risk tolerance, 302–308
rolling techniques, 169–178

s

seller, 69–70, 90–96
short hedge, 272–273,
    275
short straddle, 285–287
spread
    bear, 252–256
    box, 256–258
    bull, 250–252
    butterfly, 269–272
    calendar, 259–260
    credit and debit,
        258–259
    defined, 248
    diagonal, 259–261,
        262–263
    horizontal, 259–262
    money, 248
    patterns, 263–272
    ratio calendar, 263–265
    ratio calendar combination,
        265–269

time, 259–260
vertical, 248, 249–259
straddle
  defined, 248–249
  long, 282–285
  short, 285–287
  strategies, 281–287
striking price, 26–27, 64

t

tax put, 243–245
terms, 63–64
time spread, 259–260
time value, 56–62
trading cost risks, 301–302

u

unavailability of a market risk, 299–300
underlying stock
  analyzing, 196–217, 224–228
  for call writing, 185–191
  identification, 65–66
  opening and closing trades, 80–82
  practical approach to, 182–185
  selection, 49–51, 53–56, 179–181,
    231–233

v

variable hedge, 277–279
vertical spread, 248, 249–259